CHASING the PEARL-MANUSCRIPT

Arthur Bahr

CHASING the PEARL-MANUSCRIPT

Speculation, Shapes, Delight

The University of Chicago Press CHICAGO AND LONDON

The University of Chicago Press, Chicago 60637
The University of Chicago Press, Ltd., London

Published 2025
Printed in China

34 33 32 31 30 29 28 27 26 25   1 2 3 4 5

ISBN-13: 978-0-226-83535-8 (cloth)
ISBN-13: 978-0-226-83536-5 (e-book)
DOI: https://doi.org/10.7208/chicago/9780226835365.001.0001

The University of Chicago Press gratefully acknowledges the generous support of the Massachusetts Institute of Technology toward the publication of this book.

Illustrations on pages ii and vi: Details adapted from Cotton Nero A.x/2 (folios 37/41r, 56/60r, 56/60v, 82/86v, 90/94v). Photographs: The British Library.

Library of Congress Cataloging-in-Publication Data
Names: Bahr, Arthur, 1976– author.
Title: Chasing the Pearl-manuscript : speculation, shapes, delight / Arthur Bahr.
Description: Chicago ; London : The University of Chicago Press, 2025. | Includes bibliographical references and index.
Identifiers: LCCN 2024020863 | ISBN 9780226835358 (cloth) | ISBN 9780226835365 (ebook)
Subjects: LCSH: British Library. Manuscript. Cotton Nero A. x. | Pearl (Middle English poem) | Sir Gawain and the Green Knight. | Patience (Middle English poem) | Purity (Middle English poem) | English poetry—Middle English, 1100–1500—History and criticism. | Manuscripts, English (Middle)
Classification: LCC PR1972.G353 B34 2025 | DDC 821/.109—dc23/eng/20240525
LC record available at https://lccn.loc.gov/2024020863

♾ This paper meets the requirements of ANSI/NISO Z39.48-1992 (Permanence of Paper).

To the makers of the Pearl-Manuscript

CONTENTS

INTRODUCTION

This is a book about a book: the small, cropped, somewhat ragged but brightly illustrated volume now known formally, and rather forbiddingly, as British Library MS Cotton Nero A.x/2.[1] The fame and beauty of its four Middle English poems have given it sobriquets beyond the shelfmark, however, which are more familiar and intimate: it is also the Gawain-Manuscript or, as I will call it, the Pearl-Manuscript.[2] The fact that *Pearl, Cleanness, Patience*, and *Sir Gawain and the Green Knight* (all of these modern editorial titles) survive here alone means that the literary character of these poems is bound up in this particular object, their material text. Although the identity, number, and intentions of those who collectively crafted it cannot be pinned down, this book will show that analyzing the Pearl-Manuscript's intersecting aesthetic effects, across linguistic, visual, and codicological acts of shaping, affords fresh appreciation of its poems' beauty—and may even transform our sense of what a medieval book can be.

For in many ways, the Pearl-Manuscript is just as strange and unique as the poems it contains. Rather plain for the vessel of such remarkable verse,

1. This designation has its own material history, which touches the concerns of this monograph. In the seventeenth century, Sir Robert Cotton had the fourteenth-century book of poems that is my subject here bound together with two apparently unrelated Latin volumes from different centuries. This composite volume of three originally separate books was disaggregated by the British Library in 1964, and the two Latin volumes rebound together as "Cotton Nero A.x/1," hence the formal designation "Cotton Nero A.x/2" for the "original" Pearl-Manuscript. As we will see, however, terms like "original" and "authentic" are especially vexed with this particular codex. On this complex postmedieval history and its resonance with *Sir Gawain and the Green Knight*, in particular, see Hines, "'The Best Boke of Romance.'" My opening formulation is indebted to Mary C. Fuller's brilliant book about a very different kind of book, Richard Hakluyt's *Principal Navigations* (*Lines Drawn across the Globe*, 1).

2. I hyphenate "Pearl-Manuscript" instead of using the more traditional "*Pearl* [or *Gawain*] manuscript" so as to register the necessary connection between poems and object—since they survive only here—and to accord them comparable status. Thanks to Kyle Stevens for helping me think through the stakes of that hyphen.

it is also very small: now less than 5 × 7 inches, with the area ruled for text smaller still at "approximately 3¾ × 5¾ inches."[3] A. S. G. Edwards has called it "the only surviving Middle English manuscript consisting solely of alliterative poems."[4] Even the scribal hand is unusual to the point of uniqueness: C. E. Wright notes its "very individualistic small, sharp, angular character," and Anthony Petti calls it "probably one of the most distinctive and easily recognizable book hands of the period, though this is the only example that has come to light."[5] Likewise unusual is its presentation of vernacular poems in a textura (or *textualis*) hand, such "woven" or "tied" letters being more often reserved for "bibles, psalters, books of hours, missals, and other scriptural and liturgical manuscripts," as Seamus Dwyer has noted in an important study of the manuscript's hand.[6] The curiosity of the text-block's visual character is heightened by hints that the scribe was "happier with anglicana than the textura he or his employer felt was called for," as A. I. Doyle suggests; Joel Fredell likewise sees a scribe "practiced in cursive anglicana but not terribly familiar with textura, trying to create a book hand."[7] Such evidence of deliberate care, coupled with occasional clumsiness of execution,

3. Edwards, "The Manuscript," 197. Malcolm Andrew and Ronald Waldron give an overall measurement of 171 × 123 mm in their introduction to the Folio Society facsimile of the manuscript (2015), 17; so does Kathleen Scott (*Later Gothic Manuscripts*, 2:66–68, cat. no. 12). This measurement is consistent with the range (165–173 × 115–125 mm) that Alexandra Gillespie and Daniel Wakelin found in measuring seven sample pages during their examination of the manuscript; I thank them for sharing their observations, which inform my analysis at several points. The 171 × 123 mm figure of Andrew and Waldron yields a "proportion" (width divided by height) of 0.72, which makes the manuscript feel slightly squat for its size since "medieval manuscripts cluster around a particular shape," with a proportion "about 0.7," as Daniel Sawyer has shown (*Reading English Verse*, 92). The manuscript's higher proportion suggests that more may have been cropped from the tops and/or bottoms of pages, which is consistent with what can be seen of its effects (e.g., top of folio 57/61r).

4. Edwards, "The Manuscript," 197.

5. Wright, *English Vernacular Hands*, 15 (quoted in Edwards, "The Manuscript," 197); Petti, *English Literary Hands*, 49 (quoted in Roberts, "Hand and Script").

6. Dwyer, "Reading the Tied Letters," 21. I join Dwyer and Roberts ("Hand and Script") in seeing the hand as basically textura, rather than a hybrid of textura and cursive as others have suggested; see further Dwyer, 18–19. At the same time, Fredell is right to note that the scribe's "yogh-like zed for final 's' [-ȝ] . . . simply is not a glyph used in textura," but rather "reflects Anglo-French writing habits, and suggests a scribe doing specifically notarial work, much of it in French still in this period" ("*Pearl*-Poet Manuscript in York," 28). The hand thus consistently gestures in at least two different directions at once, another aspect of the manuscript's multiplicity.

7. Doyle, "English Books," 166; Fredell, "*Pearl*-Poet Manuscript in York," 13.

resonates with other highly wrought, slightly imperfect shapes that we will find across the codex.[8]

Moreover, and uniquely among surviving Middle English literary manuscripts from this period, it features twelve illustrations, nearly all of them full-page: four of *Pearl*, two each of *Cleanness* and *Patience*, and four of *Sir Gawain and the Green Knight*. Kathleen Scott calls this the earliest such pictorial program extant in the Middle English corpus, another facet of the Pearl-Manuscript's outlier status.[9] Long disdained for their supposed crudeness, the images were added some while after the poems were copied and, as Maidie Hilmo in particular has demonstrated, constitute an important early set of interpretations of them.[10] Yet while its illustrations may be innovative, the manuscript's old-fashioned decorative motifs complement its "quirkily homespun" feel.[11] This two-way temporal pull creates historical and aesthetic tension in the object itself.

As this brief description suggests, the Pearl-Manuscript has many makers even if it contains the work of only one poet (and this itself is not a fully settled question, or one likely to be so): the scribe and possible later corrector,[12]

8. Such clumsiness can be seen in the scribe's occasional challenges with the ruling, especially early in the manuscript, e.g., the bottom of folio 54/58v; and in the awkwardly scrunched execution of the bottom lines of multiple pages (e.g., 46/50r), as if the scribe has mismanaged the text-block above but remains committed to the manuscript's rule of thirty-six lines to the page. (Some few exceptions to this rule will inform chap. 5.)

9. "[N]o other manuscript with a Middle English text had, so far as is known, been illustrated with pictures in this [full-page] format, and only a few others . . . had been illustrated at all" (Scott, *Later Gothic Manuscripts*, 2:66, cat. no. 12).

10. Among Hilmo's important series of essays are "Creating a Visual Narrative," "Did the Scribe Draw," and "Re-Conceptualizing." See also Queen, "Negative Affect," and McGillivray and Duffy, "New Light."

11. Dwyer, "Reading the Tied Letters," 16. Roberts notes that the manuscript's "simple pen-flourishing, usual from Romanesque book production onwards but by this time perhaps less fashionable, may help create an old-fashioned feel" ("Hand and Script," 2–3). Kathryn Kerby-Fulton concludes: "The *Gawain* scribe, even if he was writing in the Ricardian period, was looking back" (*Opening up Medieval Manuscripts*, 57).

12. In her edition of *Cleanness*, Kenna Olsen notes a "corrector's hand, in darker ink than the original, . . . evident in some passages throughout the manuscript with some important interventions in the text of *Cleanness*" (5). Edwards also notes the corrections but is less confident that they are necessarily later or in another hand ("The Manuscript," 197). Whether later or not, the otherness of the corrector's practice from the main scribe's is clear in cursive features like the final *-s* of *weldes* on folio 80/84r, which contrasts pointedly with the usual textura final *-s* at the ends of lines just above and below.

illustrator (if different from the scribe),[13] colorist(s), medieval patron(s), and later owners, all the way through to its modern editors, curators, and digitizers, whose choices shape our interpretive affordances.[14] These extra-authorial agents have not always been guided chiefly by the poems' literary qualities, and some of their decisions invite interpretation more obviously than others. Nevertheless, they all exist on a spectrum of interpretability and can thus legitimately be approached from multiple methodological perspectives, with a range of scholarly goals. Building on that premise, one overarching argument of this book is that the Pearl-Manuscript rewards close reading for its creative interplay of text, image, and matter.

Crucially, this invitation inheres not just in codicological features such as decorated initials, ruling and quiring structures, and marginal paraph marks, but also in the poems' own frequent references to elements of medieval manuscript culture, which reinforce the concrete, often idiosyncratic "thinginess" of the book in which they singularly survive.[15] Paper and parchment, stylus and *glayre* ("the clarified white of an egg . . . used in the illumination of manuscripts"), and the fluttering leaves of a book torn in two all form the basis of powerful similes in the poems.[16] Such imagery suggests a strong sense of the dual significance, moral and aesthetic, that the *materia* of literary production could convey, and of their complex mediating effects. The poems and the manuscript thus create a feedback loop, each encouraging analysis in terms of the other: the poems display what I will call a scribal or bookish sensibility, which recalls the book in our hands and reinforces how uncannily it shapes its poems.[17]

13. Hilmo argues that the scribe also produced the original, pen-and-ink drawings in "Did the Scribe Draw," and "Re-Conceptualizing."

14. On digitization and remediation in this context, see Foys, "Remanence of Medieval Media," and "Medieval Manuscripts." Michelle Warren uses the evolution of a single fascinating textual object as a powerful lens for such questions, among others, in *Holy Digital Grail*.

15. On "thinginess": this project owes an ambient but important debt to Brown, "Thing Theory," and the scholarly conversations generated by that provocative essay.

16. On *glayre* in *Pearl*, see Griffin, "Instruction and Inspiration." Thanks to Michael Johnston for this reference.

17. In imagining "the book in our hands," I do not dispute that these poems may likely have been performed aloud along the lines famously proposed by Joyce Coleman (*Public Reading*). The sonic richness of *Pearl* begs to be heard, and we will see that *Patience*, in particular, makes important appeals to aurality. But interest in the visual unites all four poems, as Sarah Stanbury in particular has shown (*Seeing the Gawain-Poet*), and since I focus chiefly on the poems as manifest in the Pearl-Manuscript, the visual and tactile will be my more usual sensory lenses.

The uncanny is too Freudian and too negative for what I really mean, however, which is more like "supereffability," a term usefully coined by Cristina Maria Cervone to describe "an understanding of sacred fullness enacted through form."[18] This formulation especially befits the aesthetic and devotional landscape of the manuscript's opening poem, *Pearl*, whose otherworldly beauty intimates the supereffability of God's grace by means of paradoxical inversions of earthly, logical hierarchies. The difficulty of its lessons is sweetened by the gorgeous lushness of its highly wrought structures, which adumbrate divine plenitude by creating meaning across many axes and in many registers: formal, lexical, mathematical, and more. *Pearl*'s aesthetic of "more," a word that organizes two of its twenty sections (one more than any other such word), invites reading for more. I will argue that this "more" is a mode of the supereffable, which expands outward into the manuscript itself, enhancing and at times even evoking its poems' own intricate construction.[19] Reading for more involves finding, and taking seriously, the complex shapes and symmetries manifest in the Pearl-Manuscript across time, media, and recoverable intention. In short, it involves *speculation*.

By speculation, I mean to reach back into that word's medieval history, which chapter 1 lays out more fully. Briefly, medieval speculation involves looking closely at what remains in order to trace the outlines of something not fully knowable, occluded but real. A midpoint between cognition and contemplation, speculation is operationally intellective, but subtended by feeling.[20] It mediates between—and therefore needs—both. More than any other medieval poem I know, *Pearl* inspires devotion, even as its coruscating patterns delight and exercise the mind.[21] By inviting speculation in this technical, historicized sense, *Pearl* turns the Pearl-Manuscript into a locus of speculation today. To so regard it is to embark on a kind of time

18. Cervone, *Poetics of the Incarnation*, 5.

19. Reichardt makes a version of this argument across a series of important essays: among them "Paginal Eyes," "Counted," and "Several Illuminations." Although he occasionally overlooks or explains away inconvenient details to help the number symbolism work, a point to which I return in chap. 5, many of the patterns he uncovers are striking enough to invite speculation.

20. On the complex, sometimes contested relation between contemplation and cognition in the Middle Ages, see in particular Despres, "Sacramentals and Ghostly Sights"; Karnes, *Imagination, Meditation, and Cognition*; and Johnson, *Staging Contemplation*.

21. Sarah McNamer, for example, calls it "the most intricate poem ever wrought in English" and "one of the most moving and beautiful poems ever composed" ("Literariness," 1433), while David Coley praises its "palimpsestic multiplicity [and] astonishing formal design" (*Death and the Pearl Maiden*, 218). Comparably eloquent encomia abound.

travel,[22] not to the as-it-really-was of the manuscript or its poems' origins but rather to a version of the multifaceted interpretive landscape initiated by *Pearl*, which is further refracted through the following poems and the codex itself.

The Pearl-Manuscript is such a remarkable outlier among the corpus of surviving books from medieval England that its broader significance to book history may seem limited. Yet for that very reason, it is also a fascinating limit-case that should expand our understanding of what a medieval manuscript may attempt or achieve. In that sense, my project neither disputes nor weakens the recent conclusion of Daniel Wakelin, that the scribes of many Chaucer, Gower, and Lydgate manuscripts "between the late 1300s and early 1500s . . . sometimes show little regard for the material form of texts," and in fact generally "wanted people to read the poem, not to look too closely at the book."[23] The Pearl-Manuscript is exceptional in rewarding both perspectives, the reader's and the viewer's: not just for its illustrations (obviously meant to be looked at) but also for its interplay of words, images, and material construction more broadly. I regard this dual perspective, reader + viewer, as one of the Pearl-Manuscript's many aesthetics of more, which as we will see are closely linked to its spiritual concerns.

Indeed, the secular focus of Wakelin's principal texts (Chaucer's *Tales* and *Troilus*, Hoccleve's *Regiment of Princes*, and Lydgate's *Troy Book* and *Siege of Thebes*) and his manuscripts' mostly later provenance may lead to different conclusions than those suggested by the Pearl-Manuscript, whose core—composition, initial construction, and copying—dates from the early part of his period and whose contents are mostly (some would say thoroughly) devotional.[24] Joel Fredell's association of the Pearl-Manuscript with religious book production in Yorkshire is apposite here.[25] So too is Jessica Brantley's analysis of British Library MS Additional 37049, an illustrated Carthusian manuscript that she has shown "collectively train[s] the reader in performative methods of devotional reading."[26] For although it is significantly earlier

22. For such asynchronous aspirations, I am indebted to the work of Carolyn Dinshaw, especially *How Soon Is Now?*, as well as to David Hadbawnik, *Postmodern Poetry and Queer Medievalisms*.

23. Wakelin, *Immaterial Texts*, 8–9.

24. Recent monographs foregrounding the theological commitments of all four poems include Campbell, *Gawain-Poet*; Hatt, *God and the Gawain-Poet*; and Spyra, *Epistemological Perspective*.

25. Fredell, "*Pearl*-Poet Manuscript in York."

26. Brantley, *Reading in the Wilderness*, 22. For a helpful introduction to Additional 37049, see Brantley, *Medieval English Manuscripts*, 276–96.

and illustrated quite differently, I will argue that the Pearl-Manuscript achieves similar effects: from its choice and sequencing of texts to its paratext and images, it is a pedagogical compilation in the art of speculation.

Speculation involves finding beauty in expanding one's perspective. It therefore offers a model for appreciating how the Pearl-Manuscript's cross-temporal, multimedia network of aesthetic effects expands beyond the intentions of its many makers. Those who deem it a mistake, or category error, to approach codicological material with a literary-critical eye should therefore "[t]urne over the leef, and chese another tale," as Chaucer advises those who may be shocked by the effrontery of the *Miller's Tale* (1.3177).[27] This book enthusiastically mixes materials and methodologies since I believe that allowing diverse modes of analysis and objects of value to jostle against one another can refresh our perspective and, in that sense, afford new knowledge. My goal is therefore to sketch some of the shapes and delights that can emerge from looking closely, for a long time, at one illustrated book of medieval poems.

BACKGROUND

Scholarship on the Pearl-Manuscript has been in a state of productive ferment recently, thanks substantially to the Cotton Nero A.x Project's publication of a digital facsimile in 2012, followed by the British Library's own version of the same.[28] These digitization projects helped spur a series of important essays that have transformed our understanding of the codex, which now emerges as a more temporally complex and artistically subtle object than could readily be appreciated from the poor-quality print facsimile of the Early English Text Society, now a century old.[29] The Cotton Nero A.x Project is not complete at the time of this writing, but it has published the first of what promise to be revelatory essays on key features of the manuscript, as well as new editions of all four poems, based on extensive

27. All Chaucer quotations come from the third edition of *The Riverside Chaucer*.

28. See https://digitalcollections.ucalgary.ca/Browse/Collections/Gawain-Manuscript; http://www.bl.uk/manuscripts/Viewer.aspx?ref=cotton_ms_nero_a_x!2_f041r. Scholars owe an immense debt to Murray McGillivray, who heads the Cotton Nero A.x Project and currently hosts it from the University of Calgary; this digital curation has been instrumental in multiplying scholarly energy around the manuscript and its poems, as have McGillivray's own scholarly essays.

29. Gollancz, *Facsimile Reproduction of Cotton Nero A.x*. This facsimile uses a grayscale that makes the handwriting—already frequently cramped and idiosyncratic—nearly illegible in places, particularly in *Sir Gawain*. The illustrations are also reproduced in shades of gray, to the obvious detriment of analysis and appreciation.

in-person study of the manuscript and recent scientific advances.[30] These editions depart significantly from earlier ones, including those of Malcolm Andrew and Ronald Waldron (long an industry standard),[31] and their notes provide comparative and historical editorial data that enable readers to reach their own conclusions about contested readings.

Such cruces are numerous because the Pearl-Manuscript's idiosyncratic scribal hand, "slowly fading" ink, and frequently poor parchment quality often make it difficult to reliably distinguish various letter forms and combinations.[32] As we will see, these challenges are enhanced by the poems' multilingual lexical heritage and enthusiasm for wordplay—and their scribe's varied orthography—which often enable multiple interpretations of any particular set of graphemes. Recent reassessments of the basis of alliterative meter, meanwhile, have contributed another lens for rereading the poems, whose very words these developments have cumulatively put into a generative state of play.[33] Digital facsimiles enhance this play by enabling readers to check the manuscript and decide such questions for themselves—albeit through a screen, darkly.

Not coincidentally, one supposes, other aspects of scholarly consensus have also been revisited recently.[34] Two of the poems' most influential commentators, Marie Borroff and John M. Bowers, have revived the argument that *St. Erkenwald*, an alliterative poem surviving in a single,

30. See gawain-ms.ca; among those available at the time of this writing, Jane Roberts's essay "The Hand and Script" is particularly valuable, and all others are eagerly awaited. As this book went to press, the main website was unavailable due to technical difficulties, but until service there is restored, McGillivray has made the core materials available at https://wpsites.ucalgary.ca/gawain-ms/.

31. Andrew and Waldron, *Poems*. Typically I cite the more recent editions of the Cotton Nero A.x Project, by McGillivray, Olsen, and others, but since I am interested in the evolution of the poems' textual existence across time, we will frequently consider other editions, too.

32. Gollancz describes the ink as "slowly fading" in the introduction of his 1922 Early English Text Society facsimile (8). On the letter forms, Roberts writes that "*n* and *u* must be interpreted according to context (the use of the *v* shape initially is helpful); moreover the straight sides of *o* may lead to its misinterpretation as *u*. In addition, *c* and *t* are not always distinct, and in bitings *b* and ɪ may present difficulties to the reader" ("Hand and Script," 5). Particular letter combinations are even harder to distinguish, as we will see in chap. 2.

33. E.g., Cornelius, *Reconstructing Alliterative Verse*; and Weiskott, *English Alliterative Verse*. Metrical considerations also inform many of the emendations made by Putter and Stokes in their edition, *Works of the Gawain Poet*. See also Weiskott, "Alliterative Metre."

34. *A Companion to the Gawain-Poet* (ed. Brewer and Gibson) offers an excellent survey of the field as it existed around the turn of the century, especially Andrew, "Theories of Authorship," 23–33; and Spearing, "Poetic Identity," 35–51.

mid-fifteenth-century paper manuscript, should be added to the works of the Pearl-Poet.[35] Since then, important studies have also suggested revising the poems' dating and geography, back toward a more midcentury, Edwardian rather than Ricardian date, and potentially northward, to Yorkshire.[36] Long-standing conundrums around questions of single authorship, biographical identification, and patronage are even now being considered afresh by leading voices in the field. Although of obvious literary-historical interest, however, such debates are not central to this book, which mostly does not depend upon precisely when or where, by whom or for whom, these poems were written.[37] Instead, my methodological framework and literary interpretations are historicized chiefly by the evolving materiality of the manuscript itself. Chasing the Pearl-Manuscript renders traditional questions of authorship largely moot, hence my title; for whether the product of one person or more, these poems survive only here, in a single scribal hand, and with illustrations whose stylistic similarities further propose this object as a complex aesthetic whole.

I emphasize the illustrations not just because they reinforce the poems' own internal emphasis on the visual, well established by Sarah Stanbury and others,[38] but also because they make the visual character of the page itself a site of reading, in two senses. The illustrations constitute interpretations, and in that sense readings, of the poems they depict; they also invite interpretation by the reader, and from there (upon reflection), perhaps rereading of the poem in question. As readings that shape further readings, they nicely perform the accretive nature of aesthetic meaning. Such play across media also prompts attention to page-shape(s), by which I mean not just *mise en page* as traditionally understood but also geometries as they emerge more multiply,

35. See Borroff, "Narrative Artistry," and Bowers, *Introduction to the Gawain Poet*.

36. E.g., Ingledew, *Sir Gawain*; McNamer, "Literariness"; and Fredell, "*Pearl*-Poet Manuscript in York."

37. Nevertheless, I can hardly write a book about the Pearl-Manuscript without offering my own opinion on authorship, however discreetly. Largely on the strength of the intertextuality displayed across the manuscript, I find the simplest and likeliest answer to be that the same person ("the Pearl-Poet") wrote all four poems. While such echoes do not prove common authorship, they reinforce the four poems' presentation as a coherent aesthetic whole. In Piotr Spyra's words: "The sheer volume of analogies and connections points to the presence of a deliberate design whose meaning can only be derived through a careful analysis of the totality of the manuscript's composite text" (*Epistemological Perspective*, 155). Jessica Brantley offers a helpful précis of how the Pearl-Manuscript suggests unity of purpose that need not depend upon single authorship in *Medieval English Manuscripts*, 217–31.

38. Stanbury, *Seeing the Gawain-Poet*.

and abstractly, upon the page and across the book. The poems' own delectation in shapes encourages such an approach, as the next section will show.

SHAPES

From *Pearl*'s perfect sphere and the "fayre forme3" of *Cleanness* to the "nobel poynt" of *Patience* and Sir Gawain's "endeles knot," the poems of the Pearl-Manuscript are famous for their shapes. Some of these appear within the poems, like Gawain's pentangle ("on his schene schelde schapen wat3 þe knot" ["the knot was shaped on his bright shield"], line 661); others take shape *as* the poems, mostly obviously *Pearl*, whose intricate stanza form and shimmering concatenation intimate the lost pearl's perfection and luster ("so rounde, so reken in vche araye" ["so richly round in each array"], line 5). These examples suggest how the word "shape," with its geometric and architectural associations, may offer a helpfully concrete subset of "form."[39] Such associations are true to the spirit of the poems, which delight in strikingly concrete depictions of material reality and physical craft: from the gorgeous ekphrasis of Solomon's sacred vessels in *Cleanness*, taken up in chapter 4, to the brittling scenes of *Sir Gawain*, which sculpt dead animals into fitting centerpieces for lordly feasts.

The poems' fascination with number and proportion, meanwhile, is both diegetic (Gawain's pentangle; *Pearl*'s obsession with the number twelve and *Cleanness*'s with three) and structural.[40] To take two famous examples: both *Pearl* and *Sir Gawain* have 101 stanzas, a suggestively not-quite-perfect number that evokes the slight-but-real climactic misstep of their respective

39. The plasticity of "form" as a concept in recent critical discourse is suggested by the wide-ranging subtitle of Caroline Levine's *Forms: Whole, Rhythm, Hierarchy, Network*. As Jessica Brantley has neatly observed, "form demands to be interpreted, and yet it means so very many different things" ("Reading the Forms of *Sir Thopas*," 438); and although she is referring to the material layout of a specific medieval poem, her point rings true more broadly. For promising paths forward, see *The Medieval Literary: Beyond Form*, ed. Meyer-Lee and Sanok.

40. Numerological analysis is a thriving subfield of Pearl-Manuscript studies. Important analyses of individual poems include Barootes, "Number Symbolism in *Pearl*"; Crawford, "Architectonics of *Cleanness*"; Fleming, "The Centuple Structure of *Pearl*"; Kean, "Numerical Composition in *Pearl*"; Kean, *The Pearl: An Interpretation*; Gilligan, "Numerical Composition"; Hieatt, "*Sir Gawain*: Pentangle, Luf-Lace, Numerical Structure"; and Käsmann, "Numerical Structure." Condren applies this approach to the four poems as a whole in *Numerical Universe*, whose conclusions Spyra adapts into a more theological (strongly Augustinian) framework in his *Epistemological Perspective*. On number play as performed by material features of the Pearl-Manuscript itself, like quiring and lineation, see Reichardt, "Counted."

protagonists: the Dreamer's mad plunge into the river that separates him from the Maiden, and Sir Gawain's more ambiguous failure at Castle Hautdesert. In each case, moreover, the seemingly imperfect additional stanza also creates a thematically resonant total number of lines as traditionally reckoned: 1212 and 2530, respectively. Such moments encourage us to find and take seriously other mathematical shapes in and around the poems.

As a physical object, the Pearl-Manuscript adds dimensions to its poems' fascination with number, geometry, and construction. This concreteness works against an idealizing, "old formalist" understanding of the poems, some of whose most celebrated literary shapes are complicated by their material realities. To take the first example cited above: 1212 seems like a perfect number of lines for *Pearl* largely because the poem thematizes the number twelve so insistently; but the manuscript actually contains 1211 lines of verse, and I believe scholars have been overconfident in attributing this anomaly to scribal corruption rather than authorial intent. As chapter 2 will show, the question's ultimate undecidability creates an enduring crux, which itself creates literary value by preventing the poem's beauties from being crystallized into static perfection; in Newtonian terms, they retain potential energy.

The 2530 lines of *Sir Gawain* would seem even more significant since the poem's 101 stanzas are further embedded within them: 2530 divided by 25 (the five squared of Gawain's pentangle) yields 101 with a remainder of 5—and 5 + 2525 = 2530. This method of reckoning, however, depends upon counting the poem's two-syllable "bobs" as poetic lines even though they never receive their own physical line in the manuscript: "a fact that not all advocates of number symbolism in the poems are disposed to discuss," as A. S. G. Edwards rightly notes.[41] Instead, the bobs are written off to the side, often one or two lines above the quatrain (or "wheel") whose *baba* rhyme scheme their *a*-rhyme initiates. I consider this complex sensory landscape, by which we usually see the bob before we hear it, in more detail in chapter 7. I mention it here as one concrete example of how the poems, illustrations, and codicological features of the Pearl-Manuscript all foreground the dynamic nature of sense perception, by which we assemble the incomplete, imperfect shapes that we encounter into some kind of provisional, evolving whole.[42] Such shapes might be letter forms, like the bobs of *Sir Gawain*, whose relation to a larger stanza we must parse; or paratextual features like

41. Edwards, "The Manuscript," 202.

42. See, e.g., Cannon's description of literary form as a process of becoming: the "*in*forming of raw materials according to the script of some idea," an inherently temporal phenomenon

decorated initials and paraph marks, both of which play important roles in shaping *Cleanness*, especially. These and other examples suggest that we may appreciate the poems more fully when we read them with attention to the manuscript's physical and visual cues.

Doing so is a necessarily subjective and interactive process, as Sonja Drimmer has shown.[43] I therefore draw inspiration from her and others including Sarah Kay, Arthur Russell, and Elaine Treharne, whose phenomenological readings of medieval manuscripts have yielded great interpretive riches.[44] As the following chapter will show, medieval speculation also concerns an evolving act of perception: that of coming to see the imprint of the Divine in the complex beauties of the sensible universe. In that sense, speculation is a form of appreciative, even devotional close reading. I will propose adapting this medieval practice into a way of reading the Pearl-Manuscript today, bearing in mind that "inherent within the book's fabric are joy, delight, and the *techne* and *poesis* of its makers as well as the spiritual hope or admonition, awe, guidance, or illumination of its contents," as Treharne has eloquently put it.[45] Such a perspective accords well with Rita Felski's observation that "interpretation can be respectful, even reverential in tone, with the critic adopting the role of a disciple or follower, aspiring to go beyond the text in service of the text, to aid in the revelation of hidden mysteries."[46]

("Form," 175). Arnheim frames the problem more concretely, and explicitly in terms of architecture, in *Dynamics of Architectural Form*. Thanks to Eugenie Brinkema for this reference and several helpful exchanges about form and shape.

43. Of the positivist lexicon in which attributional paleography, in particular, has tended to cloak itself, Drimmer writes: "Rather than anchoring our conclusions in a spurious rhetoric of conviction we might nurture the candor of a lyricism that describes the cognitive encounter with the apparently individualizing mark on the page." Doing so, she continues, must acknowledge "two ineluctable features of attribution: the scholar's embodied subjectivity and its essence as an act of response to a physical object" ("Connoisseurship," 458).

44. Kay writes: "By focusing on the page itself, as much as on what is written, drawn, or painted on it, I sketch a speculative phenomenology of the parchment book," which shows how "the page itself interferes in the reading experience" (*Animal Skins*, 3). This formulation will prove especially resonant when we turn to *Patience*. Russell proposes "a more meditative and iterative approach to the material . . . to realize the accumulative effects of slow and repetitious habits, of touch- and time-sensitive modes of meaning-making" ("Praying by Hand," 203). Treharne shows that medieval manuscripts "are archetypally phenomenal objects, dependent on sensory engagement for their fullest interpretation" (*Perceptions of Medieval Manuscripts*, 6); her concept of "architextuality" is congruent with my own interest in page-shape.

45. Treharne, *Perceptions of Medieval Manuscripts*, 122.

46. Felski, *Limits of Critique*, 57.

Doing so involves resisting the normative posture of critique, which as Felski has shown "proves a poor guide to the thickness and richness of our attachments."[47] Exhaustion with disenchantment helped animate the New Formalist movement that has shaped much of my scholarly practice, and insofar as "shape" is a subset of "form," reading for page-shape(s) is a kind of formalism.[48] As this book will show, the forms of the Pearl-Manuscript can sometimes best be approached like the forms of Middle English poems: with minute attention to the relation of part to whole, and with comparably engaged interest in their evolution across time.[49] Thus read, the Pearl-Manuscript's complex interplay of visual, textual, and material form sometimes constellates into arresting strangeness, turning its very page-shapes into literary art.[50]

Such moments are rare; most of the Pearl-Manuscript is made to be read, not looked at, to use Wakelin's terms. When speculative constellations do emerge, however, their rarity does not detract from their power. On the contrary: by offering to interrupt, or punctuate, our apprehension of an "immaterial text," they reground us in the material, which is one way the Pearl-Manuscript—like speculation itself—mediates between abstract ideal and sublunary reality. Wakelin has suggested that unadorned, unannotated pages may "evoke a history of reading as an imaginative process that lives in the mind as much as on the page: reading as mental, emotional absorption or attachment."[51] The Pearl-Manuscript absolutely inspires and rewards this kind of reading, but its poems' delight in material craft and artefactual

47. Felski, *Limits of Critique*, 17.

48. For an important early assessment of the movement, see Levinson, "What Is New Formalism?"

49. On the diachronic dimension of literary meaning, see in particular Dimock, "A Theory of Resonance," Holsinger, "'Historical Context' in Historical Context," Simpson, "Not Yet: Chaucer and Anagogy," and Strohm, "Historicity without Historicism?" For a compelling analysis of this process as manifest across a particular medieval book through time, see Warren, *Holy Digital Grail*.

50. Throughout, I use metaphors of constellation in the sense outlined by Walter Benjamin: "It's not that what is past casts its light on what is present, or what is present is light on what is past: rather, image is that wherein what has been comes together in a flash with the now to form a constellation. In other words: image is dialectic at a standstill" (*Arcades Project*, 462). See further Anderson, "Studies in Medieval Star-Gazing." The interactive nature of the constellation—we must choose to perceive the pattern in the stars, or on the page—resonates with Drimmer's comments on the subjective nature of paleographic analysis in "Connoisseurship."

51. Wakelin, *Immaterial Texts*, 184.

construction suggests that we should also take seriously its idiosyncratic blending of media, shape, and matter. I believe that coming to perceive the complex dialectic between these two modes of apprehension—the "immaterially" textual and the visual-material—constitutes an important component of the bookish delight that the Pearl-Manuscript affords.

Some of this complexity is perceptible immediately, while some emerges only upon reflective rereading. I therefore regard the poems' shapes as accumulative, in the sense that *Pearl* vitally informs *Cleanness*; *Patience* invites reading as an echo, reflection, or trace of the previous two poems; and *Sir Gawain* offers a delightful final trial of our speculative capacities as honed by the first three. Accordingly, I bear in mind both continuous through-readers, whose understanding evolves as they unpack the poems for the first time in their material context; and devoted rereaders, who bring some sense of the whole to whichever particular moment they happen upon or choose in returning to the manuscript. By imitating its structure, *Chasing the Pearl-Manuscript* seeks to offer an experience of reading its poems by (speculatively) turning their pages.[52] I therefore treat the four poems in the order they now appear, paying particular attention to how each one ends and the next begins. Such moments of suture are inherently interesting, and they often provoke the manuscript's multilayered temporal existence to flash into prominence.

THE CHASE

Chapter 1 offers a brief history of medieval speculation, proposing that a speculative sensibility seems to underwrite both *Pearl* and the poet's aesthetics as a whole; and, further, that an adapted form of medieval speculation might help us read the Pearl-Manuscript today. This is so partly thanks to its many forms of unknowability: anonymous author(s?), lost holograph, uncertain patronage and reception, and more. Chapter 2 uses *Pearl* to argue that such forms of lack (of other copies, certain knowledge, etc.) can prove interpretively fruitful by enabling the poem's "manifold singularity," as I have elsewhere termed it, to expand as modern scholars read into existence new versions of its literally incomparable words. The poem's own paradox-loving dreamscape especially invites such counterintuitive modes of analysis.

52. "Speculatively" because the Pearl-Manuscript is both book and museum piece: the vast majority of its readers will never turn its pages. I did so only after drafting all but one of this book's chapters.

Chapter 3 reads the four pages by which we turn from *Pearl* to *Cleanness*, folios 55/59v–57/61r, whose verbal and visual echoes create the kind of connective tissue by which this manuscript starts to cohere into a wrought, imperfect, temporally layered whole.[53] Chapter 4 focuses on one small piece of this connective tissue: marginal paraphs, which mark stanzas in *Pearl* and *Sir Gawain*, but in *Cleanness* and *Patience* instead reinforce an underlying, generally four-line syntactic rhythm. I argue that in *Cleanness*, the paraphs' interplay with the poem's syntax offers a handhold by which to grasp the contours of this strange and difficult poem. Its final page, folio 82/86r, amplifies this strangeness, for it is the only one in the manuscript to prominently feature both text and image: the last eleven lines of *Cleanness* run headlong into the depiction of Jonah being thrown to the whale, a scene central to the following *Patience*. Chapter 5 suggests that the complex move from *Cleanness* to *Patience* subtly reinforces the kind of intertextuality likewise perceptible across the Pearl-Manuscript as a whole; that it does so across multiple, sometimes overlapping midpoints further binds the book's two halves together.

The first poem of its second (approximate) half, *Patience*, performs this binding function by echoing the two previous poems in ways both obvious and subtle. The subtler echoes continue a motif developed earlier, of challenges to our speculative faculties. In *Cleanness*, these perceptual challenges emphasize the visual, most obviously God's writing hand, which inscribes judgment into the walls of Belshazzar's Feast; *Patience* instead dramatizes God's speaking voice, which Jonah perversely tries to ignore. This focus on aurality makes *Patience* something of an outlier in the manuscript, as Dwyer has noted.[54] Yet this very apartness enables its famous *poynt* to serve as the center (one meaning of the word in Middle English) of the manuscript's aesthetic and spiritual geometry. For even as it echoes *Pearl* and *Cleanness*, *Patience* also sets the stage for *Sir Gawain and the Green Knight*, in multiple dimensions.

These dimensions constellate remarkably across the opening of *Sir Gawain and the Green Knight*, folios 90/94v+91/95r. Chapter 7 argues that the poem's fascination with geometry, and the manuscript's broader fascination with

53. The manuscript includes two sets of foliation: an earlier set in pen, which numerates the first folio 37, and a later one in pencil, which numerates it 41. (These numerations date from the manuscript's inclusion, from the early modern period, in the tripartite volume described in n. 1.) The British Library uses the later, pencil numeration, but since scholars have not been consistent in which foliation they use when they cite only one (as they often do), I cite both sets in the interests of clarity.

54. Dwyer, "Reading the Tied Letters," 3.

time, are embedded within the beheading scene depicted on 90/94v. It also suggests that creative counting may shed new light on an enduring crux: how to construe the (non)lineation of the bobs within the manuscript, noted earlier. Rather than imposing a singular denouement upon the endless knot of *Sir Gawain*, chapter 8 reads the poem through three, occasionally overlapping threads that look outside the poem proper: back in the codex to *Cleanness*; outward to Chaucer's *Squire's Tale*; and through the Pearl-Manuscript's complex concluding pages, 124/128v–126/130v. Brief final reflections propose the kaleidoscope as a metaphor for the Pearl-Manuscript, for its delights are likewise refreshable and interactive.

DELIGHT

Delight is also the lexical hinge on which the denouement of *Pearl* unfolds. As the concatenating word of the penultimate section, it traces the descent of the Dreamer's spiritual delight from the Celestial Lamb and Procession of Virgins into the natural if misguided human desire to hold his lost beloved once more, "for luf-longyng in gret delit" ("for love-longing in great delight," line 1152). It drives him into the stream that separates them:

> **Delyt** me drof in yȝe and ere,
> my maneȝ mynde to maddyng malte.
> Quen I seȝ my frely, I wolde be þere
> byȝonde þe water þaȝ ho were walte.[55]

A few stanzas later, expelled from his vision for this error, the Dreamer reflects ruefully that he might have seen more if only he hadn't wanted more:

> To þat Prynceȝ paye hade I ay bente
> and ȝerned no **more** þen watȝ me geuen . . .
> to **mo** of His mysterys I hade ben dryuen.
> Bot ay wolde man of happe **more** hente
> þen moȝten by ryȝt vpon hem clyuen. . . .[56]

55. "Delight drove in through my eyes and ears, melting my man's mind into madness. When I saw my lovely one, I wanted to be there, though she was cast beyond the water" (lines 1153–56).

56. "Had I always bent to that Prince's pleasure, and yearned for no **more** than was given to me, . . . I would/might have been led to **more** of His mysteries. But people always want to seize **more** favor than is rightly allotted to them" (lines 1189–90, 1194–96, emphasis added).

The association of delight with desire for "more" seems homiletic here, but it also recalls the poem's own exuberant aesthetic of more, reinforced by the word's repetition above.

Pearl thus performs a version of literature's traditional association with forms of excess: unlike a phone book, say, a "literary" text offers more than can be paraphrased.[57] In the Pearl-Manuscript especially, this "more" is often aligned with visual forms of delight.[58] *Pearl*'s luminescence is the lure that draws us into the manuscript, enticing us through the less obviously gratifying textures of *Cleanness* and *Patience* before rewarding (and testing) us with the alluring, shape-shifting chivalric otherworld of *Sir Gawain*. There is a potential analogy, in other words, between the Dreamer's delight and the reader's; and just as the former is morally ambivalent, so too the pleasures of literature have often been regarded with suspicion.[59] The term "pleasure" itself carries unavoidably Freudian and psychoanalytic associations in literary scholarship, which is one reason I adopt "delight" as a leitmotif instead: it seems less entangled in discourses not central to this project and thus offers a blanker slate to work with. Without minimizing pleasure's frequent importance in these poems, I therefore propose *delight* as a broader and less technical term.[60]

"Less technical" is a feature, not a bug here, for in foregrounding delight, I am conscious of being an amateur; I am no affect theorist. Yet the amateur's perspective can offer queer insights, as Carolyn Dinshaw and others have shown.[61] I have also been inspired by Myra Seaman's compelling account of

57. Defining the literary in terms of "words [that] are in excess of their abstractable meaning," to quote Terry Eagleton, has a long history; he is channeling the early twentieth century's Russian formalists (*Literary Theory*, 2). This definition is certainly open to criticism (including by Eagleton, just a few pages later), but I continue to find it useful, particularly in such deft hands as Nolan, "Lydgate's Worst Poem," and Otter, "Aesthetics in All Things," among many others.

58. On the period's pervasive association of desire with the visual, and the reformist anxieties this association provoked, see Stanbury, *Visual Object of Desire*. More generally, and with greater focus on optics per se, see Akbari, *Seeing through the Veil*, and Biernoff, *Sight and Embodiment*.

59. See Felski, *Limits of Critique*, 14–51.

60. On pleasure, see Staples, "Pure Pleasure." Thanks to him for fruitful conversations about these terms.

61. E.g., Dinshaw, *How Soon Is Now?* and "All Kinds of Time." See further Halberstam, *Queer Art of Failure*. Indeed, there is something queer about the Pearl-Manuscript's many curiosities, intricacies, and slight imperfections, a point Queen makes of its illustrations in particular ("Negative Affect"). It feels earnest, like a passion project, in spite yet also because of the occasional awkwardness of its construction.

"the emotional allure" of Oxford, Bodleian Library MS Ashmole 61, which informs her "aim to discern this single manuscript's multiplicity, to document and appreciate the whole ecology of the book-in-time."[62] Finding multiplicity in singularity is one of my chief aims as well. It was delight in the verbal artistry and intricate patterns of *Pearl* and *Sir Gawain* that first drew me to medieval literature, as they have so many others. All four poems clearly delight in their own craftsmanship and thereby make that delight central to their devotional aesthetics: not just the supereffable glories of *Pearl* but also *Cleanness*'s reverent ekphrases of artefactual construction, both of which embody versions of the "more" thematized in the passage from *Pearl* quoted above. Delighting in the capacity of language "to express *more* than it says" is one feature of an "incarnational poetic" as described by Cervone, which "entice[s] readers to notice, ruminate, delight in, and wonder at the capaciousness of metaphor, at how a figure may express *more* than the sum of its parts."[63] The poems of the Pearl-Manuscript are not all equally "incarnational" in Cervone's sense, but her evocative terms nicely capture their delight in testing the boundaries of form, language, and signification itself.

This delight serves to instruct, for it invites readers to find beauty in paradoxical modes of thought and expression—even in logical contradiction. As Laura Ashe has shown, the many irresolvable paradoxes of Christianity meant that much "medieval thought was continually pushed toward the possibility of true contradictions, despite the constant reaffirmation of their impossibility imposed by classical logic."[64] She argues, and I agree, that "this tension gives rise to extreme creativity in thought, and to a moral and ethical epistemology that has a great deal to teach us," since our acceptance or refusal of the logical existence of true contradictions ("dialetheism") cannot dispel our experience of them in life.[65] The tension caused by such contra-

62. Seaman, *Objects of Affection*, 1, 38. The "affective literacy training" Seaman finds in Ashmole 61 is consonant with some of the pedagogical effects we will find in the Pearl-Manuscript (*Objects of Affection*, 2).

63. Cervone, *Poetics of the Incarnation*, 4–5, emphasis added.

64. Ashe, "How to Read Both," 131. She notes that Christian belief in the incarnation, for example, "appears inherently contradictory, for man and God are subjects with negative relation: man is not God and God is not man. . . . The only resolution to this contradiction is the miraculous mystery at the center of the faith" (114)—hence the appeal of an "incarnational poetics" as described by Cervone.

65. Ashe, "How to Read Both," 131. She concludes: "Very few philosophers accept dialetheism, the existence of true contradictions. No one disputes, however, that life as it is lived can seem overwhelmed by them," noting Gayatri Chakravorty Spivak's insistence on "the

dictions can cause crisis, as Ashe's acute analysis of the pardon-tearing scene in *Piers Plowman* makes clear.[66] Yet tension (literally "stretching," from Latin *tendere*) can also expand our understanding by stretching our perspective beyond its usual or daily capacities; and like many forms of challenging exercise, this process can ultimately be pleasurable.[67] As many fine studies have shown, the poems of the Pearl-Manuscript especially invite such perspectival expansion. I hope to add angles to these perspectives, and further to show that the manuscript itself, in how it sequences and packages its poems, deepens their spiritual and literary power.

So, if "the literary" and its delights are best conceived as participants in an axiological process of valuing, as Robert Meyer-Lee has recently proposed, then one argument of this book is that the Pearl-Manuscript's many forms of artful complexity—most obviously that of its four poems, but also of its illustrations and material construction—merit investment in its literary value today.[68] I take such value-creating literary effects to include multiple and shifting meanings, allusiveness and elusiveness, resistance to denotative paraphrase, and openness to a wide range of conflicting, even contradictory interpretations and interpretive modes: all versions of "literary-as-excess" consonant with the aesthetics of "more" of the Pearl-Manuscript itself.[69] Many of these objects of value—complexity, ambivalence, multiple meanings held in tension—overlap with those of New Criticism, whose ghost literary

urgent necessity, in a global age, of 'learning to live with contradictory instructions.' Medieval thinkers were much better than we are at seeing these contradictions as the nature of reality" (146, quoting Spivak, *Aesthetic Education*, 1).

66. Ashe, "How to Read Both," 134–37.

67. Here we should recall St. Augustine's observation, "both that it is pleasanter in some cases to have knowledge communicated through figures, and that what is attended with difficulty in the seeking gives greater pleasure in the finding" (*On Christian Doctrine*, bk. 2, 6.8).

68. In *The Problem of Literary Value*, Meyer-Lee describes "literary value as emerging by means of an activity coextensive with its conception as a quality, an activity performed by actors within a network . . . and an activity that is a social fact integral to the phenomenon of the literary and yet . . . neither singular nor necessarily stable in character" (70–71). His position is thus "a reversal of the common conception of literary value as a function of the nature of the literary, proposing instead that the category of the literary is a function of the activity of valuing," by which "we register a text as literary when we ascribe value to some aspect of its perceived manner" (81).

69. Such objects of value are most often regarded as textual phenomena, but as demonstrated by considerable scholarship over the past decade, in particular, they can also emerge from the relation between literary and codicological form. This scholarship has often drawn in various ways on the "New Philology" of the 1990s, on which see Sarah Kay, "Analytical Survey 3."

scholarship has not yet fully appeased, as Meyer-Lee rightly notes.[70] Yet valuing such phenomena is not necessarily anachronistic, as Mary Carruthers has shown in important studies of medieval beauty and of "sweetness" (*dulcedo* or *suavitas*) in particular, whose "most interestingly medieval aspect . . . is that it is not just one thing, but has a contrarian nature that includes within itself its opposites: bitter, salt, and sour."[71] Such aestheticization (or "valuing," in Meyer-Lee's terms) of opposition recalls Ashe's account of the prominence of "true contradictions" in medieval philosophy.

As Cervone and others have shown, delight in metaphor and wordplay offered medieval writers a way of approaching such contradictions, which the poems of the Pearl-Manuscript perform with exquisite beauty. I believe that studying such beauty has the potential to make us more sensitive, ethical actors. Certainly that is one argument of *Pearl*, whose narrator's instruction takes shape across verbal and formal patterns whose beautiful complexity intimates the more capacious, less narcissistic perspective he must try to embrace. As the following chapter will show, medieval speculation proposes something comparable: that delight in the intricate beauties of the sensible universe can conduce to higher spiritual understanding. It is therefore striking that the design of the Pearl-Manuscript itself—the sensible universe in which these poems' intricate beauties singularly survive—should often work in concert with the poems it contains, adding more to their meaning today.

Delight features prominently in the following chapter's discussion of speculation as well, so I conclude here by recalling Glending Olson's observation that "literary delight makes something happen."[72] One thing delight in the Pearl-Manuscript makes happen is the sort of "reading as mental, emotional absorption or attachment" that Wakelin plausibly associates with plain pages, whose "emptiness might reflect a latent feeling that too complex a page was detrimental to the text."[73] Such respectful deference is suggested by the Pearl-Manuscript's long stretches of perfectly regular, minimally adorned verse. The relatively few suggestive or arresting exceptions to this rule create a dialectic between rule and exception that offers a resonant material analogue to the poems' own, often "perfectly imperfect" structures

70. Meyer-Lee, *The Problem of Literary Value*, 19–69.

71. Carruthers, "Sweetness," 1000. See further her *Experience of Beauty*.

72. Olson, *Literature as Recreation*, 232. See further Fradenburg, "Living Chaucer."

73. Wakelin, *Immaterial Texts*, 184–89.

(101 stanzas, etc.). Whether such imperfections are intentional or accidental is impossible to know; contemplating them therefore requires speculation. Speculation is thus the means, and delight the motive, by which I chase the Pearl-Manuscript. Speculation shapes my delight, and the delight I hope others may find in this remarkably crafted, ever-elusive book of poems.

ONE

IN PRAISE OF SPECULATION

This chapter draws inspiration from Bernard Cerquiglini's attempts to find value in a disparaged phenomenon.[1] For him, this was textual variance, long dismissed as so much scribal corruption; for me, it is speculation, with its unsavory whiff of intellectually irresponsible guesswork. Speculation played an important role in medieval philosophy and theology, however, and I believe that drawing on its practice, by understanding its evolution, may offer a refreshed perspective on medieval literature. It may also have methodological implications for engaging with the many forms of unknowability that readers of medieval books and texts so often face. The brief history of speculation that follows will lay the groundwork for my broader argument, pursued across the book as a whole, that the poems of the Pearl-Manuscript display a strongly "speculative" sensibility, which the manuscript itself complements and enhances.

The negative associations of speculation in English are generally post-medieval: the word first designates mere surmise or underinformed supposition in 1575, for example, and unscrupulous financial wheeling-and-dealing in the eighteenth century.[2] Chaucer gives us its earliest surviving English attestation when he has Lady Philosophy opine that "the soules of men moten nedes be more fre whan thei loken hem in the speculacioun or lokynge of the devyne thought."[3] By adding *lokynge* to his otherwise quite literal translation from Boethius's Latin, Chaucer foregrounds his neologism's connection with vision, emphasizing this addition by means of its punning similarity

1. Cerquiglini, *In Praise of the Variant.*

2. *Oxford English Dictionary* (accessed July 2023, https://doi.org/10.1093/OED/5095878118), s.v. "speculation, n.," meaning II.6.c, II.8.

3. "Human souls are necessarily freer when they lock themselves in speculation, or gazing upon the divine mind" (*Boece*, 5.pr.2.26–28, *Riverside Chaucer*; emphasis added). Boethius's original reads: "Humanas uero animas liberiores quidem esse necesse est cum se in mentis diuinae speculatione conseruant."

to the earlier verb *loken*.[4] Speculation derives from Latin *specere* (to look at, behold), also the root of *speculum* (mirror), *specula* (watchtower), and *species* (appearance, form, or beauty). In addition to the sense of spiritual contemplation that it has in the *Boece*, other attested meanings in Middle English include the power of sight; a show or spectacle; theory, or theoretical reasoning; and, by extension, a discipline or branch of knowledge.[5]

Why should any of these various, largely obsolete meanings be of practical import today? My answer is that they offer a powerful way of learning from the past: of finding in past words, texts, and practices unanticipated ways of reimagining and reshaping our present activities. Such learning *from* the past is an activity both more difficult and, I believe, more vital than simply learning *about* the past. In the discussion that follows, I draw on Nicholas Watson's argument, in a pair of important articles, that we should be willing to use "the past's words," as he puts it, to inform scholarly method today.[6] I will argue that medieval speculation offers one model for intellectual and affective engagement with a perceptible but not-fully-knowable Other. For the medieval philosophers and theologians discussed here, that Other was the Christian God. It need not be so for us, however, since the medieval history of speculation is one of continual adaptation and reinvention to serve changing intellectual norms and objects of value, as we will see.[7] Speculation offered a way of coming to grips with (cognitively), by finding beauty in (affectively), the never-fully-knowable patterns of the cosmos. As such, it

4. In context, *loken* must mean "lock" here, but it looks identical to the Middle English word for "look" that yields *lokynge*. It is additionally clever, given the passage's emphasis on sight, that this is a visual pun: the two meanings of *loken* have different vowel lengths but are spelled the same. On the potential power of this *loken*/*loken* pun in the poems of the Pearl-Manuscript, see Dwyer, "Reading the Tied Letters," 8.

5. *Middle English Dictionary* (accessed August 14, 2023, https://quod.lib.umich.edu/m/middle-english-dictionary/dictionary/MED42048), s.v. "speculation, n."

6. Watson, "Desire for the Past," 97. On the question of affect and empathy in scholarly writing and medieval mysticism, he argues that we should "be open to adapt the hermeneutics of empathy as described by these medieval mystics, and of course by many others, to our own ends as modern historians: a project that, taken seriously, will force us to think over and over again about our investments in the past, but in a manner that can include those investments as part of our study, as traces of the past in the present" (93). A subsequent essay demonstrates how "medieval imaginative theory . . . with its intense focus on the complexities of any act of mediation, might serve as a guide to our work as historians" (Watson, "Phantasmal Past," 4).

7. Some scholars use italicized Latin *speculatio* to designate the concept and practice whose history I trace here, presumably to inoculate it from the unsavory associations of its modern reflex. Since I wish rather to emphasize connections between past and present, I use modern English "speculation" throughout.

may be useful for a field, like ours, that is always grappling with the unknown: nameless authors, lost holographs, defaced miniatures, uncertain variants.

Such a theorized and historicized speculation represents my attempt to move beyond the sternly detached, "critical" mode whose limits Rita Felski has persuasively urged us to recognize.[8] Within manuscript studies, empiricism is comparable to critique in that it has long exerted normative force upon the field. This is understandable, for many important questions about old books have right and wrong answers that should be sought out and respected. Its importance can sometimes lend empiricism undeserved hegemony as method or object of value, however, which is why I propose speculation as a positive, noncompetitive alternative: a kind of interpretive "close looking" that, like many forms of literary scholarship, is informed yet not wholly circumscribed by original intent or recoverable data. The Pearl-Manuscript is a good object on which to test this method since it has long inspired speculation of many sorts, through both artistic design and inscrutable chance, or Providence.

The prominence of speculation in medieval thought derives substantially from two Pauline passages: 1 Corinthians 13:12 and Romans 1:20. The former is more famous today, thanks to the haunting beauty of the King James version: "for now we see through a glass darkly; but then, face to face." In the Vulgate of St. Jerome, we see by means of a mirror, enigmatically: *per speculum in aenigmate*. The force of Paul's metaphor becomes clear when we recall that premodern mirrors were much less faithful than those to which we are accustomed. Generally made of polished metal, which reflects less precisely than glass, they were also usually quite small and less than perfectly flat. As a result, they further distorted the (small, fuzzy) image that they reflected.[9] Paul's use of the mirror therefore suggests not just mediation but also the inherent imperfection of human perspective on the Divine.

In his important account of medieval speculation, Jeffrey F. Hamburger demonstrates the complementary importance of the (today) less well-known Romans 1:20:

8. Felski, *Limits of Critique*. See further introduction, pages 12–13.

9. Glass mirrors became common in Europe only in the sixteenth century, and technical challenges meant that they were generally extremely small and less than perfectly flat—like the small, curved wall-mirror in Van Eyck's famous *Arnolfini Portrait* of 1434. Whether metal or glass, therefore, the premodern mirror was inherently distorting. See further Frelick's introduction to *The Mirror in Medieval and Early Modern Culture*; Grabes, *The Mutable Glass*, 71–73; Melchior-Bonnet, *The Mirror*, 9–34; and Schmidt, "Miroir."

> Invisibilia enim ipsius, a creatura mundi, per ea quae facta sunt, intellecta, conspiciuntur: sempiterna quoque ejus virtus, et divinitas: ita ut sint inexcusabiles.
>
> For those things of his that cannot be seen, having been understood by way of what was created [*per ea quae facta sunt*], are clearly seen from the creation of the world, even his eternal power and Godhead: thus it is that they are without excuse.[10]

Reading with the Neoplatonist perspective that dominated early Christianity, we can readily see how the "created things" of Romans 1:20 might complement or even constitute the mirror of 1 Corinthians 13:12, since it is only by means of these imperfect devices (*per speculum; per ea*), that we can reach higher knowledge. With their clear evocation of the Platonic theory of forms, these passages naturally appealed to St. Augustine, who helped infuse early Christianity with the Neoplatonism of his youth. He also greatly popularized the metaphor of the mirror (*speculum*) that would be central to medieval speculation, several times proposing the Bible as the "mirror of knowledge" in which to reflect upon the *imago Dei* (image of God) that lies within each of us.[11]

In commentary on 2 Corinthians 3:18, Augustine reinforces this inwardness by emphasizing that its use of the participle *speculantes* should be understood in terms of *speculum* (inward-looking mirror), not *specula* (outward-facing watchtower).[12] Such moments attest to his broader mistrust of the material universe: for Augustine, the "created things" of Romans 1:20 are not the physical stuff of the world but rather "the image of God in the soul, namely the vestiges of the Trinity represented by the intellect, will, and memory. . . . Only by turning inward, not out towards the natural world, could man hope to recover the original *imago Dei*."[13] Any such recovery will be

10. Hamburger, "Speculations on Speculation." Thanks to my Latinist colleagues Will Broadhead and Stephanie Frampton for thinking through the linguistic complexities of this passage with me.

11. Ritamary Bradley cites as exemplary Augustine's *Enarratio in Psalmum 103*, "in which Holy Scripture is said to be a mirror: a mirror of knowledge, when it is said that all which has been written is our mirror; and a paragon for right living, when it is said that God's commands, whether read or recalled in memory, are seen as in a mirror" ("Backgrounds of the Title *Speculum*," 103). See also Grabes, *The Mutable Glass*, 95.

12. Augustine, *De trinitate*, 407.

13. Hamburger, "Speculations on Speculation," 369. As Michelle Karnes puts it, for Augustine "God is visible above all through the divine image that is the human mind" (*Imagination, Meditation, and Cognition*, 18).

imperfect, however, and its operation impossible fully to articulate, as suggested by his gloss on the *speculum* of 1 Corinthians 13:12: "If we ask what kind of mirror this might be, the thought occurs to us that the only thing ever seen in a mirror is an image. So what we have been trying to do is somehow [*utcumque*] to see him by whom we were made by means of this image which we ourselves are, as through a mirror."[14] Well into the twelfth century, Peter Lombard echoed the uncertainty of Augustine's *utcumque*: "The soul is a mirror in which *in some way* we know God."[15] For them, the precise mechanics of speculation are necessarily occluded because this form of vision is inward and devotional, not outward or empirical.

Also in the twelfth century, however, scholars affiliated with the Abbey School of St. Victor in Paris signaled the start of a shift. The Victorines were still largely Neoplatonist but made more room for appreciating the particulars of God's creation, partly by adducing "external" modes of vision to complement the inward gaze of self-reflection that had been emphasized by Augustine—adding a *specula* to his *speculum*, as it were. Thus, a follower of Hugh of St. Victor (the admirably named "Pseudo-Hugh") proposed speculation upon the natural world as the external complement to natural reason:

> Nota, in magnitudine universitatis notatur divina potentia, in pulchritudine sapientia, in utilitate bonitas, unde constat, quod non solum in universis, sed in singulis relucet quaedam imago et vestigium Trinitatis.[16]

> Take note: divine majesty can be perceived in the greatness of the universe, wisdom in its beauty, goodness in its utility, from which it is clear that not only in universals but also in particular things [*singulis*], a certain image and trace of the Trinity is reflected [*relucet*].

The mirror metaphor of 1 Corinthians 13:12 is echoed in the verb *relucet*, but this more positive depiction allows the *ea quae facta sunt* of Romans 1:20 to refer to material objects in the world, which even in their particulars (*singulis*) reflect traces of the Divine.

In making speculation "the process by which perception of the natural leads to perception of the supernatural," the Victorines did not regard it as

14. Augustine, *De trinitate*, 407.
15. Bradley, "Backgrounds of the Title *Speculum*," 112 (emphasis added).
16. Quoted by Hamburger, "Speculations on Speculation," 373; my translation.

an end in itself; rather, it was preparatory to the higher act of contemplation.[17] Yet the two concepts are often linked, as in Richard of St. Victor's definition of contemplation as "the free sight of the mind into the manifestations [*spectacula*] of wisdom, supported by admiration."[18] So while speculation remains part of a broader devotional program oriented around self-reflection, it acquires an anagogical, mediating function as well, by which coming to perceive beauty in the visual and material world conduces to higher spiritual awareness.

Similar understandings emerge in other contexts around this time. As Sara Ritchey and others have shown, twelfth-century monastic reformers argued "that their labor altered the secular character of the physical world, endowing it with divine presence, and that God would reward their labor by providing them with the ability to see the divine harmonies in the created world around them." This is the broader context for Ritchey's brilliant reading of how the *Speculum virginum*, a twelfth-century German manual for female religious and their priests, "introduced into women's communities a reformed sense of positive affirmation in speculation, training religious eyes to see the divine imprint in the material world."[19] In this context, we should recall the Pearl-Poems' much-remarked skill and delight in depicting the natural world: *Sir Gawain*'s shiver-inducing descriptions of animals and the seasons; the chastising power of God in *Cleanness* and *Patience*, often manifest through Nature; even the paradisal dreamscape of *Pearl*, whose beauty is simultaneously natural and supernatural.

The twelfth-century reinterpretations of Pauline theories of perception described above proposed the coimplication of Creation with Creator, thereby setting the stage for the thirteenth century's still more dramatic revolution in religious and intellectual life: outward and into the world. In his foundational study of medieval optics and theology, Dallas G. Denery nicely summarizes this shift as it took place in the nascent university system:

> During the course of the twelfth century, the activity of *speculatio* underwent a reinterpretation. For eleventh-century Benedictines such as Anselm of Bec, and even for twelfth-century Cistercians, *speculatio* meant "a gazing upon the

17. Hamburger, "Speculations on Speculation," 364.

18. "Contemplatio est libera mentis perspicacia in sapientiae spectacula cum admiratione suspensa," quoted in Karnes, *Imagination, Meditation, and Cognition*, 18. See further Palmén, *Richard of St. Victor's Theory of Imagination*, 141–57.

19. Ritchey, *Holy Matter*, 38, 25. On the *Speculum virginum*, see further Kumler, *Translating Truth*, 59–63.

> divine" and was essentially a devotional exercise related to *contemplatio*. . . . These connections were loosened during the course of the twelfth century. As the cathedral school supplanted the monastery as the center of intellectual activity, *speculatio* became disentangled from *contemplatio*. It came, instead, to refer to a teachable activity of the mind independent of religious emotion. Theology, in turn, became a professional academic discipline, a body of knowledge to be mastered and taught to others in the environment of the university classroom. While thirteenth-century scholars and theologians continued to condemn curiosity as a sin, the realities of university training made it all the easier to treat speculation as an end in itself.[20]

Yet while its intellectualizing effects are undeniable, Aristotelianism never wholly supplanted the Augustinian "symbolic tradition," which "survives and coexists . . . with the Aristotelian description of the properties of things," as Mary Franklin-Brown has shown.[21] Even this brief and simplified history of speculation suggests that many of the neat binaries we use as shorthands (Neoplatonist vs. Aristotelian, cognitive vs. affective) oversimplify a fluid period in intellectual history.[22] Chaucer's introduction of speculation into English ("lokynge of the devyne thought"), for example, sounds like the earlier tradition as outlined above by Denery ("a gazing upon the divine"), for the simple reason that it translates the Neoplatonist Boethius, who retained his *auctoritee* well after the arrival of Aristotelianism. This case reinforces how the powerful medieval impulse to find authority in earlier texts and authors—to learn from the past, as Nicholas Watson put it—created an inherently multifaceted and temporally complex intellectual culture.

Thus archscholastic St. Thomas Aquinas's generally Aristotelian understanding of speculation, as a process grounded in sensory perception, is nevertheless infused, via citation, with the more mystical and Neoplatonist perspectives of many of his sources.[23] His use of Augustine in linking

20. Denery, *Seeing and Being Seen*, 20–21.

21. Franklin-Brown, *Reading the World*, 54. As she puts it, "too many conflicting paradigms of knowledge and order were circulating during the scholastic period for any one paradigm to dominate" (215).

22. Groundbreaking studies by Eleanor Johnson (*Staging Contemplation*) and Michelle Karnes (*Imagination, Meditation, and Cognition*) support this point by demonstrating that medieval mystical and contemplative literature, whose links to the affective are obvious and important, nevertheless depend on the cognitive as well. Such syntheses further suggest the cultural relevance of practices, like speculation, that mediated between these modes.

23. Hamburger summarizes Aquinas's perspective as follows: "Whereas angels can see God intuitively by simple apprehension, man must proceed through and from the multitude

speculation to the mirror is especially noteworthy: "To see something by means of a mirror is to see a cause in its effect wherein its likeness is reflected. From this we see that speculation leads back to meditation."[24] He then quotes Richard of St. Victor in defining meditation as "the survey of the mind when searching for the truth."[25] Speculation thus becomes a visually oriented way of mediating between different ways or kinds of knowing (cognitive and contemplative), which in Aquinas's hands likewise mediates between different theories of the sensible universe (Neoplatonist and Aristotelian).

The Franciscan St. Bonaventure differs more in tone than substance from his Dominican contemporary in describing speculation as the outwardly directed and cognitive analogue to prayer: "desires are inflamed in us in two ways, to wit, through the outcry of prayer . . . and through the refulgence of speculation by which the mind most directly and intensely turns itself toward the rays of light." Yet Bonaventure clearly saw thought and feeling as linked, for he quickly moves to chastise the reader who wrongly supposes that "mere reading will suffice without fervor, *speculation without devotion*, investigation without admiration, observation without exultation."[26] Speculation thus became increasingly distinct from, yet still paired with, the fervor, devotion, admiration, and exultation of Bonaventure's doublets above, which shape this book's interest in delight. Indeed, Bonaventure's own delight in wordplay, puzzle, and paradox, "meant not to be understood but instead to be marveled at," as Karnes notes, is consonant with the aesthetics of the Pearl-Manuscript as a whole—a point to which we will return.[27]

The medieval history of speculation therefore supports Felski's argument that one can read "without opposing thought to emotion or divorcing intellectual rigor from affective attachment."[28] We cannot speculate exactly like the authors considered here, for obvious reasons; but that simply reinforces the dialectical nature of our relation to the past, which is necessarily constructive,

---

of impressions gathered through the senses, a process Aquinas defines as speculation" ("Speculations on Speculation," 380). He also outlines Aquinas's debts to Augustine, Bernard of Clairvaux, and the Victorines in that portion of his essay.

24. Aquinas, *Summa theologiae*, pt. II.II, q. 180, a. 3, ad 2, quoted in Melchior-Bonnet, *The Mirror*, 113–14. (For Augustine's original, see *De trinitate*, 407.) See also Leisegang, "La connaissance."

25. Aquinas, *Summa theologiae*, pt. II.II, q. 180, a. 3, ad 1.

26. Bonaventure, *Journey*, 2 (Prol. 3); Prol. 4, emphasis added.

27. Karnes, *Imagination, Meditation, and Cognition*, 108; see also her fuller discussion, 99–110.

28. Felski, *Limits of Critique*, 154. See further her discussion of French theorists Marielle Macé and Yves Citton (175–80).

not reconstructive.[29] Moreover, we have seen that medieval thinkers readily adapted speculation to fit changing times and needs. Bonaventure writes of speculating upon God "in vestigiis suis in hoc sensibili mundo."[30] If we adapt this formulation to allow other objects of value than the Divine, then it powerfully evokes a goal shared by many medievalists, across methodologies: namely to look "among traces in this sensible world" for the outlines of lost perspectives and unexpected beauties; to "locate missing stories," in Elizabeth Scala's potent words.[31] A reforged speculation that did so by infusing thought with feeling, rigor with attachment, would represent a powerful way of learning from the past—perhaps even that "tiger's leap into the past" that Walter Benjamin once proposed, to blast loose of the deadening effects of purely successive, linear historicity.[32]

Beyond any potential application to medieval literature generally, speculation of this sort offers an especially generative lens onto the Pearl-Manuscript, whose poems' delight in the complex beauty of God's craftsmanship recalls Hamburger's account of speculation, as a "concept of cosmological plenitude and order, sympathetic to the interpenetration of Creator and Creation."[33] Indeed, in his extensive discussion, Hamburger's one reference to English literature is to *Pearl*.[34] Over the course of this book, I will propose that all four poems of the Pearl-Manuscript invite speculation in the capacious sense outlined above. Moreover, as the interstitial chapters (3, 5, and 7) in

29. I adopt this distinction as articulated in *The Arcades Project* and across the essays of Walter Benjamin, e.g.: "For while the relation of the present to the past is a purely temporal, continuous one, the relation of what-has-been to the now is dialectical: it is not progression but image, suddenly emergent" (*Arcades Project*, 462). See further Bahr, *Fragments and Assemblages*, 47–48, 112, and 160–61.

30. "De speculatione Dei in vestigiis suis in hoc sensibili mundo" ("On the 'speculation' of/upon God in his traces within this sensible world") is the title of chap. 2 of the *Itinerarium*.

31. Scala, *Absent Narratives*, 1.

32. Benjamin, "On the Concept of History," 395.

33. In endorsing Hamburger's Aristotelian-sounding formulation ("Speculations on Speculation," 373), I do not deny that these poems also have important Augustinian or Neoplatonist elements—on which see, e.g., Spyra, *Epistemological Perspective*. Yet the poet's visceral delectation in craftsmanship seems at odds with the most austere version of Augustinian skepticism of the created world. For a helpful summary of the debate, see Staples, "Poynts and Spots," 36–39.

34. Hamburger, "Speculations on Speculation," 380. He draws on Stanbury's groundbreaking account of the poet's strongly visual sensibility (*Seeing the Gawain-Poet*), which has been formative to my understanding of these poems. Hsin-Yu Hu has expanded upon Stanbury's argument in "Delineating the Gawain-Poet," which contends that "the Gawain-poet dramatizes the act of looking and various forms of gaze in different emotional, religious, social,

particular will show, the manuscript itself deepens this invitation by means of physical features that enhance, and at times seem even to evoke, aspects of the poems.

These arguments do not require any of the manuscript's makers to have consciously drawn on speculation in the sense outlined above, or even to have heard of it; but it is not difficult to imagine how one or more of them might have. To outline just one possible avenue: Niklaus Largier has recently explored the importance of what he calls "speculative sensuality" to the religious writings of Heinrich Seuse (Henry Suso) and Meister Eckhart, among others.[35] Ritchey also emphasizes the former's "speculative worldview," and Hamburger's own "Speculations on Speculation" are motivated by that concept's centrality to Seuse and St. Gertrude of Helfta.[36] Fourteenth-century German mysticism thus offers a nexus of speculative theory and practice that might easily cross into England thanks to the immense popularity of Seuse, in particular. Steven Rozenski has demonstrated links between Seuse and Yorkshire mystic Richard Rolle, for example,[37] and the vastly influential Rolle, in turn, may share theological and artistic sympathies with the Pearl-Poet.[38] In this context, and considering how powerfully the codex itself deepens the speculative invitations of its poems, Joel Fredell's argument that the Pearl-Manuscript was produced in York may be significant, since fourteenth-century devotional literary production in Yorkshire went far beyond Rolle.[39]

My purpose is not to argue affirmatively for such connections, though they might fruitfully be pursued by others. Rather, it is to highlight the challenge of pinning down the many historical possibilities eddying around these poems, which suggests that some form of speculation may be inevitable when

and romantic contexts to explore the desire, anxieties and consequences of looking, and by analogy, poetic making" (2). Hu's study also valuably draws attention to the poet's theretofore little-noticed Ovidianism.

35. Largier, *Spekulative Sinnlichkeit*. Thanks to Jeffrey Hamburger for this reference.

36. Ritchey, *Holy Matter*, 178. On Seuse's insistent visuality, see also Falque, "'Daz Man Bild Mit Bild Us Tribe.'"

37. Rozenski writes: "Despite the history of nationalistic impulses separating medieval writers into discrete language groups, the artificiality of these categories might be seen most clearly in the exceedingly mobile, international and interlingual culture of late-medieval devotional literature" ("Authority and Exemplarity," 95). See further Rozenski, *Wisdom's Journey*; and Bynum, *Wonderful Blood*.

38. See further Staples, "Poynts and Spots," 189–258.

39. Fredell, "*Pearl*-Poet Manuscript in York."

faced with objects of great value about which little can be securely known. This can be seen in how frequently the charge of speculation attaches even, and perhaps especially, to conclusively historicizing interpretations of the poems.[40] Even for those who imagine that a single person wrote all four poems, "the Pearl-Poet" (like "the Gawain-Poet") remains a speculative construct.[41] The Pearl-Manuscript and its poems thus offer an exciting opportunity to "maken vertu of necessite," as their near-contemporary Chaucer put it, by asking how we might reconceive speculation as an affirmative good.[42]

This opportunity seems especially worth seizing since traditional literary history has sometimes found it hard to reckon with these poems, despite their beauty and a receptiveness to close reading that borders on insistence. The challenge posed by their dearth of securely recoverable, contemporaneous data proved particularly acute during the heyday of New Historicism, when the field's sense of "historical context" often became narrowly synchronic even as the range of texts it sought to engage expanded dramatically.[43] Thus *The Cambridge History of Medieval English Literature* devotes whole chapters to "Classroom and Confession," biblical translation, and post-1400

40. Trigg, for example, notes that one prominent proposal of a single clarifying historical context for *Sir Gawain and the Green Knight* "depends on layers and sequences of speculation. . . . In the absence of definitive dates, such discussions can easily become circular; and even when the dates all add up, suggestive allusions often resist the final click of certainty" (*Shame and Honor*, 59–60). Fredell seems to have such debates in mind when he argues that "we should recover the manuscript from generations of speculation about the poet's origins and patronage" by focusing squarely on the object before us ("*Pearl*-Poet Manuscript in York," 2). I agree, although I obviously regard "speculation" as less inherently negative than his phrasing implies.

41. As Davenport put it, "Though the *Gawain*-poet may not have existed, it has proved necessary to invent him" (*Art of the Gawain-Poet*, 1); or, in Stanbury's words, "Middle English poetry probably offers no more impressively fictional persona than the *Gawain*-poet" (*Seeing the Gawain-Poet*, 1). The author's anonymity affords yet another opportunity for affective identification, by quasi-obligating scholars to pick Team Gawain or Team Pearl in naming the poet.

42. Chaucer, *Canterbury Tales* I.3042. This memorable line is part of Theseus's attempt, at the end of the *Knight's Tale*, to make sense of the death of Arcite and of human suffering more generally. For another, rather different approach to speculation that overlaps slightly with my own, see Tom Eyers, *Speculative Formalism*.

43. Even so gifted a practitioner as Paul Strohm has acknowledged, looking back on the movement, that "however unruly or internally chaotic or contradictory a text was found to be, it was still treated as *synchronous* and 'self-present' in its situation within its own time and place and its lateral connections with other texts and events of its historical moment" ("Historicity without Historicism?," 381, emphasis added). See also Holsinger, "'Historical Context' in Historical Context."

romance, as well as to various named authors, but none to the Pearl-Poet.[44] *Pearl* itself merits just one incidental mention across its approximately thousand pages.[45]

Thanks to some trenchant theoretical interventions, we can now appreciate a more generously conceived historicity than the implicitly singular historicism that once held sway.[46] Paul Strohm's call for "a refined appreciation of the unruly multiplicity of ways in which history can manifest itself within a text" nicely accords with the kind of speculation that I propose: not just a more affectively forthright mode of intellectual engagement, but also one that opens onto the many different, potentially contradictory ways in which history "can manifest itself within a text."[47] Strohm's choice of modal is significant: the goal here would not necessarily be to determine the sharply delimited, internally consistent, and empirically demonstrable set of ways that history *did* manifest itself, but rather to see in speculative historical potentialities, and the literary interpretations that they afford, a version of the aesthetic excess that has often been associated with the literary itself.[48] The fissiparous nature of historicity, in other words, may yield aesthetic force as it plays kaleidoscopically across texts—and encourages play from us in our turn.

Two models of this play with historical potentiality are apposite here. In an uncannily prescient recent book, David Coley reads the Pearl-Poems in terms of the "unspeakable horror and . . . unavoidable truth" of the Black Death—a counterintuitive lens since English literature generally treats the

44. Wallace, *Cambridge History*, 376–406 (by Rita Copeland and Marjorie Woods); 454–82 (by David Lawton); and 690–719 (by Helen Cooper), respectively.

45. Wallace's index lists two references to *Pearl*, but one of these (315) is to the Pearl-Poet, not *Pearl* itself. The other briefly notes *Pearl*'s "use of the Apocalypse" in the context of biblical translation (479).

46. Pollock, for example, notes that "historicism carried too far can underwrite the ideology of singular meaning; the point of production of a text is fetishized to the complete disregard of the plurality of textual meaning at any given moment and a fortiori of its changeability over time" ("Future Philology," 955). Strohm is characteristically astute on the way forward: "Militating against historicism's synchronicities is another view of time and history, in which synchronicity is unattainable, owing to the fractured and divided nature of time itself. In this view, a text may or may not express its 'time,' but will certainly express multiple and contradictory temporalities. . . . [F]or the analyst who abandons the disciplinary regimes of 'historicism' but retains an interest in 'historicity,' the textual moment gains, rather than relinquishes, complexity, interest, and excitement" ("Historicity without Historicism?," 381–82).

47. Strohm, "Historicity without Historicism?," 382. See further Ashe, "How to Read Both."

48. See further introduction, pages 16–17.

plague so slightly, especially in contrast with the searing accounts of continental authors like Boccaccio and Machaut. Coley's project is "speculative by its very nature," as he notes, but he makes this characteristic a feature, not a bug; for with its careful scaffolding on "patterns of suggestion and implication, on cultural and textual context, on semantic and narrative parallel, even on informed conjecture," his argument evokes the kind of speculative energies we have seen in this chapter, mediating between seen and unseen, knowable and unknowable, to find the outlines of something occluded yet real.[49] The power of his speculation was clarified in the spring of 2020, when I taught *Pearl* during the first, frightening weeks of the COVID-19 pandemic, as we were all struggling to live through a world suddenly bereft of human touch. The students intuitively understood it as a plague poem, although I had not assigned or mentioned Coley's reading of it as such. His speculation thus sounds a deeper resonance within *Pearl* and its fellow poems that has echoed hauntingly through our own global pandemic.

I have also been inspired by Sarah McNamer's account of *Pearl* as a source ("in the generative sense—as font, wellspring") for the history of emotion, and her concrete answers to inherently speculative questions like: "How . . . does *Pearl* script consolation? How does it serve as an instrument for engaging in, training, and refining feeling?"[50] Guiding her readers through the poem's extraordinary music, McNamer argues that its "polyphonic complexities aspire to sensory and aesthetic appreciation by a listener credited with princely capacities to hear. . . . Given its acoustic subtlety as well as its subject matter, we might further deduce that *Pearl* is a form of chamber music, designed to be read aloud, not in the bustle of the hall, but in the more intimate setting of the *camera* . . . that distinctive late medieval form of public-private space."[51] Careful argumentation of this sort, grounded first in poetic detail and then in historical data about Edward III and his family, gradually leads McNamer to a specific patron for *Pearl*; but she does not present her identification as the solution to a problem.[52] Instead, her speculation offers a generative context for the poem, shaping but also leaving space for other readings, other histories.

49. Coley, *Death and the Pearl Maiden*, 7.

50. McNamer, "Literariness," 1436. For one powerful answer to the question that she poses, see Kline, "The *Pearl*, a Crayon, and a Lego."

51. McNamer, "Literariness," 1438.

52. McNamer suggests "Edward's son Lionel, Duke of Clarence, as the likeliest candidate for the father in need of consolation" ("Literariness," 1441), but also notes that "to offer history as ground and poem as embellished product of that ground . . . would be a mistake"

McNamer's account of *Pearl*, read aloud as a kind of "public-private," royal chamber music, seems entirely plausible: one way that history "can manifest itself within a text," as Strohm put it.[53] The extremely small size of the Pearl-Manuscript, however, suggests a more private history for this particular book, and therefore also—at some point, for someone—for its poems. Now just under 5 × 7 inches, it is "easily portable and so particularly suitable for private reading," as Maidie Hilmo points out.[54] Even more: so small a book is inherently intimate. It is naturally held close to the body, almost cradled, rather than declaimed from to an audience. Yet I believe that both McNamer's history of *Pearl* (as shared, princely, sonic experience) and the one I propose in the following chapter (as solitary, meditative, repeated reading-matter) can be simultaneously faithful to the artistry being contemplated. More broadly, I suggest that we try to find in the traces of the Pearl-Manuscript ("in vestigiis suis"), from which all understanding of these poems ultimately derives, as many of these speculative histories as we can.

Such desire for more, and the openness to unknowability and contradiction that it entails, may prompt reasonable questions about the limits of speculation as I conceive it. One criterion I propose is delight, in the capacious sense outlined in the introduction. Does a speculative reading make the object of inquiry more generative, resonant, or exciting, and in that sense add to the bookish delight at work in the world? Does it stretch or expand our perspective? Such questions invite discussion and debate, not objective answers, but I draw inspiration from Maura Nolan's argument, "that in order to genuinely grasp the historicity of a medieval poem we must first identify its excesses, the ways in which it solicits meanings that seem, at first glance, to be unauthorized or illicit, and to exceed the brief of the manuscript or the words on the page."[55] Subsequent chapters will show that such an aesthetics

---

since no good poem will remain tethered to that ground; on the contrary, "the results would be open to the generative effects of literary art and its capacity to shape and refine feelings 'beyond the given'" (1440).

53. Strohm, "Historicity without Historicism?," 382.

54. Hilmo, "Creating a Visual Narrative," 138. The cropping to which the manuscript was later subject means that we cannot be certain of its original size, but its tight text-block of "approximately 3¾ × 5¾ inches" (Edwards, "The Manuscript," 197) indicates that it can never have been large. See further introduction, n. 3.

55. Nolan, "Lydgate's Worst Poem," 82. She acknowledges, as do I, that "[T]hose excesses have to be evaluated, of course, and some we must reject as fanciful . . . mere castles in the air built by our own modern preoccupations. Others, however, exist in the spaces between past authority and present desire, and these meanings are perhaps the most significant, and the best indices to the power of the aesthetic within history and culture" (82). Of course, one

of supereffable excess informs both *Pearl* and the Pearl-Manuscript, which is why I see fewer limits to their speculative potential than might be appropriate for other texts or objects.

Indeed, such perspectival shifts are precisely what medieval speculation sought to effect, as Ritchey's powerful account of the *Speculum virginum* makes clear. This work usefully reinforces that manuscripts as well as texts have speculative potential; so too does the relation between them: "As a self-proclaimed *speculatorium* that insisted, on every one of its nearly two hundred folios, that the reader 'look' into its pages, its pictures, its songs, and text, the *Speculum* called attention to its own construction, to its function as a 'paradise seeing aid' [*paradisum speculatorium*]."[56] But this *speculum* is no modern, passively reflective mirror, for "it becomes evident that each image bore a multiplicity of meanings, with ever changing referents," such that (for example) a flower, "whether as an artistic rendering or a verbal picture, might refer to Christ, Scripture, virtue, enclosure, the treatise itself, or Theodora's virgin body." Moreover, the value of the book-as-*speculum* lies partly in its multiplicative properties, for the challenge of reading Peregrinus's complex imagery, "saturated with multiple referents," is what prepares Theodora for the deeper challenge of "learn[ing] to see Christ among" the virgins for whom the text was written, and from there of seeing the world itself, in all its multiform complexity, as a manifestation of God.[57] Such themes resonate in *Pearl*, as the following chapter will show.

The Pearl-Manuscript's twelve illustrations, which are such an unusual and prominent feature of the experience it proposes, also suggest private, devotional readership. For although highly uncharacteristic of vernacular English literary manuscripts in this period, comparably large, often full-page illustrations typify the books of hours that circulated so widely at the time. Nor is that these devotional books' only similarity to the Pearl-Manuscript, for Jessica Brantley notes that "in addition to being illustrated, these volumes are usually recognizable by size and shape: they are small physically and intended to be portable," a description consonant with Hilmo's of the Pearl-Manuscript, quoted above. Brantley further demonstrates that, although

reader may see "indices to the power of the aesthetic" that look to another like "mere castles in the air," which is why I offer "net increase of bookish delight" as one way of approaching the issue, however partially.

56. Ritchey, *Holy Matter*, 40–41. The work consists of a dialogue between a priest-teacher, Peregrinus, and a female religious, Theodora, which gradually emerges as a "curious constitution as a composite of text and image, spiritual significance and literal referent" (35).

57. Ritchey, *Holy Matter*, 43–44, 45–48.

these prayer-books "have seemed insufficiently *literary* to fit into a scholarly model that would include—for example—Chaucer's poetry, . . . their contents shaped the *literate* understanding of many, if not almost all, medieval readers."[58] The Pearl-Manuscript's evocation of such volumes, by means of its intimate size, full-page images, and homiletic content, suggests that we should pay particular attention to its complex interplay of word and image—and, further, of word-*as*-image, an idea that *Cleanness* in particular will develop, and which informs the entire manuscript's construction.[59]

I therefore speculate that the Pearl-Manuscript served as a devotional object whose visual character—by which I mean its interplay of letter forms, paratext, and illustrations—solicits repeated, meditative reading.[60] Such extensive handling is suggested by the amount of dirt in its gutter.[61] Yet while this small book feels deeply personal, even private ("privy," like the pearl of its opening poem), it is also a collaboratively produced object that has taken a wide variety of shapes over the years. As we will see in chapter 3, its (in)famous illustrations took shape gradually: first pen-and-ink drawings, then paint—often rather sloppily applied and possibly in multiple stages.[62]

58. Brantley, "Forms of the Hours," 65, 62 (original emphasis). Christopher de Hamel makes a similar point still more starkly: "For many medieval families it was the only book they ever owned, and for many of our ancestors it was the only book they had ever seen" ("Books of Hours," quoted in Brantley, "Forms of the Hours," 62). For a sensitive reassessment of these books' importance to the devotional lives of their readers, see Eamon Duffy, *Marking the Hours*. Eric Flanders also suggests the Pearl-Manuscript's resemblance to books of hours in "Resetting *Pearl*."

59. In this, I draw on such seminal accounts of the medieval "image-text" as Brantley, *Reading in the Wilderness*; Gayk, *Image, Text, and Religious Reform*; and Rust, *Imaginary Worlds in Medieval Books*. More recently, see Fein and Raybin, *Chaucer: Visual Approaches*; and Hamburger, *Script as Image*.

60. In thus proposing the Pearl-Manuscript as a devotional object, I have been inspired by Seeta Chaganti's seminal account of *Pearl* as reliquary in *The Medieval Poetics of the Reliquary*, 95–129.

61. Thanks to Gillespie and Wakelin for pointing out this feature of the manuscript; see further introduction, n. 3.

62. On the two-stage process of illustration, see Hilmo, "Re-Conceptualizing," and "Did the Scribe Draw," as well as McGillivray and Duffy, "New Light." Kathleen Scott dates the manuscript ca. 1375–1400 and its illustrations ca. 1400–1410 (*Later Gothic Manuscripts*, 2:66), though Hilmo's suggestion that the scribe also made the pen-and-ink drawings might suggest an earlier dating of the pen-and-ink illustrations, at least. Edwards notes additional codicological features that confirm a period of separation between script and image, specifically "the traces of offset from fol. 86 on fol. 85v and of fol. 95 on 94v. Hence these leaves were placed on top of each other while the ink was still damp, indicating that they had not yet been painted. That illustrations were not intended for all the pages that now contain

The four images that now precede *Pearl* appear on a separate bifolium that may be a later addition to the codex, and some illustrations appear on pages that were earlier ruled for text.[63] This suggests at least one change in plan after initial construction of the manuscript began, which makes that construction's undeniable intricacy additionally remarkable. Indeed, the Pearl-Manuscript's very mutability, as much as any theoretical points raised earlier, argues that we should not think solely in terms of original intentions or contexts. In that sense, the manuscript's evolution itself becomes an object of speculation.

The illustrations of *Pearl* that now begin the manuscript constitute an important part of this evolution, for they introduce visually a theme that will resonate throughout the manuscript: conspicuous yet imprecise mirrorings, or echoes. The most familiar deployment of this motif is textual: the fact that three of the four poems conclude with a slightly modified version of their beginning.[64] *Pearl* and *Sir Gawain*, first and last poems, also mirror each other's 101 stanzas across the "inner" poems, *Cleanness* and *Patience*, which themselves resemble one another in obvious though often distorted ways. Tracing such shapes will be one leitmotif of this book, so I conclude by very briefly outlining several forms of visual mirroring suggested by the bifolium preceding *Pearl*. The first of its four illustrations, figure 1.1, especially deserves consideration here, for its depiction of the Dreamer, collapsed in grief and exhaustion, does not use the contemporary convention of placing a hand beneath the head to indicate dreaming. Instead, both hands stretch awkwardly downward toward a shape that has been variously interpreted, generally as either the flowery mound into which the lost pearl tumbled or a prefiguration of the stream that appears in the following three images. Chapter 3 will consider the layers of this shape in more depth; here, I note simply that its contours almost mirror those of the Dreamer.

This form of mirroring suggests others. For example, Joyce Coleman has shown that the composition of this opening page, folio 37/41r, mirrors that of Narcissus's Fountain in several fourteenth-century manuscripts of the

them is further confirmed by the fact that some of the original blank leaves or pages had been ruled and bounded. There would have been no point in ruling them if illustration was planned" ("The Manuscript," 213–18).

63. Edwards notes that the illustrated bifolium preceding *Pearl*, folios 37/41r–38/42v, "is codicologically distinct and anomalous in terms of the manuscript's collation. It could easily have been added at some later time" ("The Manuscript," 213).

64. The importance of this circularity is one theme of this book; I consider *Cleanness*'s exception to it in chap. 5.

vastly influential *Roman de la Rose*.[65] There, within the Garden of Love, the Dreamer sees the reflection of the rosebud that becomes his obsession. This is the only piece of vernacular literature cited by the Pearl-Manuscript (at *Cleanness*, line 1057), a point to which chapter 4 will return. For "certainly a professional although probably a regional artist . . . demonstrably aware of conventional compositions," as Scott puts it,[66] to abandon the conventional pose for dreaming in favor of one that evokes a much-copied, much-illustrated poem that the Pearl-Manuscript later quotes may suggest a particular interpretive perspective on the Dreamer's grief, as Coleman argues.[67] The mirroring that she notes is further significant, I believe, because it visually prefigures many other instances of comparably "conspicuous but inexact" mirrorings across the Pearl-Manuscript as a whole. The fact that 37/41r's compositional mirroring imperfectly reflects a scene, Narcissus's Fountain, that itself depicts a fraught moment of reflection is additionally striking: a sort of *mise en abyme* or hall of mirrors that recalls Guillaume de Lorris's own description of the crystals within the fountain.[68] That such speculative invitations should appear on the Pearl-Manuscript's very first page makes them additionally powerful.

Complex, often imprecise mirrorings are just one form of the Pearl-Manuscript's obsession with highly wrought, slightly flawed shapes. These shapes may be literary or material or mathematical, but not-quite-perfection that just misses the ideal—what I will call an aesthetics of anti-exactness—is central to *Pearl*, as the following chapter will show. It is therefore noteworthy that a comparable visual aesthetic now introduces us to the poem. The next three images display different forms of inexact mirroring: most obviously the water near the Dreamer, which takes slightly different shapes in each: in figure 1.2, it is confined to the lower right, and the far shore is not depicted; in figures 1.3 and 1.4, by contrast, it appears as a stream or river, across which the Dreamer sees first the Maiden alone, then the Maiden enclosed within

65. "A large proportion of the fourteenth-century miniatures that show Narcissus or l'Amant at the fountain place him lying on the ground parallel to the water, with his arms stretched out to it. . . . If one flips figure 9.6 ["Narcissus reaching longingly toward the fountain," detail of Paris, Bibliothèque Nationale de France MS fr. 802, folio 11r], it and the *Pearl* image look like the same scene interpreted by different artists, with some details switched out" (Coleman, "Translating Iconography," 185–86). On the image's resemblance to French manuscripts, see also Richards, "Picturing Desire and Desiring Pictures."

66. Scott, *Later Gothic Manuscripts*, 2:67 (cat. 12).

67. Coleman, "Translating Iconography," 187.

68. On the *Roman de la Rose* and medieval optics, see Akbari, *Seeing through the Veil*, 45–113; Eberle, "The Lovers' Glass;" and Kay, "*Roman de la Rose* and the Inverted Bouquet."

a walled Heavenly Jerusalem, complete with inner turret. Clearly there is a progression here, even "the sense of a jump-cut animation" if we flip the pages quickly; yet as Eric Flanders also notes, all three illustrations are "'marred'—the first through a deliberate rubbing out [of the Dreamer's face], the second by a careless painting over (the pointing finger is occluded by the water), the third by what appears to be the cracking away of paint around the dreamer's hand and face."[69] However they emerged, such imperfections resonate with the poem they depict, whose opening lines appear opposite this fourth illustration. So let us turn to *Pearl*.

69. Flanders, "Resetting *Pearl*," 20, 57. On reformist anxieties that may help explain the deliberate defacement of the Dreamer in fig. 1.2, see Hilmo, "Creating a Visual Narrative," 150.

FIGURE 1.1. (*opposite*) Folio 37/41r of Cotton Nero A.x/2. Photograph © 2024 by The British Library Board. *Following pages*: FIGURE 1.2. Folio 37/41v of Cotton Nero A.x/2. Photograph © 2024 by The British Library Board. FIGURE 1.3. Folio 38/42r of Cotton Nero A.x/2. Photograph © 2024 by The British Library Board. FIGURE 1.4. Folio 38/42v of Cotton Nero A.x/2. Photograph © 2024 by The British Library Board.

TWO

THE EXPANDING SINGULARITY OF *PEARL*

As the most otherworldly of the manuscript's four poems, *Pearl* especially rewards speculation of the imaginative, meditative sort outlined in chapter 1. Such an approach is suggested both by *Pearl* itself—its words, themes, and images—and by how the poem takes shape in its sole surviving manuscript. Indeed, its material uniqueness demands some form of speculation in order to engage with its many textual cruces, which provocatively blur the boundaries between scribal error and literary art. Does a surprising or strange word in the manuscript represent a flaw to be emended, for example, or should we consider more closely how it might participate in the poet's complex lexical world? Is a particular exception to the poem's highly ornate structure accidental or authorial, and how should the fact that we cannot securely know inflect our reading?

Pearl is not unique in prompting such questions, but its status as a single-manuscript text means that we have fewer data with which to support our preferred answers. As I have argued elsewhere, its material uniqueness imbues *Pearl* with wide-ranging forms of interpretive potential that it would not otherwise have, and in ways evocative of the poem's own themes and structure.[1] Here, I expand that analysis by showing how an extra decorated initial at line 961 reinforces codicologically a phenomenon also manifest textually: what I call "more-and-less"-ness, inspired by a cluster of concatenating words related to sufficiency and value (more, less, enough). The poem's pattern of slight imperfections to its ornate shapes first emerges formally, by inviting the reader to reflect on whether it matters to encounter one letter, line, or stanza more or less than we would expect. For a decorated initial to offer comparable effects visually suggests how closely poem and manuscript, text and object, collectively shape their interpretive potential.

A similarly accretive process emerges in my final section, on the expanding

1. Bahr, "Manifold Singularity." Thanks to the editors of *ELH* for permission to draw on that material here.

literariness of the first letter of the last word of line 616 of *Pearl*. This letter has been read so variously that it earlier served as my illustration of the poem's manifold singularity.[2] Since then, two other editions have read this word differently still, further expanding *Pearl*'s textual existence.[3] This "expanding singularity" blurs the boundaries between medieval and modern, authentic and anachronistic, in ways that evoke the poem's own paradox-loving logic, exemplified by the Maiden's exposition of the parable of the vineyard. There, she rejects the Dreamer's scarcity-based understanding of value in favor of a heavenly economics by which it suffices to repeat: "þe grace of God is gret inoghe" ("the grace of God is great enough," around which section 11 of the poem concatenates). Comparably, she praises the wise merchant who sells all that he has for a single priceless pearl that he shares with all the righteous: the Pearl of Price that is the centerpiece of the Maiden's transfigured raiment. This Pearl is simultaneously unique and available to all, a paradox that the Dreamer's indignant insistence upon earthly notions of degree, propriety, and value cannot comprehend. I begin by exploring how this tension around value and uniqueness manifests textually, which will lay the groundwork for the remaining two sections' engagement with the poem's materiality.

VALUE, UNIQUENESS, AND PEARL(S)

Pearl spends considerable energy exploring the tension between earthly and celestial understandings of value, as seen in its use of two parables from the Gospel of Matthew: that of the laborers in the vineyard (Matt. 20:1–16, adapted at lines 501–76), and of the Pearl of Price (Matt. 13:45–46, adapted at lines 729–39). In the first of these, the penny paid for a day's work becomes a metaphor for salvation, showing that even the humblest laborer can earn the ultimate reward. Like some of the laborers, however, the Dreamer insists that it is unfair for everyone to receive the same payment, regardless of how long they have worked; such a poor assessment of value, he insists, is unworthy of the Lord whom the Psalms praise as the "hyȝe Kyng ay pertermynable" who "quyteȝ vchon as hys desserte."[4] The Maiden responds to the Dreamer by shifting the concatenation word from one of relative

2. Bahr, "Manifold Singularity," 746–53.

3. McGillivray and Stook, *Pearl* (2017); Putter and Stokes, *Works of the Gawain Poet* (2014).

4. The "high King, always supreme in judgment . . . [who] rewards each one according to his desert" (lines 595–96).

degree—"more," in the tenth section—to one of absolute sufficiency in the eleventh: "þe grace of God is gret inoghe" ("the grace of God is great enough"). I will consider the broader significance of this shift more fully in due course. Here we should simply note the sharply contrasting images that she uses in these lines: initially, free-flowing streams and watercourses characterize God's liberality (lines 607–8), but these natural images of unpaid-for plenitude are then juxtaposed with the man-made monetary image of the penny from the parable (lines 612–16). The tension between these two kinds of images reinforces the challenge of depicting something—salvation—whose value is so absolute as to make it priceless.

The problem of pricelessness is highlighted even more explicitly by the poem's depiction of the Pearl of Price, for which the wise merchant of Matthew's parable sells all his worldly possessions. This pearl defies earthly understandings of economics. Tangible goods are given to acquire it, but the purchaser does not consequently own the pearl in the normal sense of the word; rather, it remains "commune to alle þat ryȝtwys were" ("common to all who are righteous," line 740). Nor does one's own stake in it diminish the value of anyone else's, as is suggested by its perfectly indivisible, endless roundness. (It is significant here that pearls, unlike most gems, are not cut into numerable and therefore finite facets; this point will recur when we consider the sharper, more angular shapes of *Sir Gawain and the Green Knight*.) The pearl is thus an ideal model for the infinitely many and yet infinitely valuable king- and queenships of heaven described at lines 433–68.

As elements of both secular and sacred economies, fitting adornments for royal crowns and venerated reliquaries alike, gems offer an appropriately complex vehicle for exploring tensions between earthly and heavenly notions of value.[5] The value of coins was fixed by strict laws against counterfeiting, and coins in their turn could serve to fix dangerously slippery social relations.[6] Establishing the value of gems, by contrast, required professional expertise, a point alluded to by the opening stanza's depiction of the narrator as a jeweler practiced in such appraisals (line 7).[7] The Dreamer's confidence in his

5. See further Chaganti, *Medieval Poetics of the Reliquary*, 95–129.

6. Bowers, for example, has argued that *Pearl*'s insistence that all laborers in Matthew's parable be paid the same wage reflects conservative reaction to the contemporary problem of agricultural labor shortages in postplague England, which threatened to enable unprecedented social and geographical mobility among workers theretofore tied to the land ("Politics of Pearl"). See further Bowers, *Politics of Pearl*, 41–49.

7. See further Barr, "*Pearl*—or 'The Jeweller's Tale.'" It is also worth noting that *Cleanness* explicitly contrasts pearls and pennies (lines 1117–18).

evaluative faculties there, however, contrasts sharply with the bewilderment that he experiences when he meets his lost pearl, now transfigured and bearing what will ultimately be revealed to be the Pearl of Price:

> Bot a wonder perle withouten wemme
> in mydde3 hyr breste wat3 sette so sure—
> a manne3 dom mo3t dry3ly demme
> er mynde mo3t malte in hit mesure.
> I hope no tong mo3t endure
> no sauerly saghe say of þat sy3t,
> so wat3 hit clene and cler and pure,
> þat precios perle þer hit watz py3t.[8]

In its pleonasm and choice of alliterating letter, line 226 ("no sauerly *saghe say* of þat sy3t") subtly recalls the expression used in the first stanza to describe the Dreamer's confident assessment of his pearl's value: he "sette hyr *sengeley* in *synglure*" (line 8; the two passages both feature verbs of "setting" as well, *py3t* and *sette*). Here, pleonasm emphasizes the ineffability of this distinct though related pearl.

By marking that shift with a second, closely parallel use of pleonasm (itself a rhetorical figure defined by repetition), this passage evokes how the image of the pearl multiplies across the poem. From a unique object securely in the Dreamer's possession, it slips away from him first physically and then metaphorically, by taking on a range of new forms that he does not control or own: the gravel beneath his feet (lines 81–82), the many beautiful adornments of an elegant lady's gown (lines 193–220), the "wonder perle" described above, whose deeper, spiritual significance he cannot yet comprehend—and, most crucially, the Maiden herself, no longer just jewel or daughter but also sharp-tongued interlocutor and honored queen in Heaven.[9]

Ironically, the Dreamer's first words to her enact that very multiplication of (the) pearl(s) whose larger significance—that "his" pearl is now

8. "But a wondrous pearl without flaw was set very securely within her breast; a man's judgment would be entirely baffled [lit. "dammed up"] before his mind might take the measure of it. I believe no tongue could confidently describe that sight in words, so clean and clear and pure it was, that precious pearl where it was set" (lines 221–28).

9. Phillips makes a similar point well: "As the heavenly and earthly interpretive paradigms slide into one another, the status of the Jeweler also shifts; the reader is never allowed to settle into one mode of reading, but instead is compelled to hold alternative hermeneutic models in mind simultaneously" ("Meeting One's Maker," 91).

different from, and more than, it/she was in life—he spends much of the poem resisting:

> "O *perle*," coþe I, "in *perleȝ* pyȝt,
> art þou my *perle* þat I haf playned,
> regretted by myn one on nyȝte?"[10]

Here the Dreamer plaintively attempts to reassert the identity of the pearl he is addressing ("O perle") with the precious and "private" pearl whose loss he lamented in the first section of the poem ("my perle"); the two instances of "my(n)" in the lines above clearly recall the poem's early profusion of possessive pronouns, which insisted on the uniqueness of the pearl itself and on the Dreamer's comparably exclusive ownership of it. The fruitlessness of his effort to reclaim his former, earthly relationship with the Maiden is suggested by the contrast between these lines' multiplication of the word *perle* (which intimates how many different functions that image serves in the poem) and the motif of singularity raised by the repetition of first-person singular pronouns (four in just three lines).

This tension between singular and plural presages the poem's attempts to move beyond earthly understandings of value. For the Dreamer, uniqueness (of the pearl) and exclusivity (of his relationship to it) create value, but the Pearl-Maiden famously proposes a perspective both more capacious and less intuitive, by which Heaven has many equally precious and mutually supportive monarchs, none of whose reigns threatens the true preeminence of the Virgin Mary:

> "Sir, fele here porchaseȝ and fongeȝ pray,
> bot supplantoreȝ none withinne þys place.
> Þat emperise al heuenȝ hatȝ— [441]
> and vrþe and helle—in her bayly.
> Of erytage ȝet non wyl ho chace,
> for ho is quen of cortaysye.
>
> "The court of þe kyndom of God alyue [445]
> hatȝ a property in hyt self beyng:
> alle þat may þerinne aryue

10. "'O pearl,' I said, 'adorned with pearls, are you my pearl that I have lamented and missed, all by myself at night?'" (lines 241–43, emphasis added).

of alle þe reme is quen oþer kyng,
and neuer oþer ȝet schal depryue, [449]
bot vchon fayn of oþereȝ hafyng,
and wolde her corouneȝ wern worþe þo fyue,
if possyble were her mendyng.
Bot my lady of quom Iesu con spryng, [453]
ho haldeȝ þe empyre ouer vus ful hyȝe,
and þat dyspleseȝ non of oure gyng,
for ho is quene of cortaysye."[11]

This passage stands out for its eagerness to emphasize the paradoxes of Christian theology. It insists upon universality: *alle* those who arrive in Heaven are king or queen of *alle* the realm (lines 447–48), even as Mary herself is empress of *al heuenȝ* (line 441). The repetition of the word "all" highlights the impossibility, in earthly terms, of this proposition; yet the Maiden intimates still greater hypothetical plenitude when she claims that each concurrently and equally reigning sovereign wishes that each of his or her fellows' crowns were worth five times as much (line 451). This ever-expanding and radically egalitarian model of spiritual value contrasts sharply, not just with earthly understandings of economics, but also with Dante's notion of Heaven as expressed in the *Paradiso*, where the Celestial Rose is presented as a hierarchical theater, with each soul's degree of remove from the Godhead reflecting the nature and fullness of their sanctity.[12]

Indeed, a Dante-like concern for degree, as social and theological concept, informs the Dreamer's objections to the Maiden's model:

11. "'Sir, many here chase and seize their quarry, but there are no usurpers within this place. That empress [the Blessed Virgin] has all the heavens—and earth and hell—in her jurisdiction. Yet she will chase no one from their heritage, for she is queen of courtesy. The court of the kingdom of the living God has a property of its own, namely: all that arrive therein is queen or king of all the realm, and shall never deprive another thereby; rather, each is pleased with everyone else's possession [of the kingdom of Heaven], and would like their crowns to be worth five times as much, if any such amendment were possible. But my lady of whom Jesus sprang holds wholly high authority over us, and that displeases none of our company, for she is queen of courtesy'" (lines 439–56). I follow Andrew and Waldron and most other editors in reading *beying* in line 446; McGillivray and Stook, whose text I otherwise generally follow, read *leyng*.

12. On Dante and the Pearl-Poet, see Bahr, "Compulsory Figures"; Ginsberg, "Place and Dialectic"; Newman, "Artifice of Eternity"; Payne, *Influence of Dante*; and Shoaf, "*Purgatorio* and *Pearl*."

"That cortayse is to fre of dede,
ȝyf hyt be soth þat þou coneȝ saye.
Þou lyfed not two ȝer in oure þede . . .
and quen mad on þe fyrst day! . . .
Of countes, damysel, par ma fay, [489]
Wer fayr in heuen to halde asstate,
oþer elleȝ a lady of lasse aray—
bot a quene! Hit is to dere a date!"

"Þer is no date of Hys godnesse," [493]
þen sayde to me þat worþy wyȝte,
"for al is trawþe þat He con dresse,
and He may do no þynk bot ryȝt."[13]

Here, the Dreamer's insistence upon precise degrees of difference dissolves in the face of the Maiden's all-embracing absolutes: there is no limit; all is truth; nothing but right.[14] Multiple monarchs of the same realm are a wholly logical consequence, in other words, of the category-smashing grace of Heaven. Significantly, this exchange hinges on the concatenation word *date*, which as deployed in this section of the poem shatters everyday expectations of what a single word can mean: rank, degree, limit, date, moment, season, beginning, end. The pressure that *Pearl*'s wordplay puts on traditional lexical categories thus proves analogous to the poem's emphasis on the radicalism of Jesus's challenge to traditional social and economic categories.

In this sense, it is quite appropriate that we move from the linking word *date* in the ninth section to *more* in the tenth, since both *Pearl* and the Maiden—and, this book will suggest, the Pearl-Manuscript itself—argue for more: here, more than one queen of heaven, a more generous understanding of value and justice, and ever more elaborate lexical, formal, and poetic play. Yet the word *more* also has negative connotations, evoking both the envy of the querulous laborers of the parable, who want to receive more payment than their fellows, and the possessiveness of the Dreamer, who wants more

13. "'That courtesy is too liberal in action if what you just said is true. You lived not two years in our land; you never learned to please or pray to God, or even your pater [noster] or creed, and made queen on the first day! . . . By my faith, damsel, it would be fair to hold the estate of countess in heaven, or else a lady of less array—but a queen! It is too precious a rank [*date*]!' 'There is no limit [*date*] to His goodness,' that worthy being said to me then, 'for all that He touches is truth, and He can do no thing but right'" (lines 481–96).

14. For an incisive treatment of this passage, see Chong, "Bot a Quene!"

from his pearl and his vision than he is destined to receive. This last constitutes the poem's denouement, anticipated by the use of "more and more" as the concatenation phrase of section 3. There, it is first the paradisal dreamscape and then his initial glimpse of the Maiden that move the Dreamer to ever greater desire for ever more delights: "and euer þe lenger, þe more and more" ("and ever the longer, the more and more," line 180). Section 10 concludes with the Dreamer dramatically echoing that earlier line but adding an element of opposition: "and euer þe lenger þe lasse þe more" ("and ever the longer, the less the more," line 600). The clear-yet-inexact nature of this echo evokes comparable moments throughout the Pearl-Manuscript, as the previous chapter began to suggest with reference to *Pearl*'s opening illustrations. The pattern is highlighted here by the curiously hard-to-translate nature of the second formulation at line 600, which, as Andrew and Waldron drily note, is "more emphatic than logical."[15]

Line 600 emphasizes both the Dreamer's indignation at the Maiden's exalted status and, more broadly, a concept I call "more-and-less"-ness, encapsulated by the concatenating elements of sections 3, 10, 11, and 15: "more and more," "more," "þe grace of god is gret inoghe," and "neuer þe les," respectively. These concepts—more, less, and enough—are central to earthly understandings of judgment and value, and clearly related to the tension between uniqueness and multiplicity discussed earlier. In that sense, their prominence as four of the poem's twenty concatenating phrases seems perfectly appropriate. Yet such words do not lend themselves to the kind of wordplay for which the poem—and in particular its concatenating elements—is famous: either the punning multivalence of words like *spot* (place/stain) in section 1, *date* (whose limitlessness we have considered) in 9, or *mote* (city/moat/stain) in 17; or others' ambivalent evocation of both sacred and secular registers, as with *blysse* in section 7, *cortaysye* in 8, or *delyt* in 19. Compared to them, the "more-and-less"-oriented concatenation phrases seem rather unpoetically literal and, to that extent, surprising.[16] Yet these words pervade the poem's crucial midpoint, even reenacting its chiastic structure in miniature: the Maiden responds to the Dreamer's "and euer þe lenger þe *lasse* þe *more*" with her own, "Of *more* and *lasse* in Godeȝ ryche" ("Of more and less in God's kingdom," lines 600–601, emphasis added), as we cross from section 10 to

15. Andrew and Waldron, *Poems*, 81.

16. See Tomasch ("'Pearl' Punnology," 16), however, for the possibility that the word "les," in the concatenation phrase "neuer þe les," includes a pun on "lesyng" or "lie."

11.[17] The structural prominence and sheer number of these concatenating elements make clear, and literal, their centrality to the poem.

These "more-and-less"-themed words and phrases also subtly draw attention to slight formal irregularities in *Pearl*'s sole surviving manuscript: one line, letter, stanza, or decorated initial "more or less" than we would expect based on the poem's intricate symmetries. The ultimate source of these irregularities cannot be determined, which helps ensure their continued debatability and thus the potential energy of the poem that they adorn. The following section will argue that cumulatively, these imperfections encourage speculation upon their aesthetic and spiritual significance. This encouragement is strengthened by the prominence of "more-and-less"-themed words and phrases, which thereby attain a degree of polysemy that their denotative nature would seem to preclude. Their significance, that is, lies not just in their content but also in how they evoke the messy particularities of *Pearl*'s unique surviving manuscript, creating interpretive pressures and opportunities congruent with those of the poem itself.

THE POTENTIAL ENERGY OF MORE-AND-LESS

Here I examine four deviations-by-one from a clearly established pattern: the absence of an expected line in stanza 40 (which editors have nevertheless designated "line 472"); the subtraction of a letter from two instances of section 13's concatenation word; the addition of an unexpected, sixth stanza to section 15; and finally, an extra decorated initial at line 961, which begins the final stanza of section 16. I consider these cases in the order they appear because they gain cumulative force: the first three examples, all textual, gradually draw attention to "more-and-less"-ness and thus prepare us to linger on line 961's anomalous initial. My argument therefore imagines a through-reader's first encounter with these four irregularities as manifest in the Pearl-Manuscript—without editorial spoilers, as it were. It is speculative in the sense outlined in chapter 1: grounded in sensory observation and describable experiences, and inspired by delight at the poem's many forms of suggestive unknowability.

I begin with the fact that the poem's fortieth stanza contains only eleven lines, rather than twelve like every other: what the rhyme scheme implies would be line 472 does not appear in the manuscript. No modern editor of whom I am aware has allowed this imperfection to stand. Rather, supposing

17. On chiastic elements of *Pearl*, see Harwood, "*Pearl* as Diptych."

that the genuine, authorial line 472 was lost somewhere in the poem's transcription history, they include this phantom line in their numeration and often also depict it visually, as below:

"Cortayse," coþe I, "I leue, [469]
and charyte grete, be yow among;
bot my speche þat yow ne greue,
* * * * * * * * * * * * * * * * * * * *
Þyself in heuen ouer hyȝ þou heue, [473]
to make þe quen þat watȝ so ȝonge."[18]

Here, the editors are imagining line 472, in both the modern sense of "supposing to [have] exist[ed]" and the medieval sense of "creating an image" with which to concretize their notes' assertion: "This line is missing from the manuscript."[19] An extended run of asterisks reinscribes the line (though not its words) into the poem, which is numerated accordingly.

David Carlson has made a powerful case, however, that "line 472" is absent from the poem, not missing from the manuscript.[20] The stanza makes perfectly good sense as written, and keeps *Pearl* just short of the total number of lines, 1212, that P. M. Kean first suggested constitutes an especially perfect number and one whose symbolism perfectly suits the poem's subject.[21] Carlson therefore reads the missing line as a form of authorial humility: the poet's performed acknowledgment that, unlike the Heavenly Jerusalem it depicts, *Pearl* is "a formally magnificent edifice but still an earthly construction," which should therefore not presume to numerical perfection.[22] This theory cannot

18. "'Courtesy,' I said, 'and great charity are among you, I believe, but—I hope my language does not grieve you—**** you raise yourself too high in heaven, to make yourself queen who were so young'" (lines 469–74).

19. McGillivray and Stook, *Pearl*, 74. They continue: "The elaborate regularity of stanza structure, concatenation, etc., suggest strongly that there did exist a line to complete the stanza structure and that it has been accidentally omitted in copying" (*Pearl*, 74). Andrew and Waldron are still more terse, asserting simply: "line missing in manuscript" (*Poems*, 76).

20. Carlson, "*Pearl*'s Imperfections," 57–60.

21. Kean, "Numerical Composition in *Pearl*." This argument has since been widely endorsed, most elaborately by Condren, *Numerical Universe*, esp. 49–73. See also Newman, "Artifice of Eternity."

22. Carlson, "*Pearl*'s Imperfections," 59–60. It seems significant in this context that *Pearl* carefully grounds its description of the Heavenly Jerusalem in "þe apostel John," the concatenating phrase of section 17: further evidence, perhaps, of the poet's anxiety about too presumptuous an imitation of divine construction.

be proven, of course, but it is consonant with the sensibility of *Pearl* and, this book will argue, of the manuscript's other three poems, too. However this irregularity first occurred, the fact remains that literally and materially, *Pearl* contains 1211 lines. Editors' long-standing determination to elide that fact, by using a phantom line 472 to "round up" to their preferred total, fundamentally reshapes the poem and so deserves more sustained and careful argumentation than it has generally received. That is especially so since this "imperfection" is analogous to many others in both poem and manuscript, and assimilable to any number of interpretive explanations.

We should therefore speculate upon this anomalous stanza's potential effects upon readers. I find it significant that the poem's one "missing" line should appear just as the debate about sufficiency and value discussed earlier begins to heat up, with the Dreamer's indignant reaction to the Maiden's exalted status. The shape of this stanza offers cues both audible (the altered rhyme scheme) and visual (one less line on the page) to attend to absence, a phenomenon already thematized by the Dreamer's loss of the pearl. By offering a concrete instance of "less" just as "more-and-less"-ness begins to shape the poem's narrative drama, the anomalous stanza 40 elegantly synthesizes form and content.

It also starts to establish a pattern of slight but conspicuous exceptions to elaborately articulated structures: a phenomenon that I will call "anti-exactness," which occurs in both *Pearl* and the Pearl-Manuscript more broadly. Any given instance of this phenomenon can be explained or emended away, or simply ignored. Cumulatively, however, this cross-manuscript pattern of highly wrought, slightly imperfect designs and mirrorings reinforces what I take to be the poems' balanced aesthetic and homiletic sensibility: of delight in verbal and material craftsmanship (wroughtness), coupled with belief in the absolute insufficiency (imperfection) of all such human efforts in the face of the Divine.

It is therefore poetic that Jesus should break *Pearl*'s elaborate system of section-linking the one and only time that happens: section 13 of the poem begins with the traditional abbreviation for Jesus, "Ihs," rather than (as we would expect) a version of the previous section's concatenating word, "right." Carlson argues that this imperfection "calls attention by formal means to the Pearl-maiden's point, perhaps her most important point, that claims of 'ryȝt' are a dead end, and that Christ's mercy makes salvation possible."[23] B. S. W. Barootes has strengthened this reading by demonstrating the rich

23. Carlson, "*Pearl*'s Imperfections," 62.

numerological significance of the fact that this exception to regular section-linking takes place across lines 720/721.[24]

More broadly, and independently of any particular literary reading such as those above (both of which I find persuasive), the "Ihs/Ryȝt" opening of section 13 offers yet another example of the "slight exception to the established pattern" pattern, like the anomalous stanza 40. It thus invites us to read section 13 attentive to any comparable irregularities that may appear. Sure enough, we find two instances of its concatenating word *maskeleȝ* ("spotless"), those of lines 733 and 757, instead written *makeleȝ* ("peerless"). This apparent violation of the poem's regular stanza-linking prompted early editors Israel Gollancz and Charles G. Osgood to emend those cases to *maskeleȝ*, thereby restoring the concatenation.[25] Yet as Andrew and Waldron point out in a footnote to the beginning of section 13 (and thus before we reach the first such anomalous case in the poem itself), *Pearl* features "some play between the similar but distinct meanings" of the two words; they therefore retain the manuscript readings.[26] What might look like scribal error is thus adjudged authorial "play."

I also find these exceptions artful, but when the first anomalous instance appears at line 733, it does not stand out for its substantively different or "playful" sense. If anything, the Maiden seems to use the words synonymously, describing the Pearl of Price first as a "perle . . . *mascelleȝ*" and then as a "*makelleȝ* perle" just one line later (lines 732–33, emphasis added). The "makeleȝ Lambe" praised in line 757 is both peerless and spotless, so either word would fit equally well there, too. The full scope of play between these words is revealed only in the section's final line, when the Dreamer juxtaposes them in addressing the Maiden as "makeleȝ may and maskelleȝ" ("peerless and spotless maiden," line 780)—only to be sharply corrected for suggesting that the two words are actually the synonyms that her own earlier usage implied them to be:

"Maskelles," coþe þat myry queen, [781]
"vnblemyst I am wythouten blot,
and þat may I with mensk menteene,
bot 'makeleȝ quene' þenne sade I not."[27]

24. Barootes, "Number Symbolism in *Pearl*."

25. See Gollancz, *Pearl*; and Osgood, *Pearl*.

26. Andrew and Waldron, *Poems*, 87.

27. "'Spotless [*Maskelles*],' said that merry queen, 'Unblemished I am, without blot, and I may maintain that with honor, but "peerless [*makeleȝ*] queen"—I did not say that'" (781–84).

Unlike the Pearl of Price and the Lamb of God, the Maiden is *not* peerless in the sense of unique: on earth, the Dreamer "ne proued . . . neuer her precios pere" ("never found her precious peer," line 4), but she has emphasized that in heaven, she is just one of many concurrently and equally reigning monarchs. A first-time reader of the manuscript, however, who meets the first anomalous occurrence of *makeleȝ* without the benefit of the Maiden's subsequent explanation (or clarifying editorial footnotes), would be in a position not unlike the Dreamer's: both must use limited data to make sense of the poem's complex lexical and theological otherworld.

This congruence between reader and Dreamer is appropriate to the poem's homiletic purpose, but it is interrupted by a scribal manicule drawing our attention to the second anomalous instance of *makeleȝ* at the top of 49/53v (line 757; see fig. 2.1). Here, a paratextual addition works pedagogically by suggesting that the reader linger upon this second exception to the rule: another miswriting (or is it?) of the concatenation-word. It thus both evinces and invites sustained, even meditative engagement with the Pearl-Manuscript as a material object, interrupting our apprehension of the poem's abstract and "immaterial" textuality.[28]

We can only speculate upon the precise intentions behind this manicule and many other elements of the manuscript analyzed in this book. Two forms of the ever-multiplying pearl, the Pearl-Manuscript and the Pearl-Maiden, thus begin to resemble one another: as beautiful survivors that we are fortunate or blessed to have found once more, they are tantalizingly proximate but leave us with more questions than answers—and the unslaked desire for "more and more." If one measure of literary value lies in a text's capacity to press us to reread and reflect, then this example suggests how *Pearl* is enhanced by its material uniqueness, which creates such unexpected parallels between manuscript and Maiden, Dreamer and reader—across time, media, and recoverable intention. I once called these parallels uncanny; now I would call them supereffable, a term Cristina Maria Cervone has usefully coined to describe "an understanding of sacred fullness enacted through form."[29]

My next case study considers a version of such superabundance, namely

28. See further introduction, pages 13–14; and Wakelin, *Immaterial Texts*.

29. "In wrestling with the problem of ineffability, medieval writers paradoxically engage a sort of supereffability," which invites us "to notice, ruminate over, delight in, and wonder at the capaciousness of metaphor, at how a figure may express more than the sum of its parts" (Cervone, *Poetics of the Incarnation*, 4–5). Cervone focuses on metaphor, but her mode of reading sheds light on the materiality of the Pearl-Manuscript as well. See further introduction, pages 18–20.

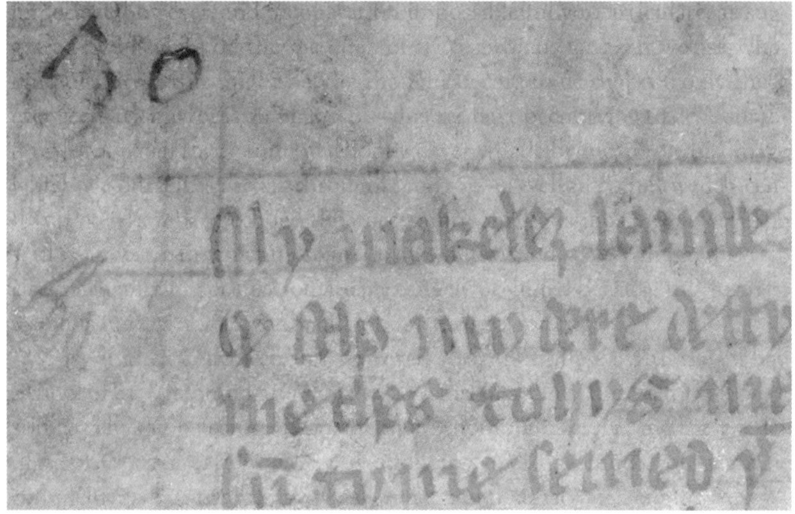

FIGURE 2.1. Folio 49/53v of Cotton Nero A.x/2. Close-up of scribal manicule at line 757 of *Pearl*. Photograph © 2024 by The British Library Board.

the fact that section 15 contains six stanzas, one more than every other section. Like the anomalous *makelez* of lines 733 and 757, this violation of the poem's regular pattern made early editors grumble, with both Osgood and E. V. Gordon suggesting that one of the six stanzas might be spurious.[30] As we have seen, however, the extra stanza makes the poem either actually reach or tantalizingly approach a symbolically significant total of 1212 lines. It also gives *Pearl* a total of 101 stanzas, the same number as in *Sir Gawain and the Green Knight*, which Andrew and Waldron rightly deem "a parallel hard to credit as coincidence."[31] It seems further significant that in *Pearl*, the extra stanza appears in a section that takes "neuer the les" as its concatenation phrase, evoking this very issue of addition and subtraction and perhaps even slyly instructing us "never" to make its six stanzas "the less" by one, despite the

30. See Osgood, *Pearl*, xvi, and Gordon, *Pearl*, 88.

31. Andrew and Waldron, *Poems*, 94. This numerical parallel seems still more significant in light of the poems' other similarities: both concern a sympathetic but flawed protagonist interacting with, and ultimately judged by, a monochromatically dressed otherworldly figure. On this logic, the slight numerical imperfection created by the addition of a single extra stanza in each poem would be congruent with the slight moral imperfection that leads to Gawain's nicked neck and the Pearl-Dreamer's abrupt eviction from his glorious vision.

anomaly. Section 15 thus conjoins "more" (the extra stanza) and "less" (its concatenating section), a multifaceted, "both-and" punning typical of this poem.

The extra stanza also anticipates, textually, an anomaly in the page layout of section 16: an extra decorated initial at line 961, which marks its final stanza.[32] To this point, only the opening stanzas of concatenating sections have received such decoration. (This pattern turns out to hold: *Pearl*'s twenty-one decorated initials appear at the beginning of each section—and line 961.) When the first-time reader encounters this line, it would therefore look like the beginning of a new concatenating section of the poem. That would mean supposing that section 16 has four rather than the usual five stanzas; but having just read section 15's six stanzas—one more than we would expect—and considering the regularity of the decoration to this point, we might well trust its suggestion that this line marks the beginning of a new section.

When the stanza at the bottom of 52/56r ends by repeating *mote* instead of taking up a new concatenation word, however, it becomes clear that line 961's decorated initial was a red herring. Turning the page, we find the next concatenating section at the top of the verso, right on cue with a decorated initial, just like the beginning of every other section: order has been restored. This visual change-up—folio 52/56r would be featureless according to the normative decorative scheme—offers another interruption of *Pearl*'s shimmering immateriality, for the poem's *mise en page* is an exception to the rule, an unexpected "imperfection" that visually complements the "more-and-less"-ness evoked by the textual shape of the poem itself: 1211 lines (not 1212), 101 stanzas (not 100), twenty-one decorated initials (not twenty).

Moreover, the fact that these are the only two consecutive stanzas to feature decoration effectively highlights them, which is significant because they establish the conditions of the Dreamer's vision-within-a-vision—and seem to be depicted in the poem's final illustration, as we will see in chapter 3:

> "Moteleȝ may so meke and mylde,"
> þen sayde I to þat lufly flor,
> "bryng me to þat bygly bylde
> and let me se þy blyssful bor."
> Þat schene sayde: "Þat God wyl schylde!
> Þou may not enter withinne Hys tor;
> bot of þe Lombe I haue þe aquylde

32. For an alternate reading of this anomalous initial's literary effects, see Condren, *Numerical Universe*, 68–72.

for a syȝt þerof þurȝ gret fauor.
Vtwyth to se þat clene cloystor [969]
þou may bot inwyth not a fote;
to strech in þe street þou hatȝ no vygour,
bot þou wer clene, withouten mote. [bottom of 52/56r]

"If I þis mote þe schal vnhyde, [973; top of 52/56v]
bow vp towarde þys borneȝ heued,
and I anendeȝ þe on þis syde
schal sve tyl þou to a hil be veued."
Þen wolde I no lenger byde, [977]
bot lurked by launceȝ so lufly leued,
tyl on a hyl þat I asspyed
and blusched on þe burgh, as I forth dreued,
byȝonde þe brok, fro mewarde keued, [981]
þat schyrrer þen sunne with schafteȝ schon.
In þe Apokalypce is þe fasoun preued,
as deuyseȝ hit þe apostel John.[33]

Both stanzas open with four-line speeches organized around an imperative ("bryng me . . . bow vp") that directs the action, and thus the reader's attention, toward the celestial city.[34] The poem's focus thus shifts from emotional turmoil and theological debate to a mediated vision of the Heavenly Jerusalem.

33. "'Spotless maiden so meek and mild,' then said I to that lovely flower, 'Bring me to that grand construction, and let me see your blissful bower.' That shining one said, 'God forbid! You may not enter within His tower; but from the Lamb I have obtained for you a sight thereof, through great favor. You may see that clean cloister from without, but not a foot within; you have no power to walk on that path unless you were clean, without spot [*mote*]. If I am to reveal this city [*mote*] to you, direct yourself [*bow vp*] to the head of the stream, and I will follow opposite you on this side, until you are brought to a hill.' Then I would wait no longer, but passed by boughs with beautiful leaves until, on a hill, I caught sight of the city and as I made my way forth, I gazed at it beyond the brook, away from me at a lower level, that shone with rays brighter than the sun. The construction is established in the [Book of] Apocalypse, as the apostle John describes it" (lines 961–84).

34. "Bow up" is an interesting locution, since although *bouen* can mean simply "come, go" (*Middle English Dictionary* [accessed August 31, 2023, https://quod.lib.umich.edu/m/middle-english-dictionary/dictionary/MED5682], s.v. "bǒuen, v." meaning 6), the word more often suggests submission and obedience (meanings 1, 2), like its modern English reflex. In this way, the Maiden's language subtly anticipates the test of obedience that the Dreamer will fail when he plunges into the water that separates them.

This speculative reorientation ends the dialogue between Dreamer and Maiden that has dominated *Pearl* since the beginning of section 5, considered earlier ("O perle," coþe I, "in perleȝ pyȝt . . . ," line 241). Like sections 1–4, which are wholly speechless, sections 17–20 contain no dialogue except the four-line conclusion of the Maiden's response to the Dreamer quoted above (lines 973–76), whose long, complex exchange thus corresponds almost perfectly to the poem's central twelve sections (5–16), yielding a *Pearl* with 4-12-4 as one of its many shapes: a central twelve-section debate enclosed by four-section units that are almost entirely speechless, oriented instead around different forms of paradisal vision. Such patterning is consonant with what chapters 3 and 5, in particular, will show to be comparable number-shaping around 12 and 4 across the codex. Just as the Pearl of Price is set "euen in myddeȝ my [the Maiden's] breste" ("even within my breast," line 740), so too this dialogue is set (or *pyȝt*, another concatenating word) almost entirely within the poem's central twelve sections.

Almost but not quite: its last four lines spill over into section 17. This is only the latest in a recurring pattern of anti-exactness, such as the poem's 1211 total lines and 101 stanzas, and I share Carlson's view that such near-misses can be read homiletically: the New Testament word for sin, *hamartia*, famously means "a missing of the mark." They also have important effects perceptually, in that they are so close to the missed ideal that both imperfection and ideal become simultaneously perceptible and, to that extent, real. "Line 472" is a good example of this phenomenon, for it is simultaneously there (in editions and scholarly citation practice, my own included) and not-there (literally), gaining a quantum-like existence. Such blurring denaturalizes our perspective, which in turn can help us find other pressure points, or fissures, out of which more (and more) of *Pearl*'s full interpretive energy can emerge. It also suggests a temporally complex approach to reading the past: one constructive rather than reconstructive, in Benjaminian terms; and attuned as much to effect and evolution as to origin(s).

This speculative appreciation of time and shape suggests a "both-and" reading of the poem's final stanza, which is a crux both formal (because section 15's six stanzas make it the "protruding" 101st) and thematic—since I am not alone in resisting its simplistic assertion that "it is very easy for the good Christian" to selflessly embrace God's will, as lines 1201–2 would have it.[35]

35. Garrison opens her appreciative reassessment of the final stanza, whose image of the elevated Host she considers in light of late medieval Eucharistic devotion, by acknowledging that "[s]ome of the best recent readers of *Pearl* have ignored or resisted its final stanza. And there is no doubt that the stanza poses difficulties" ("Liturgy and Loss," 294). Aers, for example, argues that these lines are "theologically superficial and psychologically superficial.

In fact, the action and diction of *Pearl*'s final section bely this blithely idealistic claim: the Dreamer's swoon at line 1180 recalls his fainting fit from the beginning of the poem (lines 57–58); he then describes his earthly existence as a *doel-doungoun* ("love-pain-dungeon," line 1187), evoking the courtly-love lexicon of his initial *luf-daungere* ("love-dominion," line 11); and shortly before the bland moralizing of lines 1201–2, he uses the intensive word *toriuen* ("reft away") to describe the loss of his joy (line 1197). These lines are also thick with the first- and second-person singular pronouns that characterized the Dreamer's early, theologically suspect exchanges with the Maiden: nineteen total in the thirty lines from his awakening to the end of the penultimate stanza (lines 1171–1200). He still refers possessively to "my perle" (line 1173) and three times rhetorically distances himself from God with the phrase "þat Prince" (lines 1176, 1188, 1189). All of this makes the universalizing, gnomic statements of lines 1195–96 and 1199–1200 seem more like a refuge from the Dreamer's own emotional drama than evidence of a truly altered perspective on "his" pearl and their relationship to God.

In the last stanza, however, something seems to have changed, for although the Dreamer recalls collapsing "for pyty" of his pearl, he puts this episode firmly in the past; only afterward (*syþen*) did he commend her to God and, he implies, actually make peace with his loss (lines 1206–7). Yet the poem has not depicted this selfless commendation. On the contrary, his last reported address to the pearl suggests reluctant acceptance at best, and at worst passive-aggressive self-pity:

"If hit be ueray and soth sermoun [1185]
þat þou so stykeȝ in garlande gay,
so wel is me in þys doel-doungoun
þat þou art to þat Prynseȝ paye."[36]

The reassuring invocation of 'þe god Krystyin' not only sets aside theological issues but also searching difficulties the poem itself has raised" ("The Self Mourning," 70), while Condren contends that "[h]ere the Dreamer sounds more like the Pharisee than the publican in the famous parable recounted by Luke (18:9–14)" (*Numerical Universe*, 73). Even one homiletically minded critic who reads the poem as "one huge typological metaphor of orthodox Christian behavior," nevertheless considered the final stanza's expressions of "resolution and reconciliation . . . gratuitous and facile" (Stern, "Approach to 'The Pearl,'" cited in Spearing, *Gawain-Poet*, 129).

36. "If it is really a true account that you are firmly set in that lovely garland, then I will manage [*so wel is me*] in this love-pain-dungeon, knowing that you are pleasing to that Prince" (lines 1185–88).

His perspective therefore seems to have changed significantly by the final stanza, for after contending with God for one hundred of the poem's 101 stanzas, the Dreamer claims in its last that "I haf founden Hym . . . / a frende ful fyin" ("I have found Him . . . a very fine friend," lines 1203–4). With its perfect-tense verb, the only one in section 20, these lines assert as completed action the spiritual awakening that would make sense of the Dreamer's (now, avowedly) perfect submission to God. That perfect tense, together with the poem's occlusion of the Dreamer's actual commendation of the pearl, hints at a temporal fissure, an almost imperceptible passage of time between the penultimate and final stanzas.

Read in light of two other aspects of *Pearl* that we have considered thus far—its play with "more-and-less"-ness and its delight in the counterintuitive, paradoxical nature of Christianity—such hints of a temporal fissure enable understanding both of the last two stanzas as "ends" of the poem. (It is worth noting here that in the manuscript, *Pearl* concludes with two Amens, rather than just one as the following three poems do—an invitation, perhaps, to speculate upon distinct yet complementary conclusions?) On this reading, the penultimate stanza would conclude the Dreamer's immediate experience of his vision and its aftermath; and those lines have a conclusive force that is reinforced formally by being the hundredth stanza.[37] Only after an intervening period of meditative self-reflection (another form of speculation), however, can the Dreamer truly claim to "have found" God a fine friend, as recorded in the final, 101st stanza.

However we theorize its existence, *Pearl*'s final stanza disrupts a formal tidiness that might otherwise be too pat for our experience of either life or poem.[38] As the only mortal character in the poem, the Dreamer sometimes serves as a stand-in for the reader, as we saw with the anomalous instances of *makeleȝ* noted earlier, which is why lines 1201–2 can feel like a betrayal

37. Andrew and Waldron (*Poems*, 110) also note the conclusiveness of these lines, pointing out that they summarize the moral presented at the beginning and end of *Patience*. A comparable view of the stanza's conclusiveness is implicit in Christopher Cannon's suggestion that it is this "penultimate stanza which (by virtue of the poem's circularity) also functions as its prologue" ("Form," 188).

38. In a similar vein to mine here, Carlson ("*Pearl*'s Imperfections," 64) contrasts *Pearl*'s 101 stanzas with the "perfectly round total of 100 cantos" in Dante's *Commedia*: "the *Pearl*-poet deployed a deliberately flawed structure, with a patently imperfect, excessive total of 101 stanzas that manages to allude to the kind of perfection embodied in the *Divine Comedy*" and thus emphasize its own refusal to make a comparably bold structural gesture.

of our shared humanity.[39] Read as I have here, however, the movement of the poem's final stanzas becomes more nuanced, for by refusing to show us the Dreamer's final surrender (of the pearl, to God), *Pearl* suggests that such moments of spiritual discovery are necessarily inward and private. Put another way: at the beginning of the poem, the Dreamer insisted that the pearl was unique and "pryuy" (line 12); at its ultimate conclusion, by contrast, he has come to accept that she is just one of many "precious *perleȝ* vnto His pay" (line 1212, emphasis added), even as the poem occludes the exact moment and nature of this realization such that we are not "privy" to it. That realization, and the analytic energy necessary to arrive at it, may in turn prompt deeper self-reflection in the reader.[40]

This speculative reading of the poem's last two stanzas is grounded in *Pearl*'s complex engagement with time: the inevitable progression of mortal time, which means that the Dreamer's pearl will never again be "his" in the same way as before; and its contrast with divine timelessness, made gloriously visible "in þe Apokalypce . . . / as deuyseȝ hit þe apostel John" ("in the Apocalypse . . . as the apostle John describes it," lines 983–84).[41] We should recall here that time was central both to the Dreamer's resistance to the Pearl-Maiden's exaltation in Heaven—she "lyfed not two ȝer in oure þede" ("lived not two years in our land," line 483)—and to the parable of the vineyard told to explain and justify that exaltation, by which there is no "date" to God's goodness.

Such play with temporal perspective is nicely enacted by the ambiguity of the poem's final conjugated (i.e., finite) verb: "He [God] *gef* vus to be his homly hyne / Ande precious perleȝ vnto his pay" ("He gave/may grant us

39. See further A. C. Spearing's observation that the poem's drama "is inflected with a first-person quality, a proximality and experientiality that the third-person terminology endorsed by narrator theory cannot fully convey" ("What Is a Narrator?," 89).

40. This reading complements Garrison's emphasis ("Liturgy and Loss," 296) on the "personal, inward-looking modes of devotion" that the late medieval form of the Mass encouraged, in large part because "the most sacred part of the Mass in which the consecration of the bread and wine takes place was inaudible—said silently by the priest in order to avoid revealing the secrets of God." There may be an analogy, in other words, between the faithful at Mass and the reader of *Pearl*, who is likewise kept at a distance from the process of spiritual growth taking place off stage, as it were: in each case, an occluded transformation (mystical at Mass, personal in the Dreamer) encourages personal and inward contemplation. See also Minnis's elegant reading of the final stanza in "Unquiet Graves."

41. On the poem's engagement with time, see further Staley Johnson, "*Pearl* Dreamer." On its evocation of medieval representations of the Book of Revelation, see Pierson Prior, *Fayre Formez*, 21–66; and Stanbury, *Seeing the Gawain-Poet*, 12–41.

to be his humble household, and precious pearls to his pleasure," lines 1211–12, emphasis added). As Andrew and Waldron note, *gef* can be both past (tense) and subjunctive (mood),[42] which means that *Pearl* ends by looking both backward and forward in time, simultaneously recalling the moment in history when God became incarnate on earth and thus "gave" humanity into his care; while also praying for a future in which "he may grant" that the whole Christian community become "precious perleȝ vnto his pay." *Pearl*'s lexical punning is famous; here, grammatical ambiguity creates a temporal pun that reinforces the poem's theological sensitivity and formal complexity.

What unites the case studies of this section is that in each, a slight formal irregularity creates interpretive potential—a literary version of Newtonian potential energy—that remains vibrant partly because no other copies of *Pearl* exist by which we can assess that irregularity's source, authorial or scribal. Such blurring of seemingly straightforward categories (author vs. scribe; accident vs. art) is consonant with the poem's own delight in the paradoxes of Christianity, which as exemplified by the parables of the vineyard and of the pearl of price upend earthly, logical distinctions. The "more-and-less"-themed concatenation phrases of sections 3, 10, 11, and 15 subtly reinforce such moments, and can thus be seen to operate at an extra-denotative and metaphorical level that their literal content would seem to resist. In the final section of this chapter, the many readings of a single contested letter in the manuscript will further confirm *Pearl*'s still-expanding literariness of the literal.

QUANTUM LETTERS

My text here is a single letter whose meaning has been multiplied by the range of modern editorial treatments it has received. Like my analysis of *Pearl*'s final stanza, this case study will highlight the poem's evolution across time: here not the speculative time of a literary persona's occluded journey toward spiritual growth, but rather the literal time across which living persons have made documented scholarly decisions. My play on two meanings of *literal*—"(f)actual" and "pertaining to a letter"—will afford a consideration of how *Pearl* embodies Derridean *différance* and even does it one better. Because the letter in question appears in the context of the Maiden's treatment of the parable of the vineyard, it will also return us to the theme of value with which this chapter began.

42. Andrew and Waldron, *Poems*, 110.

Below I reproduce Andrew and Waldron's apparatus (textual note and footnote) as well as the passage that contains the letter in question:

"Bot now þou motez, me for to mate, [613]
Þat I my peny haf wrang tan here;
Þou sayz þat I þat com to late
Am not worþy so gret fere*."[43]

* here (Gollancz and Osgood) MS lere
616 *fere*: "dignity, reward." The MS reading *lere* is incomprehensible; Gordon's emendation *fere* is more convincing than that adopted by Gollancz and Osgood, *here* "wages."

Manuscript *lere* can mean cheek, face, or flesh,[44] and this abrupt shift to physical appearance after a monetary metaphor has led nearly all editors to emend. Doing so is perfectly reasonable, but Andrew and Waldron's categorical framing of their decision is striking, for although they call their emendation to *fere*, adopted from Gordon, simply "more convincing" than the earlier one to *here*, that word's meaning of "payment" makes perfectly good sense given the Maiden's reference to the penny in line 614. Their emendation is thus more convincing only to the extent that the more genteel lexicon of "reward," or the more abstract register of "dignity," seems better suited to the refined Maiden than the grubbiness of a contractual "payment." But since the question of payment figured so prominently in the central parable of the vineyard, that meaning seems at least equally plausible here.

Furthermore, while manuscript *lere* may be less intuitive than either of those proposed emendations, it should not be branded "incomprehensible." It would simply suggest that the poet is using the Maiden's transfigured beauty (the Dreamer does not initially recognize her, we should recall) as a metaphor for the transformative grace she has received. Moreover, the same word *lere* has already twice described the Maiden, first in a compound that appears to mean "wimple" (line 210, though here McGillivray and Stook emend), then

43. "But now you claim, in order to confound me, that I have wrongly taken my penny here; you say that I, who came so/too late, am not worthy of such great **ere* [***contested word with many possible meanings***]" (lines 613–16). I cite Andrew and Waldron's edition here, rather than McGillivray and Stook's as generally in this chapter, for reasons that will become clear.

44. See the *Middle English Dictionary* entries for *ler* (primary meaning "cheek, face") and *lire* (primary meaning "flesh"). The scribe spells both of these words variously *ler(e)*, *lire*, and *lyre*, further complicating the situation.

later when she is called "lufsom of lyth and lere" ("lovely in comportment and visage," line 398). By the editorial maxim of *lectio difficilior potior* ("the more difficult reading is the stronger"), the counterintuitive nature of the manuscript reading here might even be a point in its favor.

Of course, that maxim is not an absolute rule; Martin L. West, for example, argues that it "should not be used in support of dubious syntax, or phrasing that it would not be natural for the author to use. There is an important difference between a more *difficult* reading and a more *unlikely* reading."[45] But our sense of the "natural" offers a highly imperfect guide for a poem that survives nowhere else, has no precise formal analogues, and everywhere exceeds the natural: in its highly wrought formal and lexical artistry, the extravagance of its paradisal dreamscape (gravel made of gems, crystal cliffs, indigo trees), and the counterintuitive (super-natural because celestial) notions of value that the Maiden both propounds and embodies. Beyond this brilliantly cultivated strangeness, other aspects of *Pearl* undermine the value of the "natural" in approaching textual cruces like this one. The poet's richly multilingual heritage (such that a given word might be argued to have any of several different sources),[46] the poet's wordplay and the scribe's varied orthography (such that a single set of graphemes often has multiple meanings and a single meaning can be represented by multiple sets of graphemes),[47] and our lack of comparative data from other manuscripts (which might help construct a fuller sense of either poet's or scribe's "natural" practice)—all of these frustrate efforts to pin *Pearl* down.

45. West, *Textual Criticism*, 51.

46. To the following examples from *Pearl* many more could be added from across the Pearl-Manuscript: MS *freles* (line 431) might mean "flawless," from ON *frýjulaust*, or "peerless," as a corruption of ME *fereles*; MS *dard* (line 609) might derive from OE *durian* ("to lurk in dread") or OE *durran* ("to dare"); MS *blose* (line 911) might be a corruption of ME *boce* ("a lump of a man") or a form of Scottish *blus* ("a boaster"); MS *walte* (line 1156) might mean "set," from OE *waldan*, or "chosen," from ON *velja*. All these possibilities are taken from Andrew and Waldron's footnotes to the words in question, and other editors propose comparably wide-ranging etymologies and ranges of meaning for other words across the manuscript. The complexity of the poet's lexical usage also animates numerous suggestive essays, such as Breeze, "A Celtic Etymology for *Glaverez*," and Donaldson, "Oysters, Forsooth."

47. On the first point: we have already considered the many significations of concatenation word *date*, but another example that is particularly relevant to the contested reading of line 616 is *fere*, which the poet uses to mean (at least) dignity, reward, martial array, company, wife, mistress, and equal. On the second point: variation in scribal orthography is of course ubiquitous in the Middle Ages, but the wide range of possible linguistic sources for the poet's usage makes it especially confounding here.

Indeed, from a single contested letter that yields three readings of the word in which it appears—*lere*, *here*, and *fere*—each of these expands outward to a still wider set of potential meanings. To take only Andrew and Waldron's chosen reading, *fere*: in addition to the far from equivalent meanings of the word that Andrew and Waldron propose ("dignity" and "reward"), the *Middle English Dictionary* lists "company," "power," and "appearance, manner" as contemporary meanings.[48] Line 616 may evoke all of these, for the Pearl-Maiden demonstrates both rhetorical and intercessory power; she will later be seen in the company of heavenly virgins ("among her fereȝ," line 1150) in the New Jerusalem; and her appearance and manner have also been lavishly described throughout the poem. (This meaning of *fere*, incidentally, would return us to the lexical world of manuscript *lere*.) Simply put: here as so often in *Pearl*, we face not a demonstrably authorial set of graphemes with a single, stable signification, but rather a dizzying range of potential meanings that ebb and flow and eddy around one another.[49] Not all of those meanings are equally apparent at all times or to all readers, and the poet cannot have consciously intended them all—but this proves only that *Pearl* has continued to gain depth and luster since its originary moment(s), in a process not unlike the gradual and accumulative one by which natural pearls are formed.

Two recent editions of the poem further attest to this accretive process, for they offer "more and more" readings of this seemingly inexhaustible word: *lowere* (Putter and Stokes) and *bere* (McGillivray and Stook). I quote the latter's helpfully thorough rationale:

> 616 *bere* So, probably, MS (bere): 'l' and lobeless 'b' before 'e' (i.e., 'b' in juncture or "with biting") are not easily distinguishable in this hand. Previous editors have read *lere*, and most have emended, Gordon (1953), Andrew and Waldron (1979+) and others to *fere* (show, array), Osgood (1906) and Gollancz (1921) to

48. *Middle English Dictionary* (accessed August 31, 2023, https://quod.lib.umich.edu/m/middle-english-dictionary/dictionary/MED15651), s.v. "fēre, n.," meanings 2, 3, and 5, respectively.

49. Gordon's rationale for emending *lere* to *fere* further substantiates this point. He suggests (*Pearl*, 68) that "ME *fere* in the phrase (*with*) *grete fere* probably derives ultimately from OF *afe(i)re*, commonly used in the phrase *de grant afeire* 'of high rank' or 'with great pomp and circumstance.' The aphetic form may have arisen in this phrase. . . . Rhymes with close *e* suggest that this word has become confused or blended with *fere* from ON *fœri* 'power, ability.' . . . Alternatively . . . *fere* may be derived from OE *gefere* 'company,' and refer to the company of Heaven's queens."

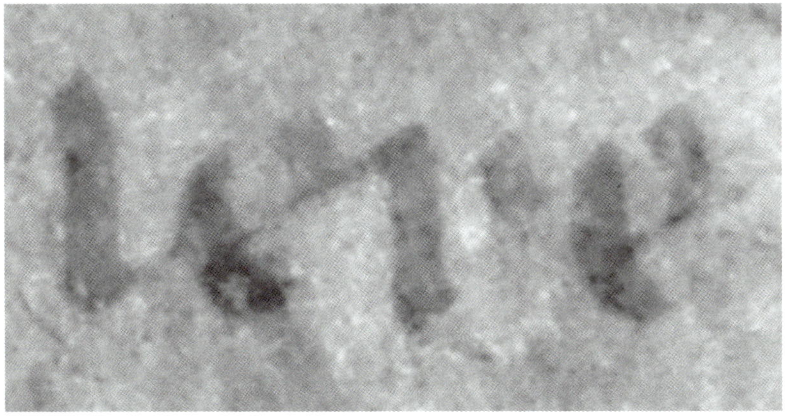

FIGURE 2.2. Folio 47/51v of Cotton Nero A.x/2.
Photograph © 2024 by The British Library Board.

> *here* (hire), Putter and Stokes (2014) to *lowere* (reward, recompense). Emerson ("Some Notes on the *Pearl*," *PMLA* 37 [1922]) read *lere* and suggested emendation to *bere*, "bearing, manner, society, position" (74), i.e. MED *bere* n9, sense b. We think this is the right word but not the right sense (since the focus of the stanza is on reward, not position) and would instead propose an attenuated use of *bere* n9 sense a ("Outcry, clamor, commotion, disturbance"); "You say that I came too late and am not worthy so great a fuss."[50]

"So great a fuss" indeed, about one letter of one word of a poem that survives in just one manuscript; yet for such lexical plenitude to emerge from a thing so small is precisely the point.

At first glance, the letter certainly looks more like an *l* than a *b* (fig. 2.2). If we look closely, however, the bottom of the initial stroke appears very slightly joined to the following *e*, especially compared to the first two letters of *late* just above, where there is (again, very slightly) discernible space between the strokes (see fig. 2.3). This difference might support the reading of *bere*; alternately, it might reflect a difference in the scribe's vowels. Perhaps he changed his mind, or realized a mistake, midstroke. A. I. Doyle's suggestion that the scribe "was happier with anglicana than the textura he or his employer felt was called for" further muddies the paleographical waters, since

50. McGillivray and Stook, *Pearl*, 76.

FIGURE 2.3. Folio 47/51v of Cotton Nero A.x/2.
Photograph © 2024 by The British Library Board.

a scribe working outside his comfort zone would seem especially prone to idiosyncratic variation in letter formation.[51]

I tend to see an *l* here, but the question's continued debatability means that we have something like a quantum letter, from which emerge a still-growing number of editorial readings with ever-expanding ranges of meaning. Indeed, it is a mark of the Maiden's otherworldliness, in systems of thought and therefore also of expression, that so many, not-at-all similar meanings can seem plausible for this particular word. In that sense, these scribal markings may signify less any particular letter, word, or meaning, than they do how thoroughly *Pearl*'s unique material situation can upend traditional understandings of the world. In that sense, *lere/bere-here-fere*

51. Doyle, "English Books," 166. See further introduction, pages 2–3.

functions much like James C. Staples's recent theorization of the *poynt*, as one means by which the poet "undermines any claims to rationalist mastery of the material or spiritual world, holding knowledge of each in perpetual tension with the other."[52] It therefore seems appropriate to represent its first letter with a *punctus elevatus*, or asterisk-as-wild-card: **ere*, with the first letter to be decided by the reader, or left undecided.[53]

The **ere* case thus highlights *Pearl*'s manifold singularity, which leads more and richer interpretations to emerge from its sole surviving manuscript. I have suggested that all of the words considered above produce meanings that are true to the poem: both individually and in the capaciousness of their (sets of) significations, which evoke the poet's wordplay and multifaceted linguistic background. I would go further and argue that we can legitimately adopt all of these readings into our understanding of *Pearl* as an evolving literary artifact. Doing so may involve expanding our notion of what a medieval poem is, or of how it exists through time. Such speculation is less unhelpfully anachronistic than it might seem, however, since the Maiden's own paradox-loving logic likewise undermines what look like comparably stable, uncomplicated categories and distinctions: between queens and lesser aristocrats, for example, or between those who have worked for a long time and those who haven't. The poet is not the author, according to any traditional understanding of the word, of the still-expanding lexical potential of **ere*. *Pearl* asks us to broaden our understanding of such traditional categories, however, and the poem survives in a form that offers this way, among many others, of doing so.

I conclude with two accounts of the literal, in its etymological sense of concerning letters: St. Paul's assertion that "the letter kills, but the spirit gives life" (2 Cor. 3:6), and Derrida's use "of the letter *a*, this initial letter which it apparently has been necessary to insinuate, here and there, into the writing of the word *difference*."[54] For Paul, literalism blinds the faithful to deeper truths that can be fully conveyed only metaphorically. Thus "real circumcision is a matter of the heart—it is spiritual and not literal" (Rom. 2:29), and the mothers of Abraham's two sons should be read as "an allegory: these women are two covenants" (Gal. 4:24). Derrida takes aim at this valorization of metaphor as part of his broader challenge to Western logocentrism, in

52. Staples, "Poynts and Spots," 5.

53. Sharon Cameron's *Choosing Not Choosing* seems relevant here; *Pearl* and Emily Dickinson converse beautifully.

54. Derrida, "Différance," 3.

which writing, as a set of "literal" signifiers, endlessly defers meaning to the originary truth-content of the spoken word. Yet rather than simply reverse the literal/metaphor binary, exalting the former at the expense of the latter, Derrida uses the pervasiveness of metaphors of writing in Western religion and philosophy to argue that "the 'literal' meaning of writing [is] metaphoricity itself."[55]

This nexus of words, ideas, and images is significant to *Pearl* in part because of the Dreamer's frequent literal-mindedness in his dialogue with the Maiden,[56] which Catherine S. Cox argues highlights the misdirected nature of his desire for "his privy" pearl, a literal and fleshly (and in that sense "carnal") body as it existed in life. As she puts it, "the carnal (that is, literal) reader, too easily satisfied with too little and thus content to stop too soon, cuts short the potential of language before fully embracing the figurative (or spiritual) connotations that signification structures represent."[57] Derrida's use of "the letter *a*, this initial letter" emphasizes the literal's capacity to sharpen the kind of semantic multivalence that we have seen animates *Pearl*'s homiletic and aesthetic action as well.[58] After discussing two meanings of *différer*, to differ and to defer, neither of which is satisfactorily conveyed by the canonical French noun *différence*, he writes that his own neologism "*différance* (with an *a*) is to compensate—economically—this loss of meaning, for *différance* can refer simultaneously to the entire configuration of its meanings. It is immediately and irreducibly polysemic, which will not be indifferent to the economy of my discourse here."[59] We have seen that in *Pearl*, individual letters—the literal, in its most literal sense—can create deeply, almost overwhelmingly polysemous effects. Furthermore, just as Derrida's wordplay is essential to his local meaning and broader project alike, so too the elaborate punning of *Pearl* is vital to its spiritual and pedagogical power.[60] That the

55. Derrida, *Of Grammatology*, 15.

56. The Dreamer's sometimes obtuse literal-mindedness has been a critical commonplace, though it has come under pressure more recently. For an argument that the two disputants are more evenly matched than has generally been allowed, see Rhodes, "The Dreamer Redeemed."

57. Cox, "*Pearl*'s 'Precios Pere,'" 379.

58. My reading here has benefited from two brilliantly provocative explorations of individual letters in the poems of Chaucer and Gower, respectively: Rust, "'Straunge' Letters and Strange Loops," in *Imaginary Worlds in Medieval Books*, 81–116; and Epstein, "Literal Opposition."

59. Derrida, "Différance," 8.

60. As Cox puts it, "because language signifies spiritually only when multiple senses obtain, the plural or polysemous character of language has theological and epistemological value" ("*Pearl*'s 'Precios Pere,'" 380). See further Largier's observation of other mystical texts,

poem continues to inspire such polysemy today, in ways unanticipated by its medieval maker(s), is one aspect of this continued vitality.[61]

In fact, *Pearl* 616's *lere* works rather more radically than *différance*, which Derrida introduces as "a kind of gross spelling mistake, a lapse in the discipline and law which regulate writing and keep it seemly."[62] *Lere* itself is a perfectly well-attested word, so it is not inherently such a "gross spelling mistake," but editors' various emendations prove that they regard it as precisely "a lapse in the discipline and law which regulate writing and keep it seemly." By being (judged to be) both of these—not a spelling mistake, yet a lapse in the discipline that regulates writing—the word gains a double meaning even before we consider its quantum other *here* or other editorial manipulations; and those manipulations, far from straightforwardly restoring the supposedly violated sense, contribute to the exuberant explosion of meaning seen earlier. This instance of polysemy is enhanced by the poem's material (literal) uniqueness, which prevents this letter from being made univocal, "literalized" in a spirit-killing way. **ere* thus shows how material history can inspire deconstructive reading.

I have argued that *Pearl*'s long-admired lexical play and elaborate poetic shaping gain still-expanding literary resonance from historical forces and actors other than the poet. As we have seen, the poem's unique survival creates multiple sources of meaning, across multiple axes, in ways that evoke the Maiden's own insistence on Heaven as a court that transcends earthly understandings of hierarchy and value. The Dreamer's initial theory of value was premised on scarcity and underwritten by envy, as his indignant expostulations made clear; the Maiden insists upon a more generous understanding, by which more (kings and queens of heaven) leads to ever more (celestial joy). We can, if we choose, regard the material uniqueness and historical uncertainties of *Pearl* as loss, and seek to restore its violated formal integrity, or to divine the singular, original historical context that would become its clearly delimited source of meaning. But "less" need not be read as "loss,"

"the figural is not opposed to the literal. Instead, it is the (hyper-)literal in its expressivity and multiplicity" (*Figures of Possibility*, 2).

61. The Maiden herself, and perhaps also the poet, would presumably take the Pauline rather than the Derridean view of the literal; Jennifer Garrison has rightly emphasized that although "figural truths appear as if they were literal . . . the pearl maiden insists that the dreamer ought to regard them as figurative" ("Liturgy and Loss," 313). But for us on that basis to dismiss the polysemous effects of the literal(ly literal) is in fact to read like the literal-minded Dreamer, rejecting wider interpretive potential in favor of the reassuringly familiar.

62. Derrida, "Différance," 3.

a literal and significant difference. We can choose instead to delight in how this instance of "less" ultimately yields "more"—not just more discrete interpretations of the text itself, but also more, and more diverse, approaches to it. The expanding singularity of *Pearl* gives the Pearl-Manuscript vectors of unknowability that have paradoxically creative force.

That may sound like exalted or even mystical language for an argument that has relied considerably upon historical contingency and codicological coincidence. It is consonant with speculation as discussed in chapter 1 and with the supereffability of *Pearl* itself, however, and further authorized by the sacral associations of the Pearl-Manuscript's *textualis* hand and its material resemblances to other devotional manuscripts.[63] This nexus of forces is productive, I believe, because it offers a partial gateway into medieval reading, by which I mean less a set of empirically demonstrable, reconstructable historical practices than an opportunity to approach this manuscript with a version of the speculative framework—at once devotional and intellectual—that helped shape so much fourteenth-century writing and reading.[64]

Such an exercise is necessarily anachronistic, a word long taboo in polite academic circles—right up there with "speculative," in fact.[65] Yet such radical perspectival shifts are precisely what medieval speculation sought to effect, as Sara Ritchey's powerful account of the *Speculum virginum* makes clear.[66] At a deeper level, then, reshaping our scholarly perspective can be faithful to the spirit of the book we are considering, even if our version of the practice, our own speculative vision, cannot re-create either the as-it-really-was of medieval readers or the precise intentions of its makers. The pages by which we turn from *Pearl* to *Cleanness* especially merit such speculation, for they shape the interpretive challenges and opportunities that this striking textual juxtaposition affords.

63. On the scribal hand, see Dwyer, "Reading the Tied Letters." Fredell notes the Pearl-Manuscript's codicological similarities with religious book production in Yorkshire ("*Pearl*-Poet Manuscript in York"). See further introduction, pages 6–9, and chap. 1, pages 31–32.

64. I draw inspiration here from Arthur Russell's comparable interpretive framework for a devotional image-text, which he calls "less an attempt to pin down the religious sentiments of the composition and more an effort to flesh out its reading experience. My drawn-out handling . . . intends to reconstitute the sort of sense methods premodern readers both learned from and brought to their everyday devotions" ("Praying by Hand," 203).

65. See Johnston and Mueller, "Kant in King Arthur's Court."

66. See further chap. 1, n. 19.

THREE

LAYERS OF TIME

The aesthetics and ethics of *Pearl* are insistently, gorgeously otherworldly. But just as *Pearl* ends with the Dreamer's sudden return to the waking world, so too we will see that its final page regrounds the reader, poignantly, within the Pearl-Manuscript as a physical object. This material turn is significant because it anticipates the extent to which turning from *Pearl* to *Cleanness* prompts reengagement with the visual and tactile nature of the written word. The vibrant colors and unusual composition of the illustrations on both sides of folio 56/60 (figs. 3.2 and 3.7), which separates the two poems, also highlight continuities between them that are deadened by reading in modern, unillustrated editions. The four pages by which we turn to *Cleanness* therefore serve as an object lesson in how all four poems are enhanced by the Pearl-Manuscript's material peculiarities and evolution across time, whose accretive layers this chapter explores.

These pages also start building the kind of connections, across texts and media, that cumulatively propose the manuscript as a compilation that rewards repeated and creative forms of reading. My analysis of 55/59v–57/61r therefore draws inspiration from Jessica Brantley's account of the *Desert of Religion* in British Library MS Additional 37049: "Each opening of the text is . . . a complex representational object to be perceived at once but perused at leisure."[1] The Pearl-Manuscript is not devotional in the same way as that significantly later, much more extensively illustrated manuscript, but I

1. Brantley, *Reading in the Wilderness*, 79.

Following spread: FIGURE 3.1. Folio 55/59v of Cotton Nero A.x/2. Photograph © 2024 by The British Library Board. FIGURE 3.2. Folio 56/60r of Cotton Nero A.x/2. Photograph © 2024 by The British Library Board.

To þat pryncez paye hade I ay bente
& ȝerned no more þen watz me geuen
& halden me þer in trwe entent
As þe perle me prayed þat watz so þryuen
As helde drawen to goddez present
To mo of his mysterys I hade ben dryuen
Bot ay wolde man of happe more hente
Þen moȝten by ryȝt vpon hem clyuen
Þerfore my ioye watz sone toriuen
& I kaste of kythez þat lastez aye
Lorde mad hit arn þat agayn þe stryuen
Oþer proferen þe oȝt agayn þy paye

To pay þe prince oþer sete saȝte
Hit is ful eþe to þe god krystyin
For I haf founden hym boþe day & naȝte
A god a lorde a frende ful fyin
Ouer þis hyul þis lote I laȝte
For pyty of my perle enclyin
& syþen to god I hit bytaȝte
In krystez dere blessyng & myn
Þat in þe forme of bred & wyn
Þe preste vus schewez vch a daye
He gef vus to be his homly hyne
Ande precious perlez vnto his pay Amen · Amen ·

56
60
BRITISH MUSEUM

will argue that comparably complex modes of image-textual apprehension emerge where poems begin and end in the Pearl-Manuscript—if we are open to speculation.

THE ENDS OF *PEARL*

Pearl is so beautiful that it is hard to see it end, as we do on folio 55/59v (fig. 3.1). In this, we may feel sympathy with the Dreamer, who first laments and then accepts the end of his vision in the two stanzas on this page: the two "ends" of the poem discussed in chapter 2. This is one of several moments when the manuscript invites us to feel with one of the main characters—acting as a script for emotion, in Sarah McNamer's words.[2] I believe this script is material and visual as well as poetic, and that the physicality of this page subtly reinforces key themes of *Pearl*: loss and absence; sufficiency and value; human imperfection. Folio 55/59v thus suggests how the Pearl-Manuscript itself can become a lens for contemplating its poems' artistry.

The last page of *Pearl* prompts such speculation because it is the only page of the poem with just two stanzas. Until now, the poem's delight in geometric precision has been evoked by the near-perfect regularity of its text-block and decoration: three stanzas per page, with a large, blue-and-red initial at the beginning of each concatenating section.[3] On 55/59v, however, the lack of a third stanza creates the first substantial, nonmarginal white space in the manuscript thus far. *Pearl*'s generous lower margins and the scribe's consistently tight text-block make the poem's last two stanzas feel physically small, as if crowded up toward the top-left quadrant of the page. The doubled "Amen" of the final line pushes out toward the right margin, reinforcing by contrast both the shortness of the lines just above and the text-block's smallness overall.

This dynamic tension between text and not-text becomes poignant when we contemplate the blank space where a third stanza has been on every page of the poem until now. By maintaining the page-shape and ruling of its recto, 55/59v nudges this visual absence toward its center, as if foregrounding the loss that opens and closes the poem: the initial loss of the pearl and the Dreamer's final, rueful recognition that his glorious vision might have continued had he adhered to his bargain with the Maiden. To quote the very first words on this page:

2. McNamer, "Literariness," 1436.

3. The sole exception to this rule is the decorated initial at line 961, discussed in chap. 2.

To þat Prynceȝ paye hade I ay bente
and ȝerned no **more** þen watȝ me geuen . . .
to **mo** of His mysterys I hade ben dryuen.
Bot ay wolde man of happe **more** hente
þen moȝten by ryȝt vpon hem clyuen.[4]

The repetition of *mo(re)* here recalls its prominence in *Pearl*, where it was the only word to feature in more than one section's concatenating structure. This repetition, coupled with the fact that the page itself offers one less stanza than every other page of the poem, means that we can add 55/59v to the instances of "more and less"-ness discussed in the previous chapter, such as the "missing" line 472, or the extra decorated initial of line 961. The continuation of the ruling pattern after the end of the poem, still faintly visible in the white space below, reinforces the potential of continuation and fulfillment (for the Dreamer, had he not transgressed; for the faithful, in Heaven) even as its doubled "Amen" emphasizes finality in the here and now.

The final stanza's importance is further highlighted by a manicule in the left margin (see fig. 3.3). This manicule is only the most obvious (though faint and possibly fading) indication that we should linger on these lines. It points toward the leftmost edge of an unusually florid capital *T*, with significant space between it and the following *o*. This unusual word-internal gap reinforces the fact that the script on this page is itself unusually large and formal, despite (and within) the physical smallness of the text-block noted earlier. As recently as the previous verso (54/58v), the scribe was missing lines (i.e., writing over the ruling) and executing a more cramped version of his *textura media rotunda*. On 55/59v, by contrast, rightward-tilting feet of minims are generally well articulated (those of *proferen* in the line above are representative), and word separation is more consistent; at times, we see significant space between words, as in the third line ("hit is ful") of the detail.

This page also sees frequent embellishment of final *-e* and the occasional, dramatically dotted *i*, both visible in figure 3.4 (here the "dot" is nearly minim-sized; final words *laȝte*, *enclyin*, and *bytaȝte*). Such ornamentation is not new to *Pearl*, but it appears more consistently and clearly on 55/59v. Significantly, these features of the script anticipate the first page of *Cleanness*, which as Seamus Dwyer notes likewise showcases "a particularly formal mode of the

4. "Had I always bent to that Prince's pleasure, and yearned for no ***more*** than was given to me, . . . I would/might have been led to ***more*** of His mysteries. But people always want to seize ***more*** favor than is rightly allotted to them" (lines 1189–90, 1194–96, emphasis added).

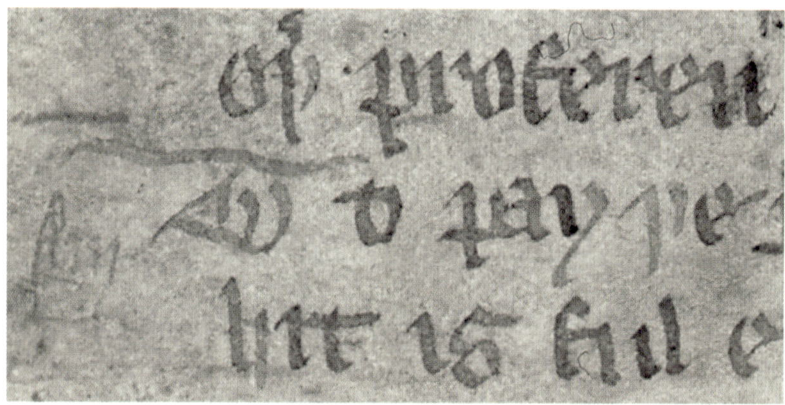

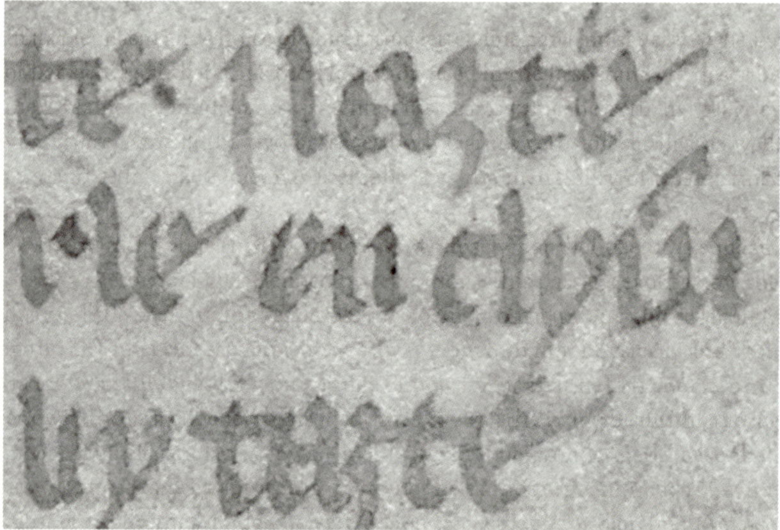

FIGURE 3.3. Folio 55/59v of Cotton Nero A.x/2. Close-up of scribal manicule at line 1201 of *Pearl*. Photograph © 2024 by The British Library Board.
FIGURE 3.4. Folio 55/59v of Cotton Nero A.x/2. Ending words of lines 1205–7. Photograph © 2024 by The British Library Board.

Cotton Nero script . . . with some of textualis's ornamentation, like the hairline tongue in **e**" and upward-tilting feet of minims visible in figures 3.3 and 3.4.[5] A first-time reader of the Pearl-Manuscript cannot anticipate this visual resemblance between the end of one poem and beginning of the

5. Dwyer, "Reading the Tied Letters," 25.

next—but that the words physically resemble one another across the pages will reinforce the verbal echoes to be discussed shortly.

Yet while the script of 55/59v draws attention to itself and anticipates the next poem, the manicule points more ambiguously: not at the text-block itself, but upward. In this it is unique; the other two, possibly three visible manicules in the manuscript point rightward, toward the line. Yet by extending leftward into the margin, the unusually florid decoration of line 1201's capital ***T*** allows this manicule to point in two ways simultaneously: both toward the first word of the last stanza, thereby reinforcing its importance and implicitly leading us rightward across the poetic line; and upward through the left margin. The manicule's verticality contrasts with the many horizontal forces around it, from the decoration of the ***T*** to the lineation itself. An unusually dark bit of the ruling even hovers over the manicule like a ceiling, pressing down and reinforcing the page's strong rightward pull.

The only previous manicule in the manuscript invited us to find meaning in an exception to the rule by pointing to the second anomalous instance of *makelez* in line 757 of *Pearl* (top of 49/53v; see fig. 2.1). This manicule signifies more ambiguously and multiply. It highlights the final stanza, as noted above, emphasizing its integrity to the poem despite the numerical imperfection (101). Yet by avoiding the text-block of this particular page, its verticality points instead back into the poem as a whole, as if *Pearl* were unfurled on a scroll, from top to bottom. The manicule thus solicits rereading, while also suggesting a theme of circularity or recursiveness that will recur through this book. In the context of this elegiac final page, its verticality might also point toward the hope of resurrection. The manifold interpretive potential of this manicule's anomalous shape participates in a larger pattern of aesthetic excess through imperfection; more locally, it invites us to slow down and reflect.

This invitation is quieter than it used to be, thanks to its fading ink and the facing page's later addition of an eye-catching illustration: a large, though not quite full-page, illustration of what we will ultimately recognize to be Noah's Flood, a key episode in the following poem (see fig. 3.2). I say "ultimately recognize" because this boat does not include any of the distinguishing features that often appear in contemporary depictions of the Ark, such as animals or living quarters for Noah and his family.[6] With its vibrant colors and bold, idiosyncratic use of the page, 56/60r draws our eye across the

6. Medieval illuminations of the Flood tend to depict the ark with a roof, for example, and often include one or more animals, whether one of the birds sent to find dry land or some of the animals in the ark itself. Kathleen Scott attributes 56/60r's lack of such elements to the artist's ignorance of "the more common models for the ark with a tiered and

opening, away from the end of *Pearl*; and by depicting an as-yet unnarrated scene whose iconography is not immediately recognizable, it creates visual tension that urges the first-time reader, especially, to turn the page and read on.

Yet it also recalls the poem we have just finished, for stylistically this illustration clearly evokes those that preceded *Pearl*. For example, the stream that appears on folios 37/41v–38/42v (figs. 1.2–1.4) features comparable, charmingly curvaceous fish to those of 56/60r's ocean (though of increasing size and aggressiveness). The final illustration of *Pearl* (folio 38/42v; fig. 1.4) is especially worth returning to, both because it is the most recent illustration in the manuscript and because it shares a number of subtle similarities with that of 56/60r. For example, the russet tower within the Heavenly Jerusalem on 38/42v contrasts sharply with the white of the Maiden and surrounding city—but is nearly the same color as the crown-like crow's nest of Noah's ark. Both structures occupy the same general area of the page (top middle) and tilt slightly to the right, adding to the unexpected similarities between the two images. Such resemblances might not be noticed at first, but they can be seen upon reflection, an activity which this manuscript encourages in readers.

Stepping back a bit, we can see the two-page opening that begins *Pearl* (38/42v+39/43r) as a mirror image of the 55/59v+56/60r opening with which it concludes: image + text . . . text + image. The poem's first and last pages also feature its most anomalous textual layouts: 55/59v for having just two stanzas, 39/43r for including by far the largest and most elaborate section-initial decoration, with extensive red foliation down the left-hand margin; the opening ***P*** of *Perle* descends fourteen lines, past the first stanza, whereas subsequent decorated initials are generally only three, occasionally four lines large. That means that the bulk of the poem (folios 39/43v–55/59r), with its extremely regular text-block and decoration, is enclosed by visually distinctive pages of text (39/43r, 55/59v), which are then further bracketed by illustrations: a bookish version of the enclosure imagined by the poem's first two lines: "Perle, plesaunte to princes paye, / to clanly *clos* in gold so clere" ("Pleasant pearl, pleasing for a prince to cleanly *enclose* in gold so clear," lines 1–2).

Because the illustrations are later additions, this chiastic enclosure evolved over time, a version of the gradual, accretive process by which natural pearls

windowed superstructure," but since (as she notes) many of the other illustrations do display "knowledge of transmitted iconography," the illustration's "vagueness" may instead be deliberate (*Later Gothic Manuscripts*, 2:68). Either way, its ambiguities contribute to the tension described above.

take shape. The "original" *Pearl*—the urtext of the author's fair copy, or imagination—is like the irretrievable grain of sand that gradually evolved into the Pearl-Manuscript, the only *Pearl* that survives. Murray McGillivray and Christina Duffy are therefore right to describe the manuscript as "a paradox and a mystery in itself," and further to suggest that "study of the illustrations emerges as one of the ways in which that paradox can be evaluated."[7] Their formulation leaves open the very *Pearl*-like possibility of multiple, concurrently valuable modes of engagement: both the empiricist demonstration of what the manuscript conclusively reveals and a more speculative mode that delights in exploring, without necessarily solving, its "paradoxes and mysteries," as McGillivray and Duffy call them.

Such language recalls Michelle Karnes's account of Trinitarian paradoxes in St. Bonaventure's *Itinerarium*, "meant not to be understood but instead to be marveled at. . . . That puzzle is not meant to be solved, but neither is it to be left uncontemplated."[8] It also recalls Dwyer's account of how even the Pearl-Manuscript's simplified version of *textualis* was "capable of illustrating the transcendence of sacred language."[9] The consonance of McGillivray and Duffy's language ("paradoxes and mysteries") with the intellectual contemplation of Bonaventure; the sacral associations of its scribal hand and its material resemblance to other religious manuscripts; even its unintended, "chosen" status as the poems' sole surviving witness: all these and more suggest how the original devotional energies of *Pearl* extend across time, media, and recoverable intention. Indeed, the British Library amplifies this energy today by severely restricting access to the manuscript, which thereby gains talismanic force. As both secular relic of literary history and much-read book of Christian art, it doubly solicits devotional reading strategies: both speculation as described earlier and image-textual appreciation of the whole page.[10]

Two broad similarities in their overall visual aspect further suggest the 55/59v+56/60r opening as a resonant juxtaposition. One is the ruling structure that continues across the top of 56/60r; the other is the blank space at the bottom of each page. I have already suggested how that emptiness might complement the ends of *Pearl* on 55/59v, but the corresponding blank space at the bottom of 56/60r is also noteworthy, for this is the first of the manuscript's illustrations that has not extended all the way to the edge of the

7. McGillivray and Duffy, "New Light," S111.

8. Karnes, *Imagination, Meditation, and Cognition*, 108. See further chap. 1, pages 29–30.

9. Dwyer, "Reading the Tied Letters," 21.

10. See further Brantley, "In Things"; Gayk, *Image, Text, and Religious Reform*; Rentz, "Holsum to Haue in Memory"; and Smith, "Taymouth Hours."

page. Here, only the water does so, presumably to signal the boundlessness of the Flood, with the lower quarter or so left blank—less than on the facing page, but a good deal more than the regular lower margin. That shared blank space at the bottom, coupled with their shared ruling structure at the top, creates a horizontal pull that further suggests this opening as a temporally evolving diptych.

For 56/60r offers numerous invitations to notice and engage with the Pearl-Manuscript's multilayered existence. This temporal residue can be so physically proximate as to overlap, as with the superimposition of the illustration over the earlier ruling pattern at the top of the page. Another, smaller-scale but recurring example is the competing sets of page numbers: here, an archaic-looking 56 in pen, stricken through and corrected by the 60 below, in modern pencil (fig. 3.5). On some pages, the earlier number has been clearly stricken through, as on the penultimate illustration of *Pearl* (38/42r; fig. 1.3), while on others (e.g., 47/51r), the correction has been made only faintly if at all, and the earlier number still dominates visually. Here, the strike-through extends well to the right of the earlier number, almost blending into the medieval ruling pattern that runs parallel below, which itself competes for attention with the later illustration that now dominates the page. Such physical traces of discrete moments in time blur into one another, recalling Deleuze and Guattari's account of the book as an object always in motion.[11]

One final temporally resonant element of this opening is the red seal of the British Museum near the bottom of 56/60r (fig. 3.2). (Until 1973, the British Library was part of the British Museum.) The seal's crown is roughly aligned with the ark's crow's nest, at the top of the page, and both tilt slightly to the right, as does the ark in between them. The seal thus helps to "seal" an impression of verticality down the middle of the page, even as it disrupts the horizontal continuity with the lower third of 55/59v, whose white space bears no such modern imprint. The crown that dominates the seal, meanwhile, recalls both the prominence of royalty within *Pearl*'s narrative and several crown-like pictorial elements of the illustrations that bookend it: the castellated Heavenly Jerusalem, enclosing a crowned Maiden and turret on 38/42v (fig. 1.4), which is complemented by the crown-like crow's nest at the top of 56/60r.

Like the illustration itself, the seal also reminds us that the Pearl-Manuscript is both book and art: unique material witness of priceless verbal art, and thus rightly safeguarded by a museum (as the seal proclaims),

11. Deleuze and Guattari, *A Thousand Plateaus*, 3–4.

FIGURE 3.5. Folio 56/60r of Cotton Nero A.x/2.
Photograph © 2024 by The British Library Board.

it is also a book made to be read from and so properly housed in a library (as it now is). Current curatorial practice reinforces this dual status, in that while part of a library and thus technically usable by the scholarly public, access to the book itself is restrictive enough to reinforce its talismanic status and make it also, effectively, a museum piece. Indeed, it is often on display, behind glass, as one of the rotating "Treasures" of the British Library. The seal reinforces the manuscript's dual status, and thus the tension between seeing and holding. This tension in turn recalls the denouement of *Pearl,* which hinged on the "look-but-don't-touch" agreement between Dreamer and Maiden (lines 961–76), considered in chapter 2.

Such interpretive readings of a medieval book's codicological and especially its postmedieval features are untraditional, but the Pearl-Manuscript reminds us that the lives of old books rarely divide neatly into simple binaries of "medieval" and "postmedieval."[12] Recent multispectral analysis of the manuscript has revealed temporal and interpretive disjunction within the illustrations themselves:

12. See further Warren, *Holy Digital Grail*; and Foys, "Medieval Manuscripts."

> Examination of the ink drawings underneath the current colored pictures is possible because the iron-gall ink that was used to draw them has its own unique response to the various spectra produced by the imaging setup . . . with the result that the iron-gall ink lines show as dark gray, while the other pigments show as shades of white or light gray. The effect is that we were able to look right through the pigment on top and see the original ink drawing.[13]

McGillivray and Duffy conclude that "the draftsperson's intention was not to draw scenes for later coloring but to create line drawings as black-and-white illustrations complete in themselves, using the illustrative vocabulary of line art rather than preparing a drawing expressly for coloring." They further deem it "likely . . . that Cotton Nero A.x had already existed as a bound volume for some time before the line drawings were added to it, and then existed as a volume with black-and-white line drawing illustrations for some time before the color was added."[14] Their phrasing emphasizes the duration of these phases ("had already existed . . . for some time . . . ; and then existed . . . for some time . . ."), as if they were different stages of life—which, in a sense, they are.

Multispectral imaging enables us to look through layers of ink and time, and this scientific speculation ("spectrometry" even features the same root) invites speculation in its more usual, interpretive sense.[15] For as McGillivray and Duffy note, "far from merely answering existing questions," such technologies allow us to "raise new ones" about how these poems' earliest

13. "McGillivray and Duffy, "New Light," S112. Hilmo makes similar arguments in "Did the Scribe Draw," and "Re-Conceptualizing."

14. McGillivray and Duffy, "New Light," S121, S123.

15. For example, McGillivray and Duffy note that several areas of color that now look monochromatic react differently to various wavelengths, which suggests that multiple pigments with different chemical compositions were used, and thus that these parts of the manuscript did not originally look as monochromatic as they now do. One such area is "the undistinguished muddy-green blob of bush to which the Dreamer's left hand perhaps points" (see fig. 1.2), which depicts his initial wandering through the poem's paradisal dreamscape. On the basis of color contrast that emerges only at the 940 nM wavelength, however, they suggest that "the currently opaque green of the bush was originally painted as a semi-transparent wash over a foundation of leaves. . . . If so, the effect would have been to give this particular bush a special illumination or glow as compared to all the other foliage, perhaps illustrating the poem's lines describing the unearthly shining of the trees in the *locus amoenus*. . . . The bush, glowing as it must have been with bright light from within, might also visually remind the viewer of the burning bush of Exodus 3 and thus signal the presence of the divine" ("New Light," S140).

commentators—the draftsperson and colorist, and perhaps the patron as well—saw and read them.[16] Far from limiting us to "original" perspectives, however, each of these new physical and temporal layers adds to the Pearl-Manuscript's interpretive potential: a bookish aesthetic of "more and more" consonant with that of *Pearl*. The manuscript's evolving shape reinforces the pull that these poems retained well after they were committed to parchment, despite surviving nowhere else and later disappearing from view for centuries.

Such reflections reinforce key themes of the poem, such as access, loss, and (in)tangibility, in ways that enhance our appreciation of text and manuscript as multidimensional objects. A concrete example will reinforce this point, drawing on Maidie Hilmo's powerful analysis of the curious shape just below the Dreamer in the manuscript's very first illustration (see detail, fig. 3.6):

> The contour of the dreamer's body parallels not only the wavy hillside above but also the prominent dark green spot below, calling attention to it. What does this "spot" contain? Is it a pond or an underground entrance? What does it signify? Since the "spot" is such an important focus of the first part of the poem, its possible meanings are as multilayered as is the visual image.[17]

As Hilmo points out, this "spot" suggests the burial mound into which the Dreamer's precious pearl fell, "þurȝ gresse to grounde" ("through grass into ground," line 10), but its curvature and color palette also anticipate the comparably wavy waterways that feature in the following three illustrations (figs. 1.2–1.4).[18]

Multispectral imaging demonstrates that until "someone, not necessarily the original artist, added the second layer of paint," this area of the page actually depicted "a continuation of the flowery meadow upon which the dreamer reclines." Significantly, however, this part of the meadow was marked off by the original draftsperson, and "the original wavy spot seems a bit darker than the surrounding area," which is presumably what encouraged someone later to heighten that contrast by adding the second layer of paint.[19] Hilmo concludes:

16. McGillivray and Duffy, "New Light," S143.
17. Kerby-Fulton, Olson, and Hilmo, *Opening up Middle English Manuscripts*, 173.
18. Kerby-Fulton, Olson, and Hilmo, *Opening up Middle English Manuscripts*, 174.
19. Kerby-Fulton, Olson, and Hilmo, *Opening up Middle English Manuscripts*, 176.

FIGURE 3.6. Folio 37/41r of Cotton Nero A.x/2.
Photograph © 2024 by The British Library Board.

> However lacking in painterly expertise and costly pigments, the person who painted these areas clearly wanted to emphasize the thematic importance of the spot even though it was previously part of the flowery meadow. . . . Whether or not this critical mind thought of the other layers of meanings it would likely have evoked in subsequent viewers is not clear, but in effect, a tantalizing mystery was created around the image of the spot.[20]

Hilmo's language here is significant, particularly the words "layers" and "tantalizing." The latter evokes the Dreamer's desire to hold his pearl once more (and many a scholar's desire to hold the manuscript), while metaphorical "layers of meanings" evoke the physical layers of paint and ink, whose accumulation explodes the idea of the Pearl-Manuscript as either temporally or interpretively stable.

One final case in point: multispectral imaging reveals that the small blobs of white and red within the "spot" below the Dreamer, visible in figure 3.6, are

20. Kerby-Fulton, Olson, and Hilmo, *Opening up Middle English Manuscripts*, 177.

flowers like those that populate the rest of the meadow; but today, with their stems painted over and nearly invisible, they also "anticipate the vision of the jeweled stream reflecting the starry skies" of lines 107–20, as Hilmo points out.[21] In that sense, they have become both flowers and gems, not unlike the Maiden herself, whom the Dreamer calls both a pearl and "so ryche a reken rose" ("so rich a lovely rose," line 906). Although modern spectrometry can lay bare its objective realities, this "spot" gains a stranger, almost quantum existence when contemplated through the lens of *Pearl*'s many inversions of traditional, earthly logic—a bit like the quantum letter of line 616's **ere*, considered in chapter 2.

The "tantalizing" complexities of this spot, as Hilmo terms it, add resonance to the contract between Maiden and Dreamer that sets up the poem's denouement. In the last stanza of section 16, she firmly rebuffs his request to join her within the Heavenly Jerusalem, but she offers to grant his second boon, to see where she lives. Section 17 begins with her repeating this offer, now conditionally:

> "If I þis mote þe schal vnhyde,
> bow vp towarde þys borneȝ heued,
> and I anendeȝ þe on þis syde
> schal sve tyl þou to a hil be veued."[22]

Here *mote* clearly means "city," but the word also frequently means "blemish" (e.g., lines 924, 948, 960), and the poem has earlier used *spot* as a synonym for this meaning (e.g., "For mote ne spot is non in þe" ["For there is neither stain nor spot in you"], line 764). The Maiden's reference to "unhiding" a *mote* thus proleptically evokes the kind of spectroscopic analysis that sees through layers of paint and ink and time, enabling Hilmo to "unhide" some of this spot's original shapes for modern viewers. Scientific advances thus enhance the resonance of both poem and manuscript in ways unintended by their medieval makers but consonant with *Pearl*'s own supereffability and accretion of meaning over time.

The Pearl-Manuscript itself thus evokes the themes of sight and touch around which *Pearl*'s denouement unfolds, beginning in these very stanzas

21. Kerby-Fulton, Olson, and Hilmo, *Opening up Middle English Manuscripts*, 174.

22. "If I am to reveal ["unhide"] this city to you, direct yourself to the head of the stream, and I will follow opposite you on this side until you are brought to a hill" (lines 973–76).

that articulate the Maiden's "look but don't touch" bargain with the Dreamer. As we saw in chapter 2, these same stanzas momentarily tested the reader's sense of section breaks by virtue of the anomalous decorated initial of line 961. They therefore make a fitting transition into the following poem, *Cleanness*, whose decorated initials appear much more irregularly than those of *Pearl*; if line 961 of *Pearl* was the exception that proved the rule (while also exemplifying "more-and-less"-ness and highlighting a key moment in the poem's drama), the decorated initials of *Cleanness* are far harder to make sense of.

That visual contrast between the two poems evokes more familiar literary ones. Whereas *Pearl* invests its theological debate with psychological depth and the suggestion, at least, of emotional and spiritual growth, the moralizing of *Cleanness* can feel grimly iterative, an extended series of dire counterexamples. *Pearl*'s human drama is enhanced by its obviously artful structures of rhyme, meter, and concatenation, whereas the comparatively unsympathetic tone of *Cleanness* is reinforced by its less gratifying poetic texture: unrhymed, irregular alliterative long-lines without obviously distinguished stanzas or sections as in *Pearl*. Yet as we will see, the less obvious shapes of *Cleanness* test our capacity to perceive its delights, spiritual and literary. Its seemingly random decorated initials, for example, actually appear at mathematically significant intervals, as Donna Crawford has brilliantly demonstrated.[23]

Thus, one final significance of the 55/59v+56/60r opening we have been considering is that its complexities and change-ups suggest reading the following poem with a sharp and careful eye—not just to the text itself, but also to how text both takes shape and creates shapes on particular pages. If *Pearl* beguiled us with the obvious beauty of its construction, *Cleanness* challenges us to find beauty—the "fayre formeȝ" memorably praised by its opening lines—in more difficult material. In that sense, the Pearl-Manuscript is amplifying the demands placed upon the spiritual, visual, and literary imagination of its readers: their speculative capacities, in short. So let us turn the page and see what this new challenge looks like.

TURNING TO *CLEANNESS*

What we see is a poem that looks nearly identical to *Pearl*: the same scribal hand and general layout, even the same thirty-six lines to the page (folio

23. Crawford, "Architectonics of *Cleanness*," to which chap. 4 will return.

57/61r; fig. 3.8). This decorated initial is smaller than the one that opened *Pearl* (eight vs. fourteen lines tall), and the marginal decoration less elaborate, but the same general decorative scheme prevails: blue and red ink (mostly red), and a tendency to curlicued, foliate ornamentation. An attentive reader may also note three small marks in the left-hand margin next to lines 13, 17, and 21, just opposite the vertical red double-line (see figs. 3.9, 3.10, and 3.11). This is especially true of *Cleanness*'s first such mark, at line 13, since it appears at the same interval we would expect from the twelve-line stanzas of *Pearl*. The first twelve lines of *Cleanness* also echo *Pearl* verbally:

Clannesse who-so kyndly cowþe comende,
and rekken vp alle þe resounȝ þat ho by riȝt askeȝ,
fayre **formeȝ** myȝt he fynde in forþering his speche,
and in þe contrare kark and combraunce huge.
For wonder wroth is þe Wyȝ þat wroȝt alle þingeȝ [5]
wyth þe freke þat in fylþe folȝes hym after,
as renkeȝ of relygioun þat reden and syngen
and aprochen to hys presens, and presteȝ arn called.
Thay teen vnto his temmple and temen to hymseluen, [9]
reken with reuerence þay rychen his auter,
þay hondel þer his aune body and vsen hit boþe.
If þay in **clannes** be **clos**, þay cleche gret mede.[24]

24. "Whoever would naturally/kindly commend cleanness, and reckon up all the reasons [for doing so] that she asks by right, might find fair **forms** in furtherance of his speech, and in [doing] the contrary, trouble and massive difficulty. For wondrous wroth is the Being that wrought all things with the man who follows after him in filth, like men of religion that read and sing and approach his presence, and are called priests. They go into his temple and praise him; pious, with reverence, they prepare his altar, where they handle his own body and also partake of it [*vsen hit*]. If they are **enclosed** in **cleanness**, they catch great reward" (lines 1–12, emphasis added). For an alternative, equally plausible reading of the first four lines, see Staples, "Pure Pleasure," 57.

Following spread: FIGURE 3.7. Folio 56/60v of Cotton Nero A.x/2. Photograph © 2024 by The British Library Board. FIGURE 3.8. Folio 57/61r of Cotton Nero A.x/2. Photograph © 2024 by The British Library Board.

Clannesse who so kyndly cowþe comende
& rekken vp alle þe resonz þat ho by riȝt askes
Fayre formes myȝt he fynde in forþering his speche
& in þe contrare kark & combraunce huge
For wonder wroth is þe wyȝ þat wroȝt alle þinges
Wyth þe freke þat in fylþe folȝes hym after
As renkez of relygioun þat reden & syngen
& aprochen to hys presens & prestez arn called
Thay teen vnto his temmple & temen to hym seluen
Reken with reuerence þay rychen his auter
Þay hondel þer his aune body & vsen hit boþe
If þay in clannes be clos þay cleche gret mede
Bot if þay conterfete crafte & cortaysye wont
As be honest vtwyth & inwith alle fylþez
Þen ar þay synful hemself & sulped altogeder
Boþe god & his gere & hym to greme cachen
He is so clene in his courte þe kyng þat al weldez
& honeste in his housholde & hagherlych serued
With angelez enourled in alle þat is clene
Boþe withinne & withouten in wedez ful bryȝt
If he nere scoymus & skyg & non scaþe louied
Hit were a meruayl to much hit moȝt not falle
Kryst kydde hit hym self in a carp onez
Þer as he heuened aȝt happez & hyȝt hem her medez
Me mynez on one amonge oþer as Mathew recordez
Þat þus of clannesse vnclosez a ful cler speche
Þe haþel clene of his hert hapenez ful fayre
For he schal loke on oure lorde with a bone chere
As so saytz to þat syȝt seche schal he neuer
Þat any vnclannesse hatz on auwhere abowte
For he þat flemus vch fylþe fer fro his hert
May not byde þat burre þat hit his body neȝe
Forþy hapel not to heuen in haterez totorne
Ne in þe harlatez hod & handez vnwaschen
For what vrþly haþel þat hyȝ honour haldez
Wolde lyke if a ladde com lyþerly attyred

The word *forme* is an obviously significant tangent point between the two poems, for as Sandra Pierson Prior and others have noted, *Cleanness*'s praise of "fayre formeȝ" evokes the literary beauties of *Pearl* in particular.[25] Indeed, this vividly tactile representation of the Elevation at the Mass—"þay hondel þer his aune body" ("they handle there his own body," line 11)—evokes the last lines of *Pearl* in particular, which commended the Maiden to Christ, "þat in þe **forme** of bred and wyn / þe preste vs scheweȝ vch a daye" ("whom in the **form** of bread and wine / The priest shows us every day," lines 1209–10). Those lines in turn anticipate the "fayre formeȝ" of *Cleanness*, line 3. The repetition of the opening word *clannes* in line 12 gives these twelve a self-contained, circular feel, which is reinforced by the word *clos* ("enclosed"), as well as the centrality of the number twelve to the previous poem. Its juxtaposition of *clannes* and *clos* also echoes the first stanza of *Pearl*: "to *clanly clos* in gold so clere" ("to cleanly enclose in gold so clear," line 2).

Such lexical connections across the first and last lines of *Pearl* and *Cleanness* recall the effect of *Pearl*'s own stanza-linking: a "passing of the baton" by which the concluding section's concatenating element is heard one last time in the first line of the following section, thus joining section N to section N + 1, whose concatenating element takes over at the end of the opening stanza of N + 1.[26] Here, it is echoes of words and word roots (*forme*, *clan-*, *clos*) across poems, highlighted by shared Eucharistic imagery, that creates this linking effect.[27] This type of linkage across poems further encourages reading the Pearl-Manuscript as an artfully conceived compilation. As Seamus Dwyer has noted, moreover, these structurally and echoically complex lines appear in "a particularly formal mode of the Cotton Nero script."[28] This visual distinctiveness further encourages the reader to linger over these lines' complex textual echoes—and, since we have seen that the last page of *Pearl* featured a comparably elaborated script, further to link the two poems.

All this interpretive energy makes their obvious dissimilarities especially striking—for by the time we reach line 12's potent evocation of *Pearl*, it will have become clear that *Cleanness* is quite a different kind of poem. This contrast operates both formally (unrhymed alliterative long-lines as against

25. Pierson Prior, *Fayre Formez*.

26. "Passing the baton" is translator Simon Armitage's helpfully concrete metaphor for *Pearl*'s concatenation in his translation of the poem.

27. On the juxtaposition of Eucharistic imagery across the transition from *Pearl* to *Cleanness*, see also Campbell, *Gawain-Poet*, 1–3.

28. Dwyer, "Reading the Tied Letters," 10.

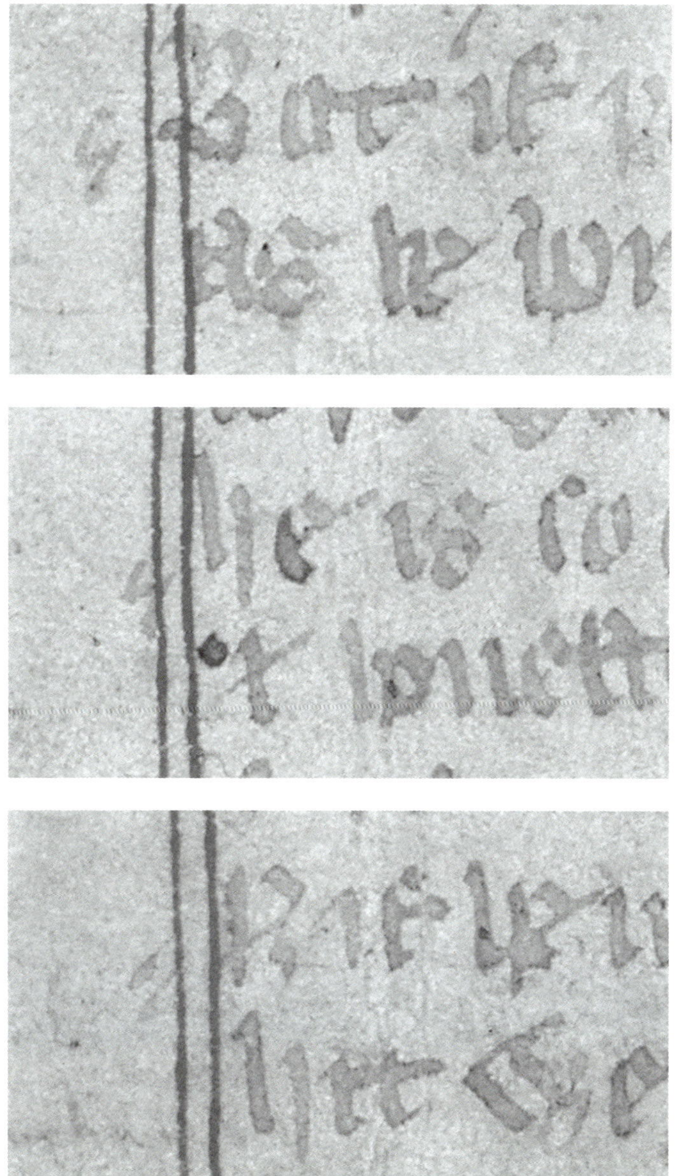

FIGURE 3.9. Folio 57/61r of Cotton Nero A.x/2. Line 13 scribal paraph. Photograph © 2024 by The British Library Board. FIGURE 3.10. Folio 57/61r of Cotton Nero A.x/2. Line 17 scribal paraph. Photograph © 2024 by The British Library Board. FIGURE 3.11. Folio 57/61r of Cotton Nero A.x/2. Line 21 scribal paraph. Photograph © 2024 by The British Library Board.

Pearl's intricately rhymed, generally alliterative twelve-line stanzas) and affectively: *Pearl* inspires devotion, as we have seen, whereas *Cleanness* asks us to embrace the discomfort of negative feelings.[29] The first twelve lines of the poem anticipate this focus, for after emphasizing praise and "fayre formeȝ" in its first three lines, the next eight turn sharply negative, especially in their comprehensive denunciation of "renkeȝ of relygioun þat . . . presteȝ arn called" ("men of religion who . . . are called priests," lines 7–8).[30] Despite line 12's conclusive elements and conciliatory content—"If þay in clannes be clos, þay cleche gret mede" ("If they are enclosed in cleanness, they catch great reward")—the brevity of its syntax almost begs a contrasting follow-up, given the second quatrain's emphasis on a wrathful God punishing filth.

Sure enough, line 13 begins a four-line attack on priests whose inner depravity means they merely "counterfeit" the craft that they alone can perform, the selfsame celebration of the Eucharist that concludes *Pearl*:

> ¶ Bot if þay conterfete crafte and cortaysye wont [13]
> as be honest vtwyth and inwith alle fylþeȝ,
> þen ar þay synful hemself, and sulpen altogeder
> boþe God and his gere, and hym to greme cachen.[31]

The first paraph mark visible in *Cleanness*, indicated above with the modern pilcrow, highlights this characterization of priestly hypocrisy as a kind of false craftsmanship, while the following *cortaysye* recalls its role as the linking-word of *Pearl*, section 8. Subsequent paraph marks appear at lines 17 and 21 (see figs. 3.9, 3.10, and 3.11), thereby beginning to suggest visually the four-line syntactic beat that generally structures the poem. This four-line rhythm is audible through the rest of 57/61r, but no more paraph marks appear until the next page, when their placement regularizes dramatically.

The apparent (speculative) logic of these marginal paraphs will be central

29. This paradox will be central to chap. 4, and is suggested by the titles of some seminal studies of the poem: Johnson, "Horrific Visions of the Host"; Queen, "Negative Affect"; Keiser, *Courtly Desire and Medieval Homophobia*; and Wallace, "*Cleanness* and the Terms of Terror."

30. As Campbell points out, "in the opening sentences [of the poem], there are no conditional words or phrases to soften the poet's critique. The 'prestez' are introduced here as an unindividuated group who will serve as the primary example of those hypocrites who trigger God's most violent wrath" (*Gawain-Poet*, 93–94).

31. "But if they counterfeit craft and lack courtesy, such as by being outwardly honest and all filth inside, then they are sinful themselves and altogether defile both God and his gear and drive him to wrath" (lines 13–16).

to the following chapter's reading of *Cleanness* as a whole, so I do not linger on them here except to draw attention to their surprising rhythm on this particular page. The first paraph mark's appearance, after twelve lines, recalls the twelve-line stanzas of *Pearl*—though it is impossible to say whether this effect is intentional or simply because the decorated initial consumes marginal space where earlier paraphs might have appeared. Two more paraphs then appear at four-line intervals, before disappearing for the rest of the page. A fourth paraph mark, at line 25, would have suggested a chiastic 12-4-4-4-12 structure to 57/61r, closer to the 12-12-12 that structures nearly every page of *Pearl*, and a mirror image of the 4-12-4 pattern of its central dialogue, discussed in chapter 2. Instead, 57/61r offers 12-4-4-16, a mixture of old and new, familiar and strange—which in turn invites readers to start playing with those numbers, testing hypotheses, trying to grasp the shape of the poem we are embarking upon.

As Sarah Stanbury has shown, comparable perceptual tests—of the visual, the verbal, and those modes' complex interaction—are central to *Cleanness*'s framing of its various biblical narratives.[32] One significance of the paraph marks here, therefore, is to suggest how the manuscript itself may join the poem in testing our ability to find the *fayre formeȝ* of *Cleanness*. On the one hand, folio 57/61r clearly evokes, and visually closely resembles, the poem we have just finished. Those textual and paratextual resemblances, however, also highlight the dramatic contrasts between *Pearl* and *Cleanness* noted above. As a conspicuously if often enigmatically crafted piece of verbal art, *Cleanness* leans into the difficulties it offers the reader, which are both textual and contextual. These challenges, in turn, are multiplied by the particularities of its codicological situation: everything from its sequencing within the manuscript to its *mise en page* and illustrations.

The first of these illustrations (folio 56/60r; fig. 3.2), opposite the end of *Pearl*, we have already considered; the second, on the verso (fig. 3.7), highlights both the sacramental focus of the lines we have been discussing and the importance of rightly interpreting visual and verbal signs. It depicts Daniel explaining the significance of God's writing to Belshazzar as his queen looks on, her body-lines mirroring his own. (This royal couple also looks much like Arthur and Guinevere in the first illustration of *Sir Gawain and the Green Knight*, a resemblance to which chapter 7 will return.) The prophet

32. As Stanbury puts it, the poet makes "the art of recognizing signs . . . a touchstone for reading the text's . . . Old Testament parables," thereby demonstrating "how the faithful can perceive divine form as it appears in physical, visual shape" (*Seeing the Gawain-Poet*, 45–47).

is visually divided from the royal couple by Belshazzar's grand feasting table, which resembles depictions of altars decorated for Mass; Hilmo notes that "the vessels include a gold monstrance with the host of the Eucharist, a chalice, and a bishop's crozier."[33] By thus emphasizing the Eucharistic resonance of the biblical episode, this image deepens the associations between the end of *Pearl* and the beginning of *Cleanness* considered above.

In the upper left (see detail, fig. 3.12), Belshazzar gestures toward God's writing hand, which remains in the tableau despite having vanished by the time Daniel appears in the accounts of the Bible and *Cleanness* alike. This illustration thus boldly assembles multiple temporal points into a Benjaminian constellation.[34] Two other significant changes to the biblical account stand out within this constellation: the fact that God writes upon an unfurled scroll or banderole, on which approximations of the three climactic words—*Mane, Techal, Phares*—clearly appear, in what looks like a display form of the main scribe's hand; and that God wields a stylus, whose tip just touches the end of Belshazzar's little finger. The poem mentions the stylus (called a *poyntel* at line 1533, a notable anticipation of the *poynt* of *Patience*), but retains the biblical account of God writing into the wall, not onto a scroll as here.[35] As Hilmo has pointed out, the illustration thus highlights and deepens the "bookish"-ness of *Cleanness*'s account of this scene, which is itself rather more bookish (or at least scribal, with its addition of the *poyntel*) than the Bible's.[36]

The uncanonical nature of these details effectively highlights them, which is significant because they present the object of interpretation within the poem—the writing on the wall—as something closer to the book in our hands than what the Bible describes. This is especially so for the attentive reader of *Pearl* who may have noticed a similar adornment just a few pages earlier. Specifically, the catchphrase at the bottom of 50/54v appears within a comparable scroll or banderole, whose curling edge extends downward to the left of the first word, *leste* (see fig. 3.13). The differences between this

33. Hilmo, "Creating a Visual Narrative," 153. See also Hilmo, "Re-Conceptualizing," 400–402.

34. See further introduction, pages 13–14, drawing on Benjamin, *Arcades Project*, 462; "On the Concept of History"; and "Paralipomena to 'On the Concept of History.'"

35. The word *pared* has associations with paper at other points in the manuscript—including in this very scene, when Belshazzar's decorations for the feast are described as "pared out of papure" (line 1408). The *parget* into which these letters are *pared* may therefore have a slightly bookish whiff that would complement the illustration. (This is the earliest attestation of *parget* in the *Middle English Dictionary*; it means "plaster" by the mid-fifteenth century.) I return to the manuscript's references to paper in chap. 8.

36. Hilmo, "Creating a Visual Narrative," 155.

FIGURE 3.12. Folio 56/60v of Cotton Nero A.x/2. Detail. Photograph © 2024 by The British Library Board.

banderole and the one bearing God's words a few pages later are numerous and important, but such visual echoes—across margins, poems, and recoverable intention—constitute another subtle form of connective tissue that binds the manuscript into a whole. Here, this resemblance visually links the physical construction of the codex itself (decorated catchphrase) with the object of pious interpretive activity in the poem to come (*Mane, Techal,*

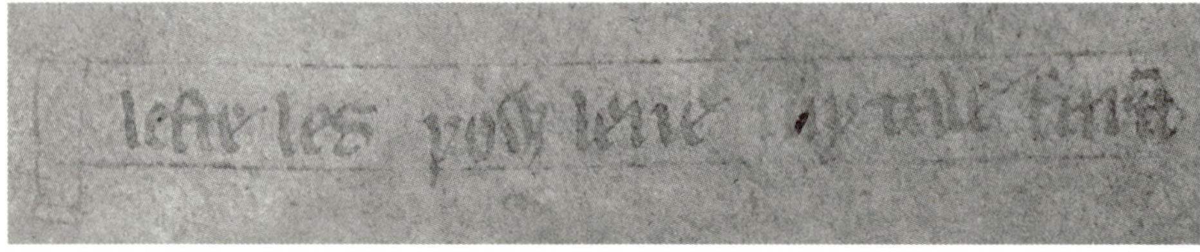

FIGURE 3.13. Folio 50/54v of Cotton Nero A.x/2. Close-up of banderole located at the bottom of the folio. Photograph © 2024 by The British Library Board.

Phares). I do not suggest that a first-time reader would likely make this connection. Most readers might not even notice the decorated catchphrase—a utilitarian bit in the margin, after all, and only slightly embellished. But this may be another point where a dedicated rereader (recall the dirt in the gutter) might see things differently. Visually linking the presentation of God's word to the performance of its own material construction is just one of many ways in which the Pearl-Manuscript presents itself as an object worthy of speculation.

I therefore note in closing the conspicuous blankness of the lower-right quadrant of 56/60v (fig. 3.7), toward which Daniel's oversized hands seem to be gesturing. The fact that each of the other three quadrants of the page is populated by a human figure (king, queen, prophet), makes the visual emptiness in the bottom right feel obtrusive, even heavy—not unlike the empty space where a third stanza might have been just a few pages ago, at the end of *Pearl*. As Robert J. Blanch and Julian N. Wasserman point out, "Daniel's movements direct the reader's gaze toward the ground and away from Belshazzar for whom the message is, within the text, lost."[37] The emptiness in the lower right suggests that we see this image from Belshazzar's perspective: just as he cannot interpret God's writing or benefit from Daniel's words, so too we see nothing where Daniel gestures. That unsettling alignment of perspective—Belshazzar's with the reader's—might come into focus only after having read the poem, for comparable play with perspective emerges when *Cleanness* narrates this scene, as the following chapter will show. In what it depicts and what it doesn't, 57/61r invites us to read with an eye to the visual and physical shape of *Cleanness*'s words.

37. Blanch and Wasserman, *From Pearl to Gawain*, 90. Their analysis of hands in the manuscript is brilliant.

Along multiple axes and in multiple media, turning from *Pearl* to *Cleanness* invites us to look with fresh eyes at the material craftedness of the poet's verbal art. This is significant since *Pearl*'s many pages of almost perfectly regular text-block and decoration may have lulled or transported us, like the Dreamer, into a less consciously embodied relationship with language and narrative. The pages considered here reorient our focus into the manuscript as a whole. As we will see in the following chapter, this renewed focus on language as a set of material signifiers allows the poet to align literary craft with those that are more obviously physical, like Noah's construction of the ark and Solomon's elaborately crafted vessels. It thereby begins to suggest that we read *Cleanness* as both a devotional offering to God, like Solomon's sacred vessels, and a test of the reader's spiritual and literary comprehension, like God's writing hand.

FOUR

SHAPING DELIGHT IN *CLEANNESS*

One overarching argument of this book is that the Pearl-Manuscript's material peculiarities enhance its poems' capacity to afford literary and bookish delight. My reading of *Cleanness* dwells on one such peculiarity, briefly introduced in the last chapter: paraph marks generally visible every four lines in the left margin.[1] As I have argued elsewhere, the paraphs' significance to *Cleanness* lies partly in the challenge of assessing that significance, for the verbal patterns that they mark are clear but inconsistent, as are the visual patterns that they create in so doing.[2] As such, they become a visual-and/as-verbal sign that we are challenged to interpret, complementing other perceptual tests central to the poem.[3]

The most famous such test occurs near the end of *Cleanness*, when a terrified and uncomprehending Belshazzar witnesses God's writing hand carve letter forms into the wall, "as a coltour in clay cerues þe forȝes" ("as a coulter carves furrows into clay," line 1547). This scene has already been forcefully impressed upon us by the illustration opposite the poem's opening lines. It

1. I call these paraph marks, or paraphs, because they closely resemble the "two diagonal lines" that Malcolm B. Parkes documents being used "to instruct a rubricator where to insert a *paraph*. But in many instances the marks were felt to be sufficient to fulfill the functions of the paraph itself. As a result they passed into the repertory of punctuation to indicate the boundaries of *propositiones* or *sententiae*" (*Pause and Effect*, 207, plate 27). Other designations for these marks in the Pearl-Manuscript include "marginal double virgula" (Olsen, *Cleanness*, 13), "double oblique stroke" (Andrew and Waldron, *Poems*, 48), and simply "two strokes" (Putter and Stokes, *Works of the Gawain Poet*, xxxii). In her diplomatic edition of *Cleanness*, Olsen uses the modern pilcrow in reproducing the manuscript's paraph marks, a practice I adopt here.

2. Bahr, "Finding the Forms of *Cleanness*." Thanks to the editors of *Studies in Philology* for permission to draw on that material here.

3. Here I draw on Stanbury's groundbreaking account of how the poet makes "the art of recognizing signs . . . a touchstone for reading the text's . . . Old Testament parables," thereby demonstrating "how the faithful can perceive divine form as it appears in physical, visual shape" (*Seeing the Gawain-Poet*, 45–47).

also features the only extended, consistent mismatch between syntax and paraphs: the first line of each "quatrain," as marked by the scribe, concludes a four-line syntactic unit, rather than initiating one as the first 1500 lines of the poem have led us to expect. By that point in the manuscript, I will argue, two other aspects of the poem have combined to suggest an interpretive reading of this mismatch between textual and paratextual form (which is so marked that some editors elect to smooth it out visually). One such suggestion is *Cleanness*'s own use of bookish and scribal imagery, which draws attention to the manuscript's physicality. Complementing this textual invitation is a codicological one: as Donna Crawford has shown, the puzzling intervals of its decorated initials weave the poem's fascination with counting ("reckoning," as line 2 puts it), numbers, and proportion into the Pearl-Manuscript itself.[4] Together with the paraphs, these features suggest a complex fusion of literary, mathematical, and spiritual meaning within the material text.

Such complexity can be perceived only gradually and with effort, and I believe that this speculative process is what *Cleanness*, as manifest in the Pearl-Manuscript, trains readers to practice. The value of such perspectival training is suggested by the poem's own initiating quotation of the sixth Beatitude: "Þe haþel clene of his hert . . . / schal loke on oure Lorde with a loue chere" ("One whose heart is clean . . . shall look on our Lord with a humble/gracious cheer," lines 27–28). As we saw in chapter 1, such speculation involves both thought and feeling, and *Cleanness* has long fascinated for its intensity of feeling: chief among them, its sensuous endorsement of (hetero)sexual pleasure, independent of procreation, and its relish in righteous destruction. Delight in material craft, and disgust at its misuse or misshaping, constitute an analogous leitmotif throughout the poem, informing its gorgeous ekphrasis of Solomon's sacred vessels, which the poet holds up for our wonderment just as they are borne to Belshazzar for desecration.[5] Such passages gradually become legible as the literary analogue of those very same vessels:

4. Crawford, "Architectonics of *Cleanness*," to which I will return. On the spiritual significance of "reckoning," see Rust, "*Arma Christi*" and, more broadly, Kaye, *Economy and Nature*, which argues that "the intensities of qualities we today consider essentially subjective and immeasurable, such as love, grace, and charity, were treated . . . as measurable and capable of relation in the same way that lines or spatial magnitudes are measurable" (166; quoted by Rust, 149). The contrast between arithmetic and geometric measurement that Kaye traces also informs Kenneth Chong's analysis of *Pearl*, considered in chap. 2.

5. Cf. Cecilia A. Hatt's instructive observation that the poet's "concern with artistic workmanship finds its most ambitious expression in *Cleanness*" (*God and the Gawain-Poet*, 75), which consistently "draws attention to itself as an artefact" (79).

masterfully crafted offerings to God, which are further enhanced by their unique material embodiment.

FINDING THE CONTOURS OF *CLEANNESS*: PARAPHS, QUATRAINS, INITIALS

I begin with the poem's representation in the Pearl-Manuscript and modern editions. Although Andrew and Waldron have influentially printed *Cleanness* in undifferentiated long-lines, two more recent editions lay it out in quatrains, as did many earlier editors.[6] *Cleanness*'s investment in the confluence of verbal and visual form makes this issue significant, so Ad Putter and Myra Stokes's account of their decision is worth considering in detail:

> The scribe marks the beginning of every fifth line with two strokes in the left margin, and since this is the same mark he uses in *Pearl* and *Sir Gawain* to signal what rhyme *proves* to be *clearly* a new stanza, we have *interpreted* the symbol as simultaneously marking off sections of text in the unrhymed poems [*Cleanness* and *Patience*]. The sense, moreover, *characteristically* falls into four-line units.[7]

The italicized words above suggest the degree of interpretation involved in finding the contours of *Cleanness*. In *Pearl* and *Sir Gawain*, paraph marks reinforce "what rhyme proves to be clearly a new stanza," but *Cleanness* and *Patience*, which lack rhyme's clarity and have only "characteristic" syntactic rhythm in its place, prompt an act of interpretation that becomes one of shaping: dividing the poem into quatrains that visually replicate the stanzas of *Pearl* and *Sir Gawain*.

I agree that the paraphs are integral to grasping the full complexity of *Cleanness*, but I am less persuaded that the traditional method of representing stanzas in modern editions, with a blank line separating each poetic unit, accurately represents that complexity. For one thing, the scribe's practice is slightly inconsistent, with visual evidence for only 85–90 percent of

6. Putter and Stokes, *Works of the Gawain Poet*; Olsen, *Cleanness*. Andrew and Waldron acknowledge that "major syntactical breaks . . . occur too often for coincidence at the ends of lines which are multiples of four" (48), but describe this as "a recurring pattern rather than a consistent structural device" (16), and therefore ignore it in their layout. J. J. Anderson and Sir Israel Gollancz also print the poem in quatrains.

7. Putter and Stokes, *Works of the Gawain Poet*, xxxii, emphasis added.

the paraphs we would expect.[8] Some of these "missing" marks may have faded over the centuries, but even if we suppose that paraphs were originally visible every four lines without fail, the shape of *Cleanness* would still be far more fluid than that of *Pearl*, since these "quatrains" are not anchored by rhyme, syllable-count, or strict adherence to the predominant four-line syntactic beat.[9] In three distinct though overlapping ways, then, the literary and material shape of *Cleanness* is difficult to pin down: its mostly-but-not-strictly four-line syntactic rhythm is usually-but-not-always reinforced by paraph marks that are frequently-but-not-uniformly visible in the left margin.

"Usually" is a hard frequency at which to find secure meaning (or *fayre formeȝ*), in contrast with the "always—or with just one exception" shapes of *Pearl*, which made its instances of "more-and-less"-ness perceptible and gave them power. The contours of *Cleanness* are comparatively fuzzy. The scribe clearly understood the paraphs to be important, for he maintains their four-line rhythm throughout despite some inconsistencies in lineation—pages with one line more or less than the manuscript's usual thirty-six—that might easily have thrown him off. (Chapter 5 will turn to these anomalous pages.) Yet the paraphs occasionally disappear for stretches of as many as twenty

8. Olsen notes that "the presence of the virgula [as she calls the mark in question] in *Cleanness* is not always consistent" (*Cleanness*, 13n3); her diplomatic transcription, upon which her excellent edition is based, notes 370 paraphs out of an implied possible total of 438, just shy of 85 percent. (The number 438 comes from dividing the poem's 1812 lines by 4 = 453, minus 15 for the space occupied by the poem's thirteen decorated initials, which never receive marginal marks in the manuscript: 15 since the larger first initial occupies space for three paraph marks, not just one.) My research assistant Madison Sneve found evidence in the digital facsimile of an additional twenty-five paraphs not noted by Olsen, however, some of which visual examination of the manuscript itself confirmed; others are clear even in the digital facsimile (e.g., at lines 349 and 353, whose paraphs are obscured but visible under the red inkwork extending down from the decorated capital of line 345). That suggests something closer to 90 percent of the paraphs we would expect. This figure may be an undercount given how faintly some of the marks now appear; just over a century ago, Sir Israel Gollancz noted the book's "slowly fading" ink and proposed that some paraphs originally marked by the scribe were even then invisible to the naked eye (*Facsimile Reproduction of Cotton Nero A.x*, 8).

9. As Andrew and Waldron point out, "no strictly metrical criteria are involved" in thus dividing the poem, and J. J. Anderson agrees despite printing in quatrains himself ("in *Cleanness* and *Patience* . . . there is no metrical confirmation of stanza division" [Anderson, *Cleanness*, 4]). In an earlier survey of scholarship on the question, J. R. Hulbert acknowledges that from a modern perspective, "it is difficult to conceive of any stanza forms not made clear by rhyme" ("Quatrains in Middle English Alliterative Poems," 81).

lines at a time. So as to represent the evidence as accurately and transparently as possible, I approximate *Cleanness*'s format in the manuscript: long-lines with the modern pilcrow, ¶, at the start of each four-line unit, which I will call "quatrains" for simplicity's sake. I use parentheses to indicate where a paraph mark would be expected, based on this four-line rhythm and the scribe's usual practice, but was not visible to me in the manuscript: (¶).

Such questions are of more than merely typographical interest; they shape our very impression of the poem, whose opening lines emphasize the links between poetic, divine, and priestly forms of craft, italicized below. Even before paraphs begin to appear in the poem, the four-line syntactic beat that they will ultimately reinforce is clearly audible:

(¶) Clannesse who-so kyndly cowþe comende,
and rekken vp alle þe resounȝ þat ho by riȝt askeȝ,
fayre formeȝ myȝt he fynde in forþering his speche,
and in þe contrare kark and combraunce huge.
(¶) For wonder wroth is *þe Wyȝ þat wroȝt alle þingeȝ* [5]
wyth þe freke þat in fylþe folȝes hym after,
as renkeȝ of relygioun þat reden and syngen
and aprochen to hys presens, and presteȝ arn called.
(¶) Thay teen vnto his temmple and temen to hymseluen, [9]
reken with reuerence þay rychen his auter,
þay *hondel* þer his aune body and *vsen* hit boþe.
If þay in clannes be clos, þay *cleche* gret mede.
¶ Bot if þay conterfete *crafte* and cortaysye wont [13]
as be honest vtwyth and inwith alle fylþeȝ,
þen ar þay synful hemself, and sulpen altogeder
boþe God and his *gere*, and hym to greme cachen.[10]

10. "Whoever would naturally/kindly commend cleanness, and reckon up all the reasons [for doing so] that she asks by right, might find fair forms in furthering his speech, and in [doing] the contrary, trouble and massive difficulty. For wondrous wroth is the Being that wrought all things with the man who follows after him in filth, like men of religion that read and sing and approach his presence, and are called priests. They go into his temple and praise him; pious, with reverence, they prepare his altar, where they handle his own body and also partake of it. If they are enclosed in cleanness, they catch great reward. But if they counterfeit craft and lack courtesy, such as by being outwardly honest and all filth inside, then they are sinful themselves and altogether defile both God and his gear, and drive him to wrath" (lines 1–16). For an alternative, equally plausible reading of the first four lines, see Staples, "Pure Pleasure," 57.

This strikingly concrete depiction of the priest's role in the Eucharist—handling and using bread that thereby becomes God's body—aligns priestly "craft" with God's own creative acts of shaping. The emphatic physicality of lines 5–16 also retroactively infuses the famous *fayre formeȝ* of line 3 with an element of concreteness that phrase might not otherwise have. "Finding" these poetic forms thus becomes more than just an Englishing of the Latin rhetorical art of *inventio*; it suggests concrete interest in visual materiality, appropriate to line 5's kenning for God: "þe Wyȝ þat wroȝt alle þingeȝ" ("the Being who wrought all things").

In this context, the paraph marks gradually emerge as visual boundaries and patterns in relation to which the poem's action unfolds. Yet the "thinginess" of the paraphs makes for a smaller, more flexible, and more elusive poetic unit than the intricate twelve-line stanzas of *Pearl*. Lines 1–32 of *Cleanness* use regular end stops to establish a strong four-line syntactic beat, but the extended image that immediately follows, introducing the parable of the wedding feast, presents a more complex relation between syntactic and paratextual form:

(¶) Forþy hyȝ not to heuen in hatereȝ totorne, [33]
ne in þe harlateȝ hod, and handeȝ vnwaschen.
For what vrþly haþel þat hyȝ honour haldeȝ
wolde lyke if a ladde com luþerly attyred,
(¶) when he were sette solempnely in a sete ryche, [37]
abof dukeȝ on dece, with dayntys serued?
Þen þe harlot with haste helded to þe table,
with rent cokreȝ at þe kne and his clutte trascheȝ,
¶ and his tabarde totorne, and his toteȝ oute, [41]
oþer ani on of alle þyse, he schulde be halden vtter,
with mony blame ful bygge, a boffet peraunter,
hurled to þe halle dore and harde þeroute schowued,
¶ and be forboden þat borȝe to bowe þider neuer, [45]
on payne of enprysonment and puttyng in stokkeȝ;
and þus schal he be schent for his schrowde feble,
þaȝ neuer in talle ne in tuch he trespas more.
¶ And if vnwelcum he were to a wordlych prynce, [49]
ȝet hym is þe Hyȝe Kyng harder in heuen. . . . [11]

11. "Therefore, do not hasten to heaven in tattered clothing, nor in the hood of a harlot and [with] unwashed hands. For what earthly man that holds high honor would like it if a

Unlike the beginning of the poem, the syntax of the passage above, especially its first half, does not coincide neatly with the four-line syntactic beat ultimately implied by the marginal paraphs. The first quatrain dramatically enjambs its question through its conclusion in line 36, but the next two quatrains open with *and*, carrying the reader along and furthering the sense of this tableau—the foully dressed man's appearance, rebuke, and expulsion from the hall—as a discrete visual sign to be read as such. Line 48 finally presents an end stop and thus distinguishes this earthly hypothetical from the biblical parable to follow, even as the beginning of line 49 recalls the identical opening of the previous two quatrains, a hint of anaphora that links these narratively and conceptually parallel episodes.

Read individually, many of these four-line units do not feel quite like stanzas—hence my reluctance to lineate them as such—but the added dimension that the paraphs create grounds these "quatrains" in a larger pattern that poetic and syntactic structure can either reinforce or complicate. Inasmuch as the scribe's paraphs create visual boundaries, for example, the quatrains that they produce can be read metaphorically. Those that systematically lack syntactic end-stopping can thus suggest the violation of natural, divinely established categories and boundaries: a frequent theme of *Cleanness*'s biblical narratives. In the following passage, for example, the tumbling of syntax across quatrain boundaries evokes the physical fall of the rebel angels:

(¶) Þaȝ þe feloun were so fers for his fayre wedeȝ [217]
and his glorious glem þat glent so bryȝt,
as sone as dryȝteneȝ dome drof to hymseluen,
þikke þowsandeȝ þro þrwen þeroute,
(¶) fellen fro þe fyrmament fendeȝ ful blake, [221]
sneued at þe fyrst swap as þe snaw þikke,
hurled into helle-hole as þe hyue swarmeȝ.

lad came wretchedly attired when he was to be solemnly set in a rich seat, above dukes on a dais, served with dainties? Then [if] the villain hastily took a place [*helded*] at the table—with leggings rent at the knee and patched, trashy shoes, and his jerkin all ripped, and his toes exposed, or any one of all these—he should be thrown outside with many a great word of blame, perhaps a buffet, hurled to the hall door and roughly shoved outside, and be forbidden ever to return to that estate, on pain of imprisonment and putting in stocks; and thus shall he be disgraced for his feeble apparel, though he never trespass further in word or deed. And if he were unwelcome to an earthly prince, the High King in Heaven is still harder on him . . ." (lines 33–50). On the difficulties posed by this parable and its articulation in *Cleanness*, see Raschko, *Politics of Middle English Parables*, 177–214.

Fylter fenden folk forty dayeȝ lencþe,
(℄) er þat styngande storme stynt ne myȝt; [225]
bot as smylt mele vnder smal siue smokeȝ forþikke,
so fro heuen to helle þat hatel schor laste,
on vche syde of þe worlde aywhere ilyche.[12]

The fiends' pride deprives them of the stability offered by God's divinely ordained boundaries, and these lines that describe their hurtling, whirling fall enact this violation formally; the end stop of line 223 and enjambment of line 224 are jarringly at odds with any underlying quatrain structure, a slight foretaste of the quatrain-syntax breakdown to come at Belshazzar's Feast.

Perhaps significantly, these quatrains also appear to lack marginal paraph marks, which by this point in the poem have otherwise become quite consistent. That invites an interpretive reading of the paraph's reappearance when the rebel angels' fall is complete, in the next quatrain:

℄ Þ/Ȝis hit watȝ a brem brest and a byge wrache, [229]
and ȝet wrathed not þe Wyȝ; ne þe wrech saȝtled,
ne neuer wolde, for wylfulnes, his worþy God knawe,
ne pray Hym for no pité, so proud watȝ his wylle.[13]

The sentence that articulates and justifies God's punishment reestablishes the poem's four-line syntactic beat, visually reinforced by the first paraph in

12. "Though the felon [i.e., Lucifer] was fierce on account of his fair raiment and his glorious glamour that shone so bright, as soon as the Lord's judgment drove upon him, teeming thousands were violently thrown out of there, inky black fiends fell from the firmament, fell like thick snow, hurled into the hell-hole like a swarming hive. Forty days' length that fiendish folk comingled, before that stinging storm might stop; but as fine meal through a small sieve smokes up quite thickly, so from heaven to hell that hateful shower stretched, on both sides of the world, everywhere together" (lines 217–28).

13. "Yes, it/This was a profound wickedness and great vengeance, and yet God was not enraged; nor did the wretch make peace, nor would he ever (for his willfulness) acknowledge God, nor pray him for pity, so proud was his will" (lines 229–32). This quatrain opens with a quantum letter that recalls the **ere* case considered in chap. 2. In her recent edition, Kenna Olsen prints "Þis," in lieu of Andrew and Waldron's "Ȝis," and writes: "My uv examination confirms Anderson (1977)'s reading [Þis], though Vantuono (1984) reports *Ȝis*, also from uv inspection" (201, referring to the editions of J. J. Anderson and William Vantuono). That different editors see different letter forms under the same specialized lighting, both of which yield plausible readings, testifies both to these poems' lexical richness and to modern readers' own coimplication in shaping them. (I was unable to decide when I examined the manuscript with a magnifying glass and normal lighting.)

sixteen lines. We cannot say with certainty, of course, what the coincidence of this reversion to syntactic, paratextual, and moral order objectively signifies or what intentions created it—a point to which chapter 5 will return. But such moments gradually combine to suggest that elements of the poem's material presentation may bear upon its literary contents: here, how the verbal and the visual work together, in laying out a poem itself obsessed with the coimplication of the verbal and the visual.

The curious placement of *Cleanness*'s decorated initials further suggests speculating upon its physical manifestation more broadly. Whereas *Pearl*'s decorated initials appear with near-perfect regularity at the beginning of concatenating sections (and once more), the thirteen initials of *Cleanness* appear at lines 1, 125, 193, 249, 345, 485, 557, 601, 689, 781 893, 1157, and 1357 of 1812 total. Yet while these intervals are obviously harder to make sense of than those of *Pearl*, as befits this more challenging poem, Donna Crawford has brilliantly demonstrated some of the mathematical logics that govern them, some of which involve relatively basic patterns of addition and subtraction.[14] Other intervals and ratios emerge if we look more closely, however, including variations on the golden section, or phi, that has influenced European aesthetics for millennia—including medieval book-construction.[15] Some of these shapes involve a kind of numerical interlocking that evokes the verbal concatenation of *Pearl*, although arguably even more complex—certainly more difficult for a casual reader to find. For example, figure 4.1 helps to explain the appearance of three initials (at lines 1, 557, and 1157) that are larger than the poem's other ten: we see that at two different points, "an interval of 556 occurs nested inside an interval of 600 lines," and these interlocking structures are "symmetrically related . . . in the manner of an overlapping mirror image."[16] We have seen that various modes of mirroring animate the poems and illustrations as well, so it is striking that a comparable structural effect should be embedded within the placement of decorated initials.

14. As Crawford discerns it, the puzzle begins with "three intervals among the line numbers—intervals of 124, 204, and 344—that simply repeat in a perfectly regular and straightforward fashion, which can be discerned by subtraction" ("Architectonics of *Cleanness*," 31).

15. Wakelin notes that "scribes, like other craftspeople, produced books that fit the Pythagorean triangle and golden ratio, because their tools of the compass, set-square and ruler were based on geometrical formulae, without the scribes needing to recalculate them for themselves—so much so that modern typographers can even extrapolate these principles from the manuscripts" (*Immaterial Texts*, 77–78). On phi as a structuring principle of the Pearl-Poems, see Condren, *Numerical Universe*.

16. Crawford, "Architectonics of *Cleanness*," 32. Fig. 4.1 is a detail from this page.

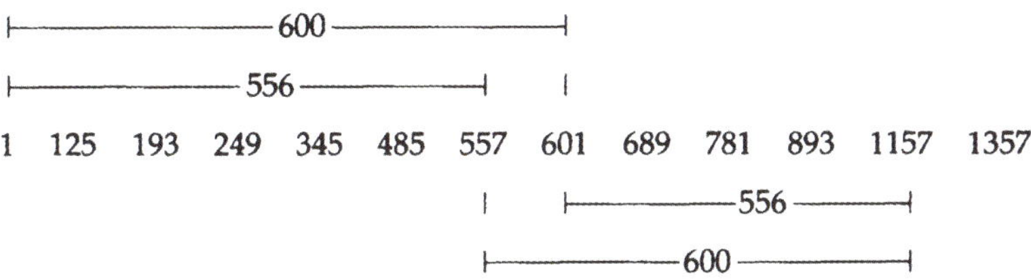

FIGURE 4.1. Nested numeric intervals of the decorated initials of *Cleanness*. From Donna Crawford, "The Architectonics of *Cleanness*," *Studies in Philology* 90, no. 1 (Winter 1993). Courtesy of the University of North Carolina Press.

The complex mathematical shapes created by these intervals thus have at least twofold significance: they reinforce *Cleanness* and the Pearl-Manuscript's shared interest in numerical patterning, while offering an extra-poetic, visual-material analogue to the perceptual challenges that the poem narrates. They thereby complement and reinforce other invitations to find meaning in potentially puzzling aspects of the manuscript, like the marginal paraphs we have been considering. Such features of the Pearl-Manuscript combine to suggest composite, cross-temporal, and multimedia "authorship" of literary complexity in ways that recall *Pearl*'s own expanding singularity. There, we saw a poem's literary existence literally multiply, as editors and scholars create new versions of its singular words, like modern scribes dealing with a tricky exemplar. Here, the Pearl-Manuscript's medieval scribe and decorator enhance a poem's resonance by means of paratextual additions (paraphs and initials), which offer additional—and additionally challenging—opportunities for speculation. So, if *Cleanness* demands that we "commit to a perpetual exercise of our interpretive faculties," as David Wallace has rightly put it, then the poem's materiality adds to the dimensions in which those faculties can be exercised.[17]

In the next section, I consider how these dimensions intersect, using the figure of the compass with which Crawford invites us to find the intervals of *Cleanness*'s decorated initials for ourselves.[18] Yet Middle English *compas*

17. Wallace, "*Cleanness* and the Terms of Terror," 97.

18. An appendix to "The Architectonics of *Cleanness*" (43–45) offers a twelve-step illustrated tutorial for "using the simple geometer's tools of a straight edge and a compass" to construct out of a rectangle the numbers whose lines receive decorated initials (36).

can mean many more things than the geometer's tool: among them, ingenuity or clever craftsmanship; figure or image; circle or sphere; and dimension, extent, or distance.[19] As we will see, the word's physical, aesthetic, and literary associations suggest analogies between forms of craft depicted within the poem and the author's own acts of poetic shaping. Such analogies reinforce the extent to which *Cleanness* delights in literary materiality as a devotional mode.

ENCOMPASSING DELIGHT

Cleanness uses the word *compas* four times, twice as a verb and twice as a noun. The first appearance figures in God's directions to Noah on the measurements of his ark:

> "And þus of lenþe and of large þat lome þou make:
> þre hundred of cupydeȝ þou holde to the lenþe,
> Of fyfty *fayre* ouerþwert *forme* þe brede,
> ℂ and loke euen þat þyn ark haue of heȝþe þretté, [317]
> and a wyndow wyd vpon, wroȝt vpon lofte,
> in þe **compas** of a cubit *kyndely* sware;
> a wel dutande dor don on þe syde."[20]

Words like *fayre*, *forme*, and *kyndely*, italicized above, recall *Cleanness*'s opening description of the rhetorical arts that the rightly intentioned poet will naturally find. They thus subtly connect divinely ordained care for number and proportion with the poet's own literary efforts. This connection between building the ark and crafting a poem becomes still more striking when we consider God's earlier characterization of the ark, as a "cofer closed of tres, clanlych planed" ("coffer enclosed by trees, cleanly smoothed," line 310). The alliteration of *closed* and *clanlych* recalls the openings of both *Pearl* ("to clanly clos in gold so clere," line 2) and *Cleanness* ("If þay in clannes be clos," line

19. *Middle English Dictionary* (accessed August 31, 2023, https://quod.lib.umich.edu/m/middle-english-dictionary/dictionary/MED8678), s.v. "cŏmpăs n.," meanings 1a, 1c, 2a, and 3c, respectively.

20. "And make the vessel of this length and breadth: hold to three hundred cubits for the length, of fifty fair across measure the breadth, and look closely that your ark has thirty of height, and a wide window made opening onto sky, the measure [*compas*] of a cubit square precisely [lit. "naturally," *kyndely*]; a well-fitting door done in the side" (lines 314–20).

12).[21] By aligning poetic art with ark-building, such echoes suggest an analogy between physical construction (measuring distances, cutting and smoothing wood) and literary craft, here centered on the word *compas*.

Cleanness further develops this analogy in the word's remaining three appearances. The next is outwardly quite unlike the matter-of-fact measurements quoted above, but is likewise spoken by God—here, to describe his invention of a natural form ("kynde crafte") of sexual pleasure, misshaped to wicked ends by the men of Sodom:

❡ "I **compast** hem a kynde crafte and kende hit hem derne, [697]
and amed hit in myn ordenaunce oddely dere,
and dyȝt drwry þerinne, doole alþerswettest,
and þe play of paramoreȝ I portrayed myseluen,
❡ and made þerto a maner myriest of oþer: [701]
when two true togeder had tyȝed hem seluen,
bytwene a male and his make such merþe schlude come,
welnyȝe pure paradys moȝt preue no better.
❡ Elleȝ þay moȝt honestly ayþer oþer welde, [705]
at a stylle stollen steuen, vnstered wyth syȝt,
luf-lowe hem bytwene lasched so hote
þat alle þe meschefeȝ on mold moȝt hit not sleke."[22]

As others have noted, the unabashed, almost performative eroticism of this speech is striking, for *Cleanness* never straightforwardly allegorizes these delights into spiritual *caritas*.[23] On the contrary, the verb *compassen* introduces a lexicon of material craft, including words like *portrayed*, *tyȝed*, and

21. Hatt notes additional instances of this alliterative pairing in *God and the Gawain-Poet*, 105–6.

22. "I designed a natural craft for them and made it known to them secretly [*derne*], and deemed it in my governance singularly precious [*oddely dere*], and placed love within, sweetest of exchanges/pains, and the play of paramours I depicted myself, and made thereto the merriest of all manners; when two true ones have tied themselves together, between a male and his mate such mirth should come, Paradise itself might well nigh prove no better. So long as they each handle [*welde*] the other honestly, at a still, stolen hour ungoverned by sight [*vnstered wyth syȝt*], the love-flame between them should lash so hot that all the mischiefs on earth might not quench it" (lines 697–708).

23. Important treatments of these lines include Keiser, *Courtly Desire and Medieval Homophobia*, 41–70; Calabrese and Eliason, "Rhetorics of Sexual Pleasure and Intolerance"; Schmidt, "Kynde Craft," 105–24; and Staples, "Pure Pleasure."

welde, that reinforces the physicality of the pleasure being described.[24] The poem intimates that pleasure with an especially lush and intricate soundscape, deepened by lexical complexity. For example, line 699—"dyȝt drwry *þer*inne, doole al*þer*swettest"—features a subtle internal rhyme on *þer* tucked within the dominant alliteration, comparable to God's own careful placement (*dyȝt*) of love within the "kynde crafte" being praised; the alliterating *doole*, meanwhile, suggests a multilingual pun on "exchange" (appropriate, given the passage's emphasis on mutuality of affection) and *doel*, a courtly form of love-pain.[25] The passage shifts almost flirtatiously in tone, from coy circumlocutions ("a maner myriest of oþer") to spicier formulations ("lasched so hote") and the bold claim that Paradise itself might well nigh (*welneȝe*) pale in comparison to such "mirth."

Such direct comparison of sexual to paradisal pleasures heightens the poet's surprising decision not to cite either childbirth or marriage as the outcome and sacrament, respectively, that circumscribe lawful, "clean" sex.[26] God's claim to have made this craft known to humanity *derne* (secretly, privately) sounds almost Promethean, and contrasts sharply with the more familiar, loudly proclaimed directive to "be fruitful and multiply" (Gen. 1:28 and repeated, with variations, at Gen. 9:1 and 9:7 and Lev. 26:9).[27] Highlighted by its successive triple alliteration, the phrase "stylle stolen steuen" ("a quiet, stolen hour") sounds more redolent of a tryst or assignation than orthodox payment of the marriage debt.[28] The next half-line—"vnstered

24. See also Queen: "The poet uses words such as 'portrayed' and 'compast' almost certainly because of their artistic valences and, arguably, indicates the poet's desire to posture God as an artist" ("Negative Affect," 129).

25. *Middle English Dictionary* (accessed August 31, 2023, https://quod.lib.umich.edu/m/middle-english-dictionary/dictionary/MED12320; https://quod.lib.umich.edu/m/middle-english-dictionary/dictionary/MED12321), s.v. "dōl," meanings 1 (from OE *dal/gedal*) and 2 (from OF *doel*).

26. Here I follow Keiser, Staples, and others; for an opposing view, that the passage should be read "as a specific reference to the union of faithful *spouses*" despite the poet's lack of explicitness, see Schmidt, "Kynde Craft," 119–22 (at 121, original emphasis). I find it telling that the poet creates clear opportunities to use the word *mariage*, by writing several *m*-alliterating lines (701, 703, 708), which the poet then declines to take. This poetic prompting to think about *m*-words almost inevitably summons up the idea of marriage, which makes the poem's failure to mention it conspicuous and suggestive.

27. Schmidt notes further that "*derne* at the end of line 697 is faintly echoed at the end of line 698 in *dere*: this divine craft or art is as precious as it is private" ("Kynde Craft," 117).

28. Keiser likewise suggests that the poet depicts "a tryst which in some sense emulates the divine nature" (*Courtly Desire and Medieval Homophobia*, 241n36).

wyth syȝt" ("ungoverned [lit. unsteered] by sight")—reinforces the emphasis on occlusion, striking in a poem that so emphasizes the visual.

As James C. Staples notes, that phrase also recalls the poem's earlier depiction of Noah's ark as lacking any form of steering.[29] There, the ship's miraculous survival despite such lack was prefigured by numerical precision and divine instruction, highlighted by the word *compas*. God's opening use of that same word in the passage above implies that it will lay out boundaries for this "natural craft" that are comparable in some sense to the dimensions of the ark; but those it outlines, chiefly mutuality of affection and open, honorable treatment of the ungendered partner (*make*, line 103), are not those we might expect from a medieval homiletic poem.[30] Even the phrase that implies marriage, of two true ones tied together (line 702), focuses more on aesthetic than sacramental qualities, "where tying forms a kind of love knot: not a jumbled tangle, but a beautiful, clever binding of bodies into a tableau of 'clean' sexual union," as Seamus Dwyer elegantly puts it.[31] This aesthetic is both physical and literary, in that it concerns not just sexual activity but also the courtly-love play that encompasses it, in whose sumptuous expression the Pearl-Manuscript so clearly delights.[32] This aspect of its aesthetic will surprise no one who has read the bedroom scenes of *Sir Gawain and the Green Knight*; line 699's *drwrye* appears there three times. Preauthorizing the reader's delectation in such material is therefore one important function of the passage in the context of the Pearl-Manuscript as a whole, for it helps

29. Staples, "Pure Pleasure," 43. *Cleanness* spends a whole quatrain (line 417–20) listing no fewer than eight steering devices that the ark lacked, among them mast, cable, rudder, and sail. The artist disregards these lines in depicting the ark on 56/60r—for what reason we cannot say, but with the effect of strengthening its resemblance to the earlier illustration of *Pearl* on 38/42v, as we saw in chap. 3.

30. Heterosexuality is famously one such boundary that the poem does make explicit—but in *Cleanness*, even heteronormativity can become queerly generative, as Staples points out ("Pure Pleasure," 42).

31. Dwyer, "Reading the Tied Letters," 13. See also Queen's argument that "the poet's description of heterosexual sex as a 'crafte that is better' here suggests an expressed interest in the aesthetics of heterosexuality—God's 'crafte' is both an artistic undertaking and the expectation of a proper appreciation of the beauty of its normativity" ("Negative Affect," 129).

32. Carolyn Dinshaw has made a similar point, though to different ends from mine here: of the passage under discussion, she writes that "the language God uses is the language of courtly love, complete with 'derne' love-craft and 'doole alþerswettest'; in fact, the 'play of paramorez' instituted by God can be nothing other than the courtly love games and the roles of courtly men and women" ("A Kiss Is Just a Kiss," 218).

to inscribe (or pre-scribe) the manuscript's last and longest poem within the spiritual framework of its first three.

Significantly, the next instance of *compas* in *Cleanness* also links courtly-love poetry—and *drwry* specifically—with spiritual self-improvement, in the Pearl-Manuscript's only citation of a nonbiblical source-text:

> ¶ For Clopyngel in þe **compas** of his clene *Rose*, [1057]
> þer he expounez a speche to hym þat spede wolde
> of a lady to be loued: "Loke to hir sone
> of wich beryng þat ho be, and wych ho best louyes,
> ¶ and be ryȝt such in vch a borȝe, of body and of dedes, [1061]
> and folȝ þe fet of þat fere þat þou fre haldes.
> And if þou wyrkkes on þis wyse, þaȝ ho wyk were,
> hir schal lyke þat layk þat lyknes hir tylle."
> ¶ If þou wyl dele **drwrye** wyth Dryȝtyn þenne, [1065]
> and lelly louy þy Lorde and his leef worþe,
> þenne confourme þe to Kryst, and þe clene make,
> þat euer is polyced als playn as þe perle seluen.[33]

As has often been noted, calling Jean de Meun's sprawling, bawdy, and satirical *Roman de la Rose* "clene" is provocative, to say the least;[34] and the third quatrain above leans into that strangeness by making Christ analogous to the "lady to be loued."[35] The self-referentiality of this passage is also striking,

33. "For Clopingel [Jean de Meun], in the course [*compas*] of his clean *Rose*, expounds there a speech to one who would be loved by a lady: 'Examine her swiftly, of what bearing she is and what she most loves, and be right such in each town [i.e., everywhere] in body and deeds, and follow in the footsteps of that companion [*fere*] whom you consider noble. And if you work in this fashion, however wicked/difficult she may be, she will like that performance [lit. "game," *layk*] which likens itself to her [*lyknes hir tylle*].' So if you wish to exchange love [*dele drwrye*] with the Lord, and loyally love your Lord and become his beloved, then make yourself clean by conforming to Christ, who is always as smoothly polished as the pearl itself" (lines 1057–68).

34. Keiser writes that this "laudatory epithet ['clene *Rose*'] has puzzled readers of *Cleanness* at least since its first editors" (*Courtly Desire and Medieval Homophobia*, 114), and Hatt notes that "slavishly (and deceitfully) copying the tastes and behavior of the beloved is ludicrously inappropriate to the idea of loving God, so much so that it throws into high relief the meaning of what copying God would actually mean" (*God and the Gawain-Poet*, 94). Ad Putter helpfully draws on Aquinas to show the danger of aiming for "likeness of equality" rather than that of "imitation" in fashioning one's likeness to God (*Introduction to the Gawain-Poet*, 213).

35. Staples acknowledges that "discursive eroticism directed at Christ, who is frequently represented as the soul's bridegroom in devotional and contemplative literature, has been a

for if line 1065's *drwrye* anticipates the Pearl-Manuscript's last poem, then the final comparison of Christ, to a perfectly polished pearl, obviously recalls its first—not least since laborious polishing was surely necessary in order to produce *Pearl*'s highly wrought, perfectly imperfect form.

The forms of *Cleanness* are less obvious than *Pearl*'s, but the passage above draws attention to itself with the same technical phrase, "expounez ... speche" ("expounds ... speech," line 1058), that Daniel will later use to introduce his reading of God's writing on the wall (line 1729). The poem thus presents these twelve lines as an interpretable verbal form, whose complex language of imitation and likeness operates clearly within the quatrain-like structure reinforced by the paraphs (though sometimes obscured by modern editorial punctuation, a point to which chap. 6 will return). I find this consonance with the underlying syntactic beat significant precisely because of the passage's challenging strangeness, for it strengthens the arguments of Elizabeth Keiser, Staples, and others that we should take its counterintuitive simile seriously. Since *Pearl* was obsessed with the number twelve, the importance of these lines is further suggested by the reference to pearls in their twelfth and final line, and *Cleanness* echoes *Pearl* elsewhere as well.[36] Moreover, because *compas* can also mean "circle" or "sphere," these twelve lines are enclosed—encompassed—by references to perfect roundness, further evoking the pearl (and *Pearl*) that its final line likens to Christ.[37]

The arresting nature of this simile also establishes the half-line "polysed als playn" in our ears, such that we are likelier to hear its chime when it recurs less than 100 lines later, comparing confession and penance to a scribe's preparation of parchment, scraping away imperfections and polishing it to a glossy luster: the shriven soul is thus "polysed als playn as parchmen schauen" ("polished as smooth as shaved parchment," line 1134), a simile that Andrew and

part of Christian devotion since the days of late antiquity, most inspired by exegesis on the Song of Songs" ("Pure Pleasure," 49), but he persuasively argues that "the poet's provocative use of sexual language, inviting the reader to 'dele drwrye' to Christ and be Christ's 'leef,' encourages a reading that takes this as more than metaphor" (51). See also Spyra, "God of the Middle English *Cleanness*."

36. Some of these echoes we considered in chap. 3, but see also, e.g., line 556, "withouten maskle oþer mote, as margerye perle" ("without flaw or blemish, like the margery-pearl"), which compares (by negation) pearls to two keywords from *Pearl*, *maskle* and *mote*; and lines 1117–18, which compare the value of pearls and pennies, two key images for value in *Pearl*.

37. *Middle English Dictionary* (accessed 31 August, 2023, https://quod.lib.umich.edu/m/middle-english-dictionary/dictionary/MED8678), s.v. "compas," meaning 2a. On the centrality of this "homiletic interlude" to *Cleanness* as a whole, see further Stanbury, *Seeing the Gawain-Poet*, 45–50.

Waldron point out "is also found (in more extended form) in a 12th c. sermon designed to appeal to illuminators of manuscripts."[38] Such moments suggest a version of the "[b]ibliophilic sensibility," inclined to "construe the world through bookish metaphor," that Martha Dana Rust has identified in late medieval literary culture more broadly.[39] A negatively expressed form of this bibliophilia also underwrites a more unsettling bookish comparison, in which the chaotic detritus of Sodom and Gomorrah's destruction is likened to "lauce leueȝ of þe boke þat lepes in twynne" ("loose leaves of the book that leaps in two/apart," line 966).[40] This is one example of the feedback loop described in the introduction, by which the poems' imagery recalls the book in our hands, thereby prompting attention to how the Pearl-Manuscript shapes and reinforces its poems.

In the twelve-line passage above, the paraphs participate in this process, not just by marking boundaries (another meaning of the word *compas*) to which the syntax broadly conforms but also by reinforcing that this is a series of three quatrains. *Cleanness*'s favorite number, three, is thus embedded within and around a single twelve-line passage that recalls *Pearl*, whose own favorite number was twelve.[41] Such play with three-in/and-one is implicitly trinitarian, and the final quatrain's use of three names for God, in three successive lines—*Dryȝtyn*, *Lorde*, and *Kryst*—also subtly suggests that theme.[42] This interweaving of material and textual form reinforces that these twelve lines occupy the middle of folio 71/75v, which, like almost every other page of the Pearl-Manuscript, has thirty-six lines of verse. That may be a coincidence, but it is aesthetically pleasing regardless, for it means that these twelve lines, which are verbally "enclosed" by circular imagery (*compas* at the beginning; *perle* at the end), are visually enclosed above and below by equal sets of twelve lines and by paraphs in the left margin. Moreover, the scribe has executed these lines in particularly sharp and sprightly fashion, with crisp

38. Andrew and Waldron, *Poems*, 159.

39. Rust, *Imaginary Worlds*, 2; see further 9–18.

40. Drawing on Ahern, "Binding the Book," Hatt (*God and the Gawain-Poet*, 119–20) persuasively suggests that this evokes Dante's image, at the end of *Paradiso*, of the heavenly light being "bound by love into a single volume" ("legato con amore in un volume," 33.86).

41. *Cleanness* uses the word "three" and its forms more than any other poem in the Pearl-Manuscript (Kottler and Markman, *A Concordance to Five Middle English Poems*, s.v. "three"; the *Concordance* includes *St. Erkenwald* as the fifth poem), and the poem's organization is explicitly threefold, as its concluding first-person summary makes clear: "Thus in three ways I have thoroughly shown you . . ." (line 1805).

42. The Trinitarian paradoxes of St. Bonaventure's *Itinerarium* resonate here; see further chap. 3, page 83.

minims and some of the same embellishments that adorned the end of *Pearl* and beginning of *Cleanness*.[43] This complex and important passage is thus artfully set, or *pyȝt*, in multiple dimensions; together, literary imagery and material page-shape stage the interpenetration of verbal and visual meaning on which *Cleanness* itself insists.

The three instances of *compas* considered thus far have had architectural, aesthetic, and literary dimensions. The final use of the word unites these senses in detailing the gorgeous construction of Solomon's sacred vessels, whose ekphrasis "seems to spring from the poet's own delight in such things," as Cecilia A. Hatt points out.[44] Seeing their beauty abused by Belshazzar inspires God's scribal intervention, which in turn provokes a sustained, highly conspicuous mismatch between quatrains and paraphs—the most significant such disjunction in the entire manuscript. I will argue that reading this mismatch homiletically reinforces both the episode being depicted and *Cleanness*'s own status as material and verbal art.

SHAPING VESSELS, WRITING IN WALLS

If the previous instance of *compas* quoted another's artistry (Jean de Meun's), then the final instance, which introduces the account of Solomon's sacred vessels, spotlights the poet's own. As we will see, these lines gain ekphrastic effect partly by using enjambment across quatrains, comparable to what we saw in the opening parable of the wedding feast. This effect is heightened by the contrasting texture of the surrounding passages, in which quatrain and syntax structure regularly correspond. Five of the six quatrains that immediately precede the ekphrasis are clearly end-stopped, for example, and the one that isn't nevertheless strongly reinforces the poem's underlying quatrain structure:

> ₵ Þat hade ben blessed *bifore* wyth bischopes hondes, [1445]
> and wyth besten blod busily anoynted,
> in þe solempne sacrefyce þat goud sauor hade,
> bifore þe Lorde of þe lyfte in louyng hymseluen,
> ₵ *now* is sette forto serue Satanas þe blake, [1449]
> bifore þe bolde Baltaȝar wyth bost and wyth pryde.

43. See further chap. 3, pages 79–81; and Dwyer, "Reading the Tied Letters," 10.

44. Hatt, *God and the Gawain-Poet*, 103.

Houen vpon þis auter watȝ aþel vessel,
þat wyth so curious a crafte coruen watz wyly.[45]

These quatrains gain structural integrity from their sharp contrast between then and now, holy and profane purpose, "Lord of the lyfte" and "Satanas þe blake." The final line, meanwhile, encourages us to read the ekphrasis that follows with particular attention to its skill and intricacy, principal associations of ME *curious*.[46]

Here, the poet's imagination takes flight in a tour de force of poetic art. In the passage below, I underline the lexicon of flora (branches, flowers, leaves), *italicize* that of architecture and castellation, [bracket] that of flying creatures, {curly bracket} that of gems and gold, and **boldface** that of shape and making. My goal is to illustrate how skillfully the poet interweaves these various image-strands into a whole greater than the sum of its parts, and thus a fitting intimation of Solomon's own devotional craftsmanship:

¶ Salamon sete him seuen ȝere and a syþe more, [1453]
with alle þe syence þat hym sende þe souerayn lorde,
for to **compas** and kest to haf hem clene **wroȝt**—
for þer wer bassynes ful bryȝt of {brende golde clere,
¶ enaumaylde with aȝer}, and eweres of sute, [1457]
couered cowpes ful clene, as *casteles* arayed,
enbaned vnder *batelment with bantelles* quoynt,
and **fyled** out of **fygures** of ferlyle **schappes**.
¶ Þe *coperounes* of þe couacles, þat on þe cuppe reres, [1461]
wer fetysely **formed** out in *fylyoles* longe;
pinacles **pyȝt** þer apert þat profert bitwene,
and al **bolled** abof with braunches and leues,
¶ [pyes and papeiayes] **purtrayed** withinne, [1465]
as þay prudly hade piked of pomgarnades;
for alle þe blomes of þe boȝes wer {blynkande perles},

45. "That which *before* was blessed by bishops' hands, and carefully anointed with beasts' blood—in solemn sacrifice that had good savor, in devotion to the Lord of the sky himself—*now* is set to serve Satan the black, before bold Belshazzar with boasting and pride. Raised up on this altar were noble vessels that were cleverly carved with so curious a craft" (lines 1445–52, emphasis added).

46. *Middle English Dictionary* (accessed August 31, 2023, https://quod.lib.umich.edu/m/middle-english-dictionary/dictionary/MED9168), s.v. "cūriŏus adj.," meanings 1b, 2, 3.

and alle þe fruyt in þo **formes** of {flaumbeande gemmes,
℃ ande safyres and sardiners and semely topace, [1469]
alabaundeirynes, and amaraunȝ, and amatsed stones,
casydoynes, and crysolytes, and clere rubies,
penitotes, and pynkardines, ay perles bitwene}.
℃ So trayled and tryfled atrauerce wer alle [1473]
by vche bekyr ande bolle, þe brurdes al vmbe;
þe gobelotes of {golde} **grauen** aboute,
and *fyoles* fretted with flores and [fleeȝ] of {golde}.[47]

This passage's creative force is so intense that several of its words, among them *enbaned* and *bantelles*, are attested only in the Pearl-Manuscript; as elsewhere, the poet is literally "finding" (i.e., inventing) words to further this devotional craft. We start at a distance, the first quatrain ending with a broad impression of brightly shining gold. From there, we focus on the cup covers and their castellated decoration. Then, we zoom in further, for a twelve-line internal set piece on the turrets and pinnacles adorning the cup covers, specifically their intricate intertwining of architectural, botanical, and begemmed embellishment (lines 1461–72). The gems prove especially dazzling, receiving their own quatrain that concludes this section with a second reference to pearls, the only gem named twice. From there we zoom back out: the last quatrain's summary ends with two references to gold that recall the end of the first quatrain and give the passage a circular, "encompassed" unity consonant with what we have seen of the manuscript's aesthetic thus far. Within that broadly chiastic and crescendo-like structure, however, the

47. "For seven years and a while longer, with all the learning that the sovereign Lord sent him, Solomon set himself to design them [the vessels] and have them made 'cleanly,' for there were bright basins of burnished gold, enameled with lapis, and ewers to match, very clean covered cups made like castles, fortified under the battlement with skillfully made bantels [projecting horizontal coursings], and carved out in marvelous shapes. The ornamented tops of the lids that sit on the cups were delicately formed into long turrets; pinnacles set at intervals protruded between, and all embossed from above with branches and leaves, magpies and parrots depicted within, as if they were proudly pecking at pomegranates; for all the blooms on those boughs were shining pearls, and all the fruit took the form of blazing gems, like sapphires and sardonyx and lovely topaz, alamandines and emeralds and amethyst stones, chalcedonies and chrysolites and bright rubies, peridots and pinkardines and pearls all between. Thus were they all entwined and trefoiled, all around the rims of each beaker and bowl; the goblets of gold engraved all about, and incense-burners adorned with flowers and butterflies of gold" (lines 1453–76).

poet achieves a remarkable degree of imagistic interweaving, as the formatting above highlights.[48]

These lines do not violate the poem's quatrains so much as they occasionally overleap them in their enthusiasm for tracing the vessels' intricacies. The paraphs nevertheless shape this passage, helping us see the quatrain-concluding reference to gold at beginning and end (lines 1456 and 1476) as well as the contours of the twelve-line detail of the lids' elaborate decoration. This twelve-line sentence is set within the larger passage just as the embellishments it describes are set (*pyȝt*, line 1465) within the vessels, enacting the analogies between poetic and sacred craft that *Cleanness* explores more broadly. (The fact that these twelve lines end with a reference to pearls, like the twelve-line "clene Rose" passage considered earlier, is additionally striking.) And while the syntax often spills over quatrain boundaries—appropriate to their subject's flamboyant ornamentation—end stops coincide with quatrains frequently enough to integrate the passage within the poem's overarching four-line beat.

The poet signals our reemergence from this ekphrastic fantasy with shorter and simpler sentences; the final quatrain above is the first of fourteen consecutive (lines 1473–1528) that consist of a single four-line sentence corresponding precisely to the manuscript's paraphs. These lines thereby gain a staccato quality, evoking the drumbeat of God's growing anger at these heathens' perverse insistence on treating dumb idols like gods:

> ¶ Alle þe *goude golden goddes* þe gaulez ȝet neuenen,
> Belfagor, and Belyal, and Belssabub als,
> heryed hem as hyȝly as heuen wer þayres,
> bot hym þat alle *goudes giues*, þat *God* þay forȝeten.[49]

The opening mention of gold recalls Solomon's vessels, which were thrice thus described; but whereas those were devotional offerings to the one true God, these objects represent a fatal misreading of the relation between creation and Creator, complementing Belshazzar's other impudently impious

48. Appropriately, this interwoven imagery is also intertextual: Stanbury notes that this passage uses "material borrowed from John Mandeville's account of the marvels of the Orient" (*Seeing the Gawain-Poet*, 61).

49. "The wretches still call on these 'good golden gods,' Belfagor and Belial and Beelzebub as well, praised them as highly as if Heaven were theirs, but the one who gives all goods—that God they forget" (lines 1525–28, emphasis added).

attempts at craft.[50] The quatrain reinforces this contrast by first sarcastically calling these "good golden gods," then closing the circle in the last line by using the same alliterating letter, and many of the same words, to denounce those who forget the God who gives all goods.

Such perverse imitation of divine making inspires God to take pen in hand and write into the wall of Belshazzar's palace:

> ¶ þer apered a paume, with poyntel in fyngres, [1533]
> þat watȝ grysly and gret, and grymly he wrytes;
> non oþer forme bot a fust, faylande þe wryste
> pared on þe parget, purtrayed lettres.[51]

Here God produces both verbal and visual form: his hand itself is a visual sign, and each of the words that he writes is later called a *fygure* (line 1726). His stylus (*poyntel*, a noteworthy anticipation of *Patience*'s famous *poynt*) is an addition to the poet's biblical source that makes God both author and scribe; it was also reinforced visually in the illustration opposite *Cleanness*'s opening lines (see figs. 3.7 and 3.12).[52]

This sight both terrifies Belshazzar and disrupts the alignment of syntax and quatrains, which as noted above has been strikingly regular in the preceding fifty or so lines:

50. For example, Putter writes: "Belshazzar, the poet leaves no doubt about it, has a sense for the dramatic and the artistic. Confident in his powers to transform matter into art, he turns concubines into ladies, guests into spectators, and finally even the sacred vessels into the stage-props of his theater. . . . In his delusions of grandeur and originality, Belshazzar copies and mimics, fashions objects and identities that are finally only supplements to God's prior act of creation, of which Belshazzar is himself the product, not the producer" (*Introduction to the Gawain-Poet*, 215–16). Reading the account of Belshazzar's own vessels at lines 1405–12, Stanbury notes that "[u]nlike the description of the holy vessels, this description is visually haphazard, proceeding as it does from the top to the bottom and then to the middle. . . . Furthermore, whereas the holy vessels are crafted from precious materials, Belshazzar's ornament is made from paper, and not 'of casteles arayed' but of little 'logges,' the Middle English term for 'tent' or 'hut'" (*Seeing the Gawain-Poet*, 64). I will return to the poet's use of paper in chap. 8.

51. "There appeared a hand, with stylus in fingers, that was grisly and great, and grimly it writes—no other form but a fist, lacking a wrist—cut into the plaster, shaped letters" (lines 1533–36).

52. Daniel 5:5 mentions God's fingers but no writing implement: "Immediately the fingers of a human hand appeared and began writing on the plaster of the wall of the royal palace, next to the lampstand. The king was watching the hand as it wrote." For astute analysis of how the spatial representation of hands in this image isolates the sinful Belshazzar, see Blanch and Wasserman, *From Pearl to Gawain*, 65–110.

¶ When þat bolde Baltaȝar blusched to þat neue, [1537]
such a dasande drede dusched to his hert
þat al falewed his face and fayled þe chere.
Þe stronge strok of þe stonde strayned his ioyntes:
¶ his cnes cachches to close, and cluchches his hommes, [1541]
and he with plattyng his paumes displayes his lernes,
and romyes as a rad ryth þat roreȝ for drede,
ay biholdand þe honde til hit hade al grauen
¶ and rasped on þe roȝ woȝe runisch saueȝ.[53] [1545]

All editions I know of agree that the final line above concludes a sentence even though it is the first line of a quatrain as marked by the paraph—an occurrence that has been vanishingly rare to this point in the poem. It seems brilliantly appropriate that Belshazzar's physical and mental breakdown—roaring like a mad bull, limbs buckling as he claws at his empty head—should be marked by a comparable breakdown in the paraph/quatrain structure.

This disruption is consistent and long enough that several editions choose to repair it. Following Gollancz, J. J. Anderson prints lines 1541–45 and 1586–90 as stanzas of five lines and 1591–92 as a separate two-line stanza, which allows the syntax and quatrain marks in that section of the poem to match up about as consistently as they do elsewhere; Putter and Stokes print 1541–45 as a stanza of five lines and 1586–88 as one of three, which achieves a comparably smoothing effect. Explaining their decision in a note to lines 1541–92, they write simply that "quatrains as marked in the MS . . . in this passage run one line out from sense divisions; we have rearranged so as to restore agreement between the two."[54] Anderson notes that "in lines 1541–85 . . . the marginal marks actually run counter to the sense," and posits that "the scribe may have made a copying error . . . perhaps retaining a line which had been cancelled in his original and thereby displacing the quatrains."[55]

53. "When that bold Belshazzar gazed at that fist, such stultifying dread struck at his heart that his face turned pale, and his countenance failed. The strong stroke of the moment strained his joints: his knees knock together and his thighs bend, and with his beating fists he displays his emptiness [i.e., foolishness], and cries out like a mad bull that roars in fear, always gazing at the hand until it had engraved everything and scratched mysterious [lit. "runish"] sayings onto the rough wall" (lines 1537–45).

54. Putter and Stokes, *Works of the Gawain Poet*, 554.

55. Anderson, *Cleanness*, 2. Max Kaluza seems to be responding in part to this passage when he writes of *Cleanness* that "the text may have fallen into more disorder [than in *Patience*], or else the poet, who also abandoned his quatrains in *Sir Gawain and the Green Knight*, here too has not executed the formation into larger stanzas with his original regularity" ("Strophische Gliederung," 178, my translation).

As with *Pearl*'s various "imperfections," such questions cannot be conclusively answered. I believe we should take seriously this tension between verbal and visual sense, however, for these very lines emphasize the confluence of verbal and visual meaning. From Belshazzar's dehumanized body, our gaze returns with his to God's writing hand:

ay biholdand þe honde til hit hade al grauen
¶ and rasped on þe roȝ woȝe runisch saueȝ. [1545]
When hit þe scrypture hade scraped wyth a scrof penne,
as a coltour in clay cerues þo forȝes,
þenne hit vanist verayly and voyded of syȝt,
¶ bot þe lettres bileued ful large vpon plaster.[56] [1549]

The homeliness of line 1547's simile combines with the previous line's rough language (*scraped, scrof*) to emphasize that God's writing is manual labor as well as mystical performance. The word *runisch* suggests not just recondite content but also graphic otherness, evoking both Hebrew script within the poem and England's pre-Christian, mostly lost system of lettering, traces of which survive in the shape of the scribe's many thorns (Þ/þ).[57] The adjective is thus a tangent point between the book in our hands, which includes literal runes, and the "runisch saueȝ" of biblical history—both of which we must read rightly, as Belshazzar demands of Daniel ("redes hit by ryȝt," line 1633). Here an attentive rereader may recall the visual echo of the banderole catchphrase of *Pearl* on 50/54v (fig. 3.13) in the *Mane-Techal-Phares* banderole of 56/60v (fig. 3.12).

The poem's earlier scribal simile, comparing the shriven soul to a finely shaven sheet of parchment, aligned smoothness with godliness, so it seems appropriate that God carves into the wall here, the stylus inscribing judgment like a blade.[58] Such vivid evocation of scribal work (the word *scrapen* also appears in line 6 of Chaucer's famous "Adam Scriveyn" lyric, for example)

56. ". . . always gazing at the hand until it had engraved everything and scraped mysterious [lit. "runish"] sayings onto the rough wall. When it had scraped this writing/Scripture with a rough pen, as a coulter carves furrows into clay, then it vanished completely and disappeared from sight, but the letters remained, very large upon plaster" (lines 1544–49).

57. As Dwyer notes, "'runisch sauez' recalls the alien nature of runes, permeating the writing with a sense of mystery and secrecy" ("Reading the Tied Letters," 24).

58. The three-dimensionality of this performance is also suggested by the earlier phrase "pared on the parget" ("cut into the plaster," line 1536). This image also evokes illustrations of scribes wielding a pen in the right hand and knife in the left (on which see, e.g., Brantley, *Medieval English Manuscripts*, 66). Such scribal imagery evokes the opposition between the right and left hands of God familiar from depictions of the Last Judgment. David Wallace's

subtly encourages the reader of *Cleanness* to attend to elements of scribal performance in the Pearl-Manuscript as well. The marginal paraphs form an important part of that performance, especially here, where they suggest artful play with our perception of quatrain boundaries. For example, line 1548 above could easily be the end of a sentence, as it is of a quatrain; our expectation that quatrain and syntactic boundaries will align, built over the poem's first 1500 lines, may lead us at first to suppose that it is. The sentence continues, however, with a powerful contrast between visual emptiness and scribal durability, emphasized by its own anomalous position ending a sentence in the first line of a quatrain. By attending to how the visual and the verbal collaboratively create meaning, we see that the bookish references to *runisch sauez* and letters cut into plaster are both highlighted by paraphs (lines 1545 and 1549), thereby reinforcing each other and the poem's broader interest in literary materiality.

Here, the tension between paraphs and syntax has artistic effects, but as this mismatch continues with near-perfect regularity for ten more quatrains, it becomes natural to wonder if something has gone awry: Are we seeing things? Do we need to emend, like modern editors? Is the fault in the writing or in our eyes? I find it significant that these interpretive challenges for readers become most pointed just as Belshazzar himself is being struck dumb by the sight of God's writing hand within the narrative. This similitude suggests a tense if temporary congruence between Belshazzar and the reader of the Pearl-Manuscript, both struggling to find meaning in the intersection of verbal, visual, and material form. Moreover, this congruence was prefigured by the illustration on folio 56/60v (see fig. 3.7), whose empty lower-right quadrant—pointed to by Daniel—likewise implied an alignment between Belshazzar and reader, both blind to the full significance of what lies before them.

This episode thus raises the disquieting possibility that the negative figures of *Cleanness* are not simply anti-exemplary but also dangerous. In a poem that has consistently emphasized the power of the visual, the fate of Lot's wife (lines 981–84) has already made clear the danger of looking at what we shouldn't. This later episode is subtler, however, since whereas she was disobeying a direct command not to look, we are witnessing a divine *warnyng* (1504) that takes the same form (written words) as the poem we are reading. Indeed, the insight into God's motives provided by that word

comments are apposite here: "So if it is God's pleasure to write the text of collective or individual history with the pen, then it is also his privilege to erase that history with the knife, or even to blow the entire book apart" ("*Cleanness* and the Terms of Terror," 98).

warnyng helps give this episode the significance that I ascribe to it. After witnessing the sacrilegious treatment of his vessels, God reflects as follows:

> ¶ So þe Worcher of þis worlde wlates þerwyth [1501]
> þat in þe poynt of her play he poruayes a mynde;
> bot er harme hem he wolde in haste of his yre,
> he wayned hem a warnyng þat wonder hem þoȝt.[59]

These lines, which have no biblical analogue, make sense only if the divine warning is meant to be an interpretable sign that viewers can make sense of. The poem does not give us the opportunity to do so within the immediate narrative context in which the words are written, but this quatrain forms part of a broader encouragement to take seriously how visual and verbal form intersect, not just on Belshazzar's wall but also in the Pearl-Manuscript itself.

Daniel reinforces this link between visual apprehension and moral exemplarity when he rebukes the king for failing to have learned from the example of his father Nebuchadnezzar, whose foolish pride he saw punished by God: "þou, Baltazar . . . / seȝ þese syngnes with syȝt and set hem at lyttel" ("you, Belshazzar, . . . saw these things with sight but paid them slight heed," lines 1709–10). Here, a pleonastic emphasis on sight ("seȝ . . . with syȝt") replaces the verb of knowing from the poet's biblical source,[60] thus representing an entire historical episode as a single, interpretable visual tableau—much like the illustration opposite the poem's opening lines (fig. 3.7). The prophet returns to this emphasis on the visual in his concluding summary to Belshazzar:

> ¶ "And for þat froþande fylþe, þe Fader of heuen [1721]
> hatȝ sende into þis sale þise **syȝtes** vncowþe,
> þe fyste with þe fyngeres þat flayed þi hert,
> þat rasped renyschly þe woȝe with þe roȝ penne."[61]

59. "So nauseated does this [Belshazzar's impiety] make the Maker of this world that at the height [*poynt*] of their play, he comes up with a plan; but before he would harm them in haste of his ire, he sent them a warning that seemed like a wonder" (lines 1501–4). Ad Putter rightly notes the strangeness of "portraying God as someone who is occasionally overcome with nausea and bouts of ill temper" (*Introduction to the Gawain-Poet*, 212).

60. "And you, Belshazzar his son, have not humbled your heart, even though you knew all this!" (Daniel 5:22).

61. "And for that overflowing filth, the Father in heaven sent these mysterious/unknown [*vncowþe*] sights: the fist with the fingers that flayed your heart, that scraped runishly in the wall with its rough pen" (lines 1721–24).

This quatrain stresses once more the rough physicality (*rasped*, *roȝ*) of God's writing, as well as its visual alterity (*renyschly*), using words that echo its initial depiction, considered earlier. That characterization helps link the pedagogical potential of narrative exempla to that of scribal activity: as performed by God within the poem, and by the scribe within the Pearl-Manuscript.

Here we should recall not just the visual but also the numerical aspect of *Cleanness*'s codicological form, which extends from the scribe, maintaining the regularity of paraphs even when the syntax or lineation makes that challenging, to the reader, untangling (with Crawford's help) the mathematical shapes of its decorated initials. The poem's narrative episodes reinforce this materially enacted emphasis on number and proportion, as seen in the precise instructions for the building of Noah's ark, considered earlier, and Daniel's explication of the three words written on Belshazzar's wall:

¶ "Þise ar þe wordes here wryten withoute werk more, [1725]
by vch fygure, as I **fynde**, as oure Fader lykes:
Mane, *Techal*, *Phares*, merked in þrynne,
þat þretes þe of þyn vnþryfte vpon þre wyse.
¶ Now expowne þe þis speche spedly I þenk— [1729]
Mane menes als much as maynful Gode
hatȝ counted þy kyndam bi a clene noumbre,
and fulfylled hit in fayth to þe fyrre ende.
¶ To teche þe of *techal*, þat terme þus menes: [1733]
þy wale rengne is walt in weȝtes to heng,
and is **funde** ful fewe of hit fayth-dedes;
and *phares* folȝes, for þose fawtes, to frayst þe trawþe.
¶ In *phares* **fynde** I forsoþe þis felle saȝes: [1737]
departed is þy pryncipalte, depryued þou worþes;
þy rengne rafte is þe fro and raȝt is þe Perses;
þe Medes schal be maysteres here, and þou of menske schowued."[62]

62. "These are the words written here, without further ado, by each figure I find, as it pleases our Father: *Mane*, *Techal*, *Phares*, marked in three, that threaten you in three ways because of your depravity. Now I intend to swiftly expound this speech to you: *Mane* means that the powerful God has counted your kingdom according to a clean number and brought it to conclusion [*fulfylled*], in faith, to its latter end. To teach you of *techal*, that term means that your exalted kingdom is chosen to hang in the balance, and has been found severely lacking in deeds of faith; and *phares* follows those faults, to lay bare the truth. In *phares* I find very truly these fell sayings: your rulership has been divided, you will be dispossessed, your

Already depicted as a scribe, God is shown here to be a reckoner as well, counting out the days of Belshazzar's reign just as the scribe has counted out the lines on each page in order to maintain the paraphs' rhythm.

Equally significant is the passage's use of the verb *fynde*, the main verb of the poem's first, quatrain-length sentence ("fayre formeȝ myȝt he *fynde*," line 3), applied both to Daniel (lines 1726, 1737) and to God (1735). From God (finding Belshazzar wanting in the balance) to Daniel (finding the meaning of God's words) to the poet (finding fair forms to further their speech), we find a set of spiritually meaningful imitations, or mirrorings, that readers are invited to join by speculating on the fair *formeȝ* of *Cleanness* and the Pearl-Manuscript as a whole. Such complex patterns of likeness and imitation recall the twelve-line "clene Rose" passage considered earlier, and it is partly on the basis of such analogies that I find significant the comparable set of resemblances that *Cleanness* presents across notions of writing and counting: from God, writing on the wall and counting out the length of Belshazzar's reign, to the scribe, writing out the poem and counting out its lines; we have also had Noah, dutifully maintaining the dimensions of the ark given to him by God, and the *compas* of Jean de Meun's *Rose*, which the poet has explicated for us in regular quatrains.

Yet such signs become harder to find as the poem progresses. The intervals between decorated initials lengthen dramatically, with the first five of its thirteen initials in the first 350 lines (1, 125, 193, 249, 345), but just two in its last half (1157, 1357), and none in its last 400 lines. Each major narrative episode also takes a bit longer than the previous one: the Flood is depicted in approximately three hundred lines (249–544), the destruction of Sodom and Gomorrah in approximately four hundred (677–1048), and the linked but contrasting examples of Nebuchadnezzar and Belshazzar in approximately six hundred and fifty (1157–1804). Such gradual expansion gives the reader more opportunities to go astray by losing the essential thrust of the exemplum at hand—particularly the last, which draws from multiple books of the Bible and takes in a wide range of years instead of confining itself to a discrete historical episode like the examples of Noah and Lot.[63]

This final episode also features a more complex moral pattern than the first two. Noah and Lot are unambiguously righteous men saved by God

kingdom is seized from you and given to the Persians; the Medes shall be masters here, and you expelled from honor" (lines 1725–40).

63. The bulk of lines 1157–1804 comes from Daniel 5, but they also draw from 2 Chronicles 36 and Jeremiah 52.

from the judgment meted out upon the unnamed, sinful multitudes. The poem's final exemplum, however, contrasts the wicked Belshazzar not (principally) with the unimpeachably virtuous Daniel but rather with his father Nebuchadnezzar, who was also punished for pride but managed to repent and reclaim his throne. His son is not given that opportunity, despite rewarding Daniel and thus presumably accepting the contours of the prophet's close reading; instead, his kingdom is invaded and he is killed that same night. *Cleanness* itself ends just a few lines after its grisly narration of how Belshazzar was "done doun of his dygnete for dedeȝ vnfayre" ("done down from his dignity for disgraceful deeds," line 1801). This abrupt conclusion contrasts markedly with that of the previous episodes in *Cleanness*, which temper the reader's consciousness of God's destructive power through Noah and Lot's concluding prayers of praise and thanksgiving. In short, although the poem's final lines insist that all three of its major exempla share the same moral,[64] their narrative forms differ substantially. Because *Cleanness* has stressed the interpenetration of form and content, that fact raises important questions about how we should interpret the text as a whole.

The poem's paratext also becomes harder to interpret in the final third of the poem. I have already discussed the extended mismatch between quatrain and syntax structure that begins with Belshazzar's reaction to the writing on the wall. The correspondence between syntactic and codicological form is largely restored during Daniel's speech to the king (lines 1641–1740), but in the conclusion of the narrative (lines 1741–1804), this relationship becomes harder to make sense of: we frequently find end stops in the middle of these quatrains (e.g., lines 1750, 1761, 1770, 1778, 1786), which has been quite rare through most of the poem. Unlike the obvious, consistent disjunction between syntax and quatrains initiated by Belshazzar's stupefaction, however, these lines' mismatch is marked enough to be odd, but not so consistent as to clearly invite interpretive explanations, such as I proposed for lines 1545–92.

The poem's first-person conclusion (lines 1805–12) restores the correspondence between quatrains and syntax, so in the context of the poem and manuscript as a whole, I read the jerky, slightly off-balance texture of its narrative ending as part of a broader resistance to the closure that comes with clear,

64. "Þus vpon þrynne wyses I haf yow þro schewed / Þat vnclannes tocleues in corage dere / Of þat wynnelych Lorde þat wonyes in heuen" ("Thus, in three ways I have thoroughly shown you that uncleanness cleaves in two the dear heart of that gracious Lord who dwells in Heaven," lines 1805–7).

straightforward meaning; but it is also, more optimistically, an opportunity for speculative engagement. As we saw in chapter 1, speculation mediates between cognition and contemplation, the knowable and the unknowable. The question of divine knowability is evoked as well by the poet's shifting characterizations of God's motives for writing on the wall—part of a challengingly anthropomorphized God more generally.[65] The Bible presents this vision as an irrevocable judgment handed down upon Belshazzar and his court, but *Cleanness* introduces it as a "warnyng" that God enacts "er harme hem he wolde in hast of his yre" ("before he would harm them, in haste of his ire," line 1503). That formulation suggests the possibility of repentance, but the poem instead draws attention to how immediately God's vengeance follows Belshazzar's reward of the prophet:

> ¶ Bot howso Danyel watȝ dyȝt, þat day ouerȝede;
> nyȝt neȝed ryȝt now with nyes fol mony;
> for daȝed neuer anoþer day, þat ilk derk after,
> er dalt were þat ilk dome þat Danyel deuysed.[66]

We have moved from warning to judgment (*dome*) without, as it were, warning. God's promise of swift punishment will take quite a different turn in *Patience*, but here the poet seems to relish this judgment, expanding two brief sentences in the Bible (Dan. 5:30–31) into fifty-two lines (1753–1804) that include graphic scenes of generalized mayhem and depict Belshazzar's fate with brutal vividness: beaten to death in his bed, "boþe his blod and his brayn blende on the cloþes" ("both his blood and his brains blended on the clothes," line 1788); his corpse fares no better than "a dogge . . . þat in a dych lygges" ("a dog . . . that lies in a ditch," line 1792).

I find the tone of these lines hard to read. On the one hand, they suggest grim satisfaction at the deserved fate of a blasphemer; but they also add a degree of brutal ugliness that contrasts sharply with the devotional delight expressed in many of the passages considered earlier. The ambiguous relationship between quatrains and syntax in lines 1745–1804 enhances the challenge of reading their tone, for it contributes to an attentive reader's sense

65. On the interpretive difficulties posed by the God of *Cleanness*, see Clopper, "God of the 'Gawain-Poet'"; Hatt, *God and the Gawain-Poet*, 73–123; Raschko, *Politics of Middle English Parables*, 178–91; and Spyra, *Epistemological Perspective*, 38–48.

66. "But howsoever Daniel was honored, that day passed; night approached at once with a great many afflictions; for another day never dawned, after that very night, before that selfsame judgment that Daniel described was meted out" (lines 1753–56).

that something may be "off" as the narrative concludes, without enabling us to reach firm conclusions about what that "something" might be, or what it might mean. Do we perceive this slight confusion between syntax and quatrains as aftershocks of the chaos besetting Belshazzar's city because of his sinful pride? Evidence of scribal corruption? Or simply normal variation within a broader, rarely wholly precise pattern? We can only speculate, and our lack of certain knowledge here reinforces the poem's broader insistence on the inscrutability of God.[67] In that sense, *Cleanness*'s presentation within the Pearl-Manuscript offers a material performance of Mary Raschko's observation that "the *Cleanness*-poet embraces the puzzling dynamics of parables and holds up paradox as fundamental to theology, as what people encounter when they strive to understand God."[68] The perspectival training of *Cleanness* suggests that we approach such challenges by attending to the confluence of visual and verbal meaning, and the poem's final page offers a dramatic invitation to do so.

67. On divine unknowability in the Pearl-Poems, see Spyra, *Epistemological Perspective*, and Clopper, "God of the 'Gawain-Poet.'"

68. Raschko, *Politics of Middle English Parables*, 189–90.

FIVE

(MID)POINTS OF INTEREST

The transition from *Cleanness* to *Patience* constitutes the approximate midpoint of the Pearl-Manuscript, and in a book whose poems evince such interest in structure, proportion, and symmetry, midpoints invite interpretation: recall the diptych-like structure of *Pearl*, for example, which hinged on the chiastic "less . . . more / more . . . less" transition from section 10 to 11.[1] That hinge—one structural midpoint—is nearly but not quite also the linear midpoint of *Pearl* (lines 600–601 of 1211/1212). We find a comparable kind of multiplication in the Pearl-Manuscript's own construction, for different midpoints emerge depending on how we measure: by poems, line numbers, page numbers, or quiring structure. Indeed, depending on how one counts the bobs of *Sir Gawain*, which do not receive their own lines in the manuscript, there are multiple midpoints even of the poems' line numbers. This chapter will suggest that some of these midpoints enhance the artistry of the poems they shape, prompting further speculation into the manuscript itself.

The asymmetries and imperfections that create these multiple midpoints are often sufficiently small or mechanical that it is easy to overlook or dismiss them. But *Patience* itself proposes that we attend to the granular, the tiny; as its opening words note, "pacience is a poynt" (line 1), a word that designates—among many, many other things—the nondimensional basis of all Euclidian shapes and, by extension, a brief moment of time.[2] *Patience* asks us to find meaning in such minutiae, so it is fitting that the pages surrounding its beginning should present so many resonant points of interest, binding the two halves of the Pearl-Manuscript together even as they radiate speculative potential outward.

1. See further chap. 2, pages 51–52; and Harwood, "*Pearl* as Diptych."

2. *Middle English Dictionary* (accessed August 31, 2023, https://quod.lib.umich.edu/m/middle-english-dictionary/dictionary/MED33862), s.v. "pointe n.(1)," meanings 3 and 4. These are just two of fifteen meanings given by the *MED* for this word, most of which have several, often quite different submeanings. On the polysemy of *poynt*, see Bernau, "Translating Form with *Patience*."

& of þyse worldes worchyp wrast out fore euer
& ȝet of lykynges on lofte letted I trowe
To loke on oure lofly lorde late bitydes
Þus vpon þrynne wyses I haf yow þro schewed
Þat vnclannes tocleues in corage dere
Of þat wynnelych lorde þat wonyes in heuen
Entyses hym to be tene telled vp his wrake
Ande clannes is his comfort & coyntyse he louyes
& þose þat seme arn & swete schyn se his face
Þat we gon gay in oure gere þat grace he vus sende
Þat we may serue in his syȝt þer solace neuer blynnez Amen

THE END OF *CLEANNESS*: CLEAVING AND BINDING

As the last chapter showed, Belshazzar's desecration of Solomon's vessels—the very impiety illustrated opposite *Cleanness*'s opening lines (fig. 3.7)—coincided with a sudden, extended, and interpretable misalignment of literary and codicological form, namely syntactic quatrain structure and marginal paraph marks. *Cleanness* has therefore primed us to find meaning in the intersection of text and page-shape, which makes the poem's ending especially arresting: its last eleven lines run almost headlong into the illustration shown in figure 5.1. Eleven is an odd number, in multiple senses; this is just the fifth page thus far whose total number of lines is not a multiple of twelve. (We will return to some of the others.)

This is also the only page in the entire manuscript to thus juxtapose text and image. Moreover, since the image below the words does not depict an episode from *Cleanness*, 82/86r combines not just text and image, but also poems: Jonah, here shown being thrown to the whale, is the flawed, often comic protagonist of the following poem, *Patience*, whose text begins on the following recto. It is striking that this unique juxtaposition should appear at nearly the textual midpoint of the codex: *Pearl* and *Cleanness* together have 3013/3014 lines; *Patience* and *Sir Gawain* combine for 3061 or 2950, depending on whether we count the latter's bobs. I will suggest that 82/86r uses its juxtaposition of text and image to unite not just *Cleanness* and *Patience* (which are often treated together by critics, for obvious reasons of form and content) but also the first and second halves of the Pearl-Manuscript, its first two and last two poems.

The image below the end of *Cleanness* (fig. 5.1) clearly echoes the image of Noah's Flood from folio 56/60r (fig. 3.2). The boat is of similar size and construction, though without the castellated mast, which would have jutted up into the text-block above. (A similarly castellated element does appear as a kind of prow, however, adding to the resemblance between the two illustrations.) Here, a sailor's harpoon descends at nearly the same angle as the oar of the ark, joined now by the figure of Jonah, whose green-and-yellow coat looks very much like that of two figures in 56/60r, including the one clasping the mast with both hands (presumably Noah), whose hair and

✣

Facing page: FIGURE 5.1. Folio 82/86r of Cotton Nero A.x/2. Photograph © 2024 by The British Library Board.

beard also resemble Jonah's. With their red and off-red tunics, the two men in Jonah's boat also look a bit like figures from Noah's Ark, though there they are crowded toward the back, behind the smaller green-clad man with the oar. The cheerfully curvaceous fish of earlier illustrations have coalesced here into a single menacing whale, rising up from the lower left of the page; but even this important difference is camouflaged somewhat by the fact that all marine life in the manuscript has been painted blue, such that it tends to blend in with the surrounding water. The whale's swallowing of Jonah is also prefigured by the larger fish eating the smaller fish on 56/60r, to the right of the swirl of water created by the oar. This visual prefiguration becomes still more resonant when we recall that Jonah was often read typologically, as a prefiguration of Jesus—including by Jesus himself, at Matthew 12:38–41.[3]

The inexactness of some of these resemblances is an important point to which I will return; read holistically, however, the image on 82/86r clearly evokes the first illustration of *Cleanness* in subject matter, color palette, and general composition. Thus 56/60r and 82/86r surround and frame the poem, recalling the thematization of wrought, morally appropriate systems of enclosure or "encompassing" discussed in chapter 4. In that sense, 82/86r gives *Cleanness* a pictorial version of the circularity that the other three poems achieve textually in their final lines: repetition with a difference.[4] The visual mirrorings across these pages thus render *Cleanness* more like its fellow poems, and the manuscript as a whole more cohesive, while also linking its inner two poems, *Cleanness* and *Patience*. These forms of linkage recall the kind of connective tissue we saw across the turn from *Pearl* to *Cleanness*. The effect here is still more dramatic, for 82/86r helps bind together the first and second halves of the codex.

The final page of *Cleanness* thus redeems the arresting simile, earlier, by which the total annihilation of Sodom and Gomorrah was likened to the leaves of a book torn in two:

> ¶ For when þat þe helle herde þe houndeȝ of heuen, [961]
> he watȝ ferlyly fayn, **vnfolded** bylyue;
> þe grete barreȝ of þe abyme he barst vp at oneȝ,
> þat alle þe regioun torof in riftes ful grete,

3. Hilmo argues that the harpoon being used on the whale reinforces this typological association between Jonah and Jesus ("Re-Conceptualizing," 387–92).

4. Famously, *Pearl* and *Patience* conclude with a slightly modified version of their opening lines, and *Sir Gawain*'s last alliterating long-line is likewise a version of its first. Chapter 8 will return to this patterning.

¶ and clouen alle in lyttel cloutes þe clyffeȝ aywhere,
as **lauce leueȝ of þe boke** þat lepes in twynne.[5]

In a powerful recent essay, Christopher D. Queen argues that "the scribe-illustrator cleverly performs this simile meta-textually and visually by having such a representation [of Sodom and its destruction] 'missing' from the illustrative program of the manuscript." He reads this lack as a kind of absent presence: "only by visually reproducing God's complete eradication of Sodom can the illustrator detail the gravity of the Sodomites' sins."[6] Yet far from a "book that leaps in two/apart," as the lines above put it, the Pearl-Manuscript gains aesthetic integrity from 82/86r, which unites its two halves by depicting what is simultaneously the first image of *Patience* (diegetically) and, more subtly, a third "illustration" of *Cleanness*—both along the lines proposed by Queen (as refusal to depict the poem's third, most absolute punishment for its most unspeakable sin) and in its evocation of the earlier illustration of Noah's Ark (thus pictorially enclosing the poem and binding the manuscript's two halves together). The image of Jonah thrown to the whale at 82/86r thus looks both backward and forward in the manuscript even as it links the manuscript's two approximate halves.

That a single page of the Pearl-Manuscript should create meaning in such multiple, seemingly contradictory ways is wholly consonant with the paradox-loving aesthetic of *Pearl*, two of whose concatenating sections were organized around "more (and more)." Folio 82/86r thus further demonstrates how constellations of page-shape—the interpretable fusion of textual, material, and visual craft—can productively punctuate our apprehension of the poems' often "immaterial" textuality.[7] Here, a division between text and image creates a rich set of connective tissues across the manuscript's two halves, thereby recalling Christ's miraculous cleaving of bread in *Cleanness*, likewise a form of division that paradoxically figures a deeper wholeness and unity:

5. "For when Hell heard the hounds of heaven, he [Hell] was wonderfully glad and immediately opened [*vnfolded*]; the great bars of the abyss he raised up at once, so that the entire region tore apart [*torof*] in great fissures; and the cliffs everywhere were split [*clouen*] into little shreds, like loose leaves of a book that splits in two" (lines 961–66, emphasis added). MS *lauce* has provoked debate among editors, with some reading *lance* instead; the manifold possibilities of these variably read graphemes evoke some of the energies we saw swirl around the **ere* crux of *Pearl* line 616, discussed in chap. 2.

6. Queen, "Negative Affect," 128, 130.

7. See further introduction, pages 6–14, and Wakelin, *Immaterial Texts*.

¶ Forþy **brek** he þe bred blades wythouten, [1105]
for hit ferde freloker in fete in his fayre honde,
displayed more pryuyly when He hit **part** schulde,
þenne alle þe toles of Tolowse moȝt tyȝt hit to **kerue**.[8]

In the supper at Emmaus to which this passage alludes (Luke 24:35), Jesus's breaking of the bread is a sign of the Divine that the apostles read correctly. In that, it offers one of *Cleanness*'s very few positive exempla.

Like other important moments in the manuscript, this miraculous cleaving of bread looks both forward and backward. It recalls *Cleanness*'s opening attack on sinful priestly celebrants and *Pearl*'s final image, of the elevated Host; it also anticipates *Cleanness*'s denouement, in which Belshazzar fails the spiritual-visual test that the disciples pass—rightly reading signs of the Divine—thereby precipitating the ruin that wraps up in the first three of 82/86r's eleven lines:

and of þyse worldes worchyp wrast out foreuer,
and ȝet of lykynges on lofte letted, I trowe,
to **loke on** oure lofly Lorde late bitydes.
¶ Þus vpon þrynne wyses I haf yow þro **schewed** [1805]
þat *vnclannes tocleues* in corage dere
of þat wynnelych Lorde þat wonyes in heuen,
entyses hym to be tene, telled vp his wrake.
¶ Ande clannes is his comfort, and coyntyse he louyes, [1809]
and þose þat seme arn and swete schyn **se** his face.
Þat we gon gay in oure gere þat grace he vus sende,
þat we may serue in his **syȝt**, þer solace neuer blynneȝ. Amen.[9]

Uncleanness breaks (*vnclannes tocleues*) the heart of the Lord, and it is a lovely grace note that, in this passage about the visual, those two words

8. "Therefore he broke bread without blades, for indeed it behaved more nobly in his fair hands, displayed more miraculously when He wished to part it, than if all the tools of Toulouse might endeavor to cut it" (lines 1105–9).

9. ". . . And [Belshazzar was] cast out of this world's worship forever, and is still deprived of pleasures on high, I believe; it will be long before he looks upon our lovely Lord. Thus, in three ways I have thoroughly shown you that uncleanness cleaves in two the dear heart of that gracious Lord who dwells in Heaven, provokes him to be angry, having aroused his wrath. And cleanness is his comfort, and wisdom he loves, and those that are seemly and sweet shall see his face. May he send us grace such that we go brightly in our apparel, that we may serve in his sight, where joy never ceases. Amen" (lines 1802–12).

FIGURE 5.2. Folio 82/86r of Cotton Nero A.x/2. Close-up of line 1806. Photograph © 2024 by The British Library Board.

should appear with prefixes separated from their root words, visually suggesting the cleavage they describe (see fig. 5.2). The verb *tocleues* even recalls the adjectival past participle *clouen* (line 965) from the description of Sodom and Gomorrah—another way in which this page subtly evokes the earlier episode. Here, the unclean are rightly condemned to spiritual blindness, reinforced with words like *schewed*, *se*, and *syȝt*. *Schewed* is used here to describe the poet's own literary and homiletic efforts; but on 82/86r, with a prominent illustration just below these lines, such vocabulary also necessarily reinforces the visual and pictorial, thus prompting further attention to this illustration's resemblances to that of Noah's Ark on 56/60r.

I have called such resemblances visual echoes because, like reverberations, they exist across time. The synesthesia of the term also seems consonant with the Pearl-Manuscript's all-sensory aesthetic. Reading its images as I have here requires flipping back and forth across pages, with an accompanying temporal gap; even now, while digital facsimiles make it easy to call up multiple images on a single screen, the eye must still move back and forth to study them. Such gaps or fissures—the impossibility of seeing everything at once, in its totality—reinforce that humanity is constrained by time and space, whereas God exists outside both those dimensions. As we will see in chapter 6, *Patience* dramatizes yet also complicates this theological commonplace; here my point is that the complexity of the Pearl-Manuscript's visual echoes grows as we move through the codex. So let us turn the page.

The second illustration of *Patience* on 82/86v (fig. 5.3) nicely encapsulates

Following spread: FIGURE 5.3. Folio 82/86v of Cotton Nero A.x/2. Photograph © 2024 by The British Library Board. FIGURE 5.4. Folio 83/87r of Cotton Nero A.x/2. Photograph © 2024 by The British Library Board.

Pacience is a poynt þaȝ hit displese ofte
When heuy herttes ben hurt wyth heþyng oþer elles
Suffraunce may aswagen hem & þe swelme leþe
For ho quelles vche a qued & quenches malyce
Ffor quo so suffer cowþe syt sele wolde folȝe
& quo for þro may noȝt þole þe þikker he sufferes
Þen is better to abyde þe bur vmbe stoundes
Þen ay þrow forth my þro þaȝ me þynk ylle
I herde on a halyday at a hyȝe masse
How Mathew melede þat his mayster his meyny con teche
Aȝt happes he hem hyȝt & vcheon a mede
Sunderlupes for hit dissert vpon a ser wyse
Thay arn happen þat han in hert pouerte
For hores is þe heuen ryche to holde for euer
Þay ar happen also þat haunte mekenesse
For þay schal welde þis worlde & alle her wylle haue
Thay ar happen also þat for her harme wepes
For þay schal comfort encroche in kythes ful mony
Þay ar happen also þat hungeres after ryȝt
For þay schal frely be refete ful of alle gode
Thay ar happen also þat han in hert rauþe
For mercy in alle maneres her mede schal worþe
Þay ar happen also þat arn of hert clene
For þay her sauyour in sete schal se wyth her yȝen
Thay ar happen also þat halden her pese
For þay þe gracious godes sunes schal godly be called
Þay ar happen also þat con her hert stere
For hores is þe heuen ryche as I er sayde
These arn þe happes alle aȝt þat vus bihyȝt weren
If we þyse ladyes wolde lof in lyknyng of þewes

the complexity of these visual echoes, for it offers a sort of mash-up of earlier illustrative motifs. The walled city of Nineveh clearly echoes the comparably enclosed Heavenly Jerusalem of folio 38/42v, and its blue-roofed structures, which almost mirror one another across the page, echo the comparable structure to the right of the Maiden in the earlier illustration (fig. 1.4). There, we see from without, like the Dreamer, rather than from above, as here; but in neither image can we see the city's full circuit, a subtle visual reminder of the limits of human perception. The preaching Jonah looks much like Daniel on folio 56/60v (fig. 3.7; similar green-and-red robe, beard, and red turban), right down to his oversized hands, thereby anticipating his role as both foil and echo—a relationship similar to that of *Patience* to *Cleanness*, as we will see.

The fact that so many discrete visual echoes constellate on 82/86v is significant because this page also concludes a larger-scale chiastic visual structure that emerges across the manuscript's twelve illustrations, as Paul F. Reichardt has shown.[10] Importantly, this structure extends across poems:

Illustration 4 (fig. 1.4): Final illustration of *Pearl*, with walled city (Heavenly Jerusalem)
Illustration 5 (fig. 3.2): First illustration of *Cleanness*, with water scene (Noah's Ark)
Illustration 6 (fig. 3.7): Belshazzar's Feast from *Cleanness*, with God's writing hand and banderole with words
Illustration 7 (fig. 5.1): First illustration of *Patience*, with water scene (Jonah thrown to the whale)
Illustration 8 (fig. 5.3): Second illustration of *Patience*, with walled city (Nineveh)

The scene of divine scribal activity and prophetic interpretation that has figured prominently in previous chapters is thus visually and materially enclosed by concentric circles of chiastic image-patterns: just the sort of complex shape that typified the poetry of *Pearl*, in particular, though here expressed in different media. This is just one of several resonant analogies to be found between the construction of the Pearl-Manuscript and that of its poems.

It is an additionally striking fillip, not noted by Reichardt, that the two images (the fourth and eighth of twelve total) enacting this enclosed illustrative shape themselves depict castellated forms of enclosure, namely walled cities. Here, we should recall that the ships in both water scenes (the fifth

10. Reichardt, "Several Illuminations, Coarsely Executed."

and seventh images) also feature elements of castellation, which is one of the main decorative features of Solomon's holy vessels as well: their ekphrasis in *Cleanness* emphasizes not just *casteles* (1458) but also *batelment with bantelles quoynt* ("battlements with cleverly constructed bantels," 1459),[11] *coperounes* ("ornamented capitals," 1461), *fylyoles* ("turrets," 1462), and *pinacles* (1463). The castellated Nineveh of 82/86v therefore recalls not just the comparably depicted Heavenly Jerusalem of 38/42v but also the holy vessels prominently displayed on Illustration 6's feasting table, which is central to the chiastic shape created by these five illustrations.[12]

This chiastic structure emerges only retrospectively, however, since a first-time reader cannot know, upon seeing Belshazzar's Feast on 56/60v, that the content and motifs of the two previous illustrations will be echoed in the two that follow. The retrospection necessary to perceive and appreciate this pattern—like so many shapes in the manuscript and its poems—helps propose the Pearl-Manuscript as a fit object for repeated study and devotion. The dialectic between through-reading and rereading thus emerges as meaningful once more, and by creating another resonant center *in* (rather than singularly or straightforwardly *of*) the Pearl-Manuscript, this cross-poem illustrative pattern invites us to speculate more deeply, now into the codicological shape of the book itself.

EXCEPTIONS TO THE RULE

Doing so reveals another significant midpoint in the manuscript, for as Reichardt has shown, its four poems are written almost entirely on seven quires of twelve folios each.[13] The codicological midpoint of these quires is the opening 80/84v+81/85r, with Daniel's climactic words leading us from the bottom of 80/84v to the top of 81/85r:

11. The *Middle English Compendium* awards all three surviving occurrences of the word *bantel* to the Pearl-Manuscript: this line, as well as *Pearl* lines 992 and 1017, where it describes the Heavenly Jerusalem's construction. See further Gordon and Onions, "Notes on the Text and Interpretation of 'Pearl.'"

12. As Reichardt notes, "the Daniel scene's centrality" to this chiastic structure "draws the attention of the manuscript's readers to what is arguably the most complex and resonant depiction in the entire sequence of illustrations" ("Several Illuminations," 125).

13. Reichardt, "Counted," 119. By the traditional lineation (i.e., including the bobs of *Sir Gawain*), only 145 of the manuscript's total lines fall outside this 7 × 12 quiring structure. According to Reichardt, quires of twelve (rather than four or eight) are unusual in this period, though by no means unheard of.

+ "*Mane, Techal, Phares*: merked in þrynne,
þat þretes þe of þyn vnþryfte vpon þre wyse.
(℄) Now expowne þe þis speche spedly I þenk: [last line of 80/84v]
Mane menes als much as maynful Gode [first line of 81/85r]
hatȝ counted þy kyndam bi a clene noumbre,
and fulfylled hit in fayth to þe fyrre ende."[14]

As Reichardt puts it, "at the very center of the manuscript, the scribe has written a passage which concerns both the act of writing (the script which appears on the wall) and the process of reading and interpretation (Daniel's explication of the mysterious script)."[15] These activities—writing, reading, and interpreting—are as metaphorically central to the poems of the Pearl-Manuscript as the passage above is literally central to the codex.[16] A "+" sign clearly visible to the left of line 1727's "*Mane, Techal, Phares*," two lines below the regularly appearing paraph, demonstrates that at least one earlier reader was also struck by this moment (see fig. 5.5).

This juxtaposition—of the Pearl-Manuscript's codicological midpoint with the height of interpretive drama in Belshazzar's hall—is just one of many suggestive peculiarities that Reichardt uses to argue that the manuscript itself is shaped around the "clene noumbre" of twelve. So symbolically and theologically important to *Pearl*, twelve and its multiples recur materially throughout the manuscript, reinforcing that first poem's insistent numerical shaping in multiple dimensions and media: not just the quires of twelve that enfold the climactic midpoint described above, but also the fact that the manuscript includes twelve illustrations; its poems are almost always written thirty-six (12 × 3) lines to the page; and it includes a total of forty-eight (12 × 4) decorated initials. These and other, similar coincidences—which is all that any of them, individually, can be called—together persuade Reichardt that "the more its numerical patterns are recognized, the more the *Pearl*

14. "*Mane, Techal, Phares*, marked in three, that threaten you in three ways because of your depravity. Now I intend to swiftly expound this speech to you: *Mane* means that the powerful God has counted your kingdom according to a clean number and brought it to conclusion [*fulfylled*], in faith, to its latter end" (lines 1727–32).

15. Reichardt, "Counted," 126.

16. Brantley notes a comparably suggestive textual midpoint in British Library Additional 37049, where the *Desert of Religion* is central not just physically but "also metaphorically to the manuscript's designs for textual and imagistic reading" (*Reading in the Wilderness*, 79, with fuller discussion in chap. 3, 354n1). Such parallels in another complex devotional image-text further suggest creative reading strategies for the Pearl-Manuscript.

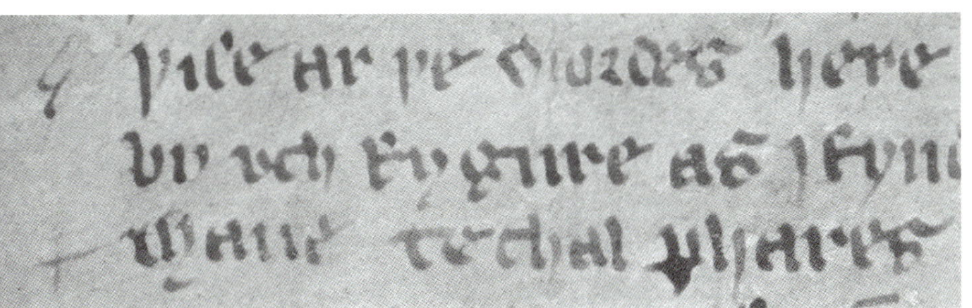

FIGURE 5.5. Folio 80/84v of Cotton Nero A.x/2. Detail of lines 1725–27 of *Cleanness*, with scribal paraph and marginal plus sign. Photograph © 2024 by The British Library Board.

manuscript's design assumes an architectonic dimension which resembles the depiction of the Heavenly Jerusalem in *Pearl*."[17]

The thrust of this argument feels intuitively consonant with the aesthetic logic of *Pearl*, which shapes the manuscript far more than its raw word count might suggest. Reichardt's reading also recalls the "architectonics" of *Cleanness*'s decorated initials as found by Donna Crawford, considered in chapter 4.[18] Yet just as Jean de Meun's "clene Rose" proves more complex than that adjective implies, so too the "clene noumbre" of the passage quoted above is more complicated, and multiple, than Reichardt's account suggests. For one thing, the 80/84v+81/85r opening asymmetrically splits the quatrains of lines 1727–32, with the first line of a quatrain left "orphaned" at the bottom of 80/84v; this has virtually never happened until now. For another, while this opening is the midpoint of the Pearl-Manuscript's principal seven quires of twelve, these are bookended by two much shorter, anomalous quires: an opening bifolium with the four illustrations of *Pearl*, and a final quire of four leaves with lines 2385–2530 of *Sir Gawain*, the last three illustrations, and other material. Since the last quire is two leaves longer than the opening bifolium, another midpoint of the manuscript (that of paginal as opposed to quiring structure) comes two pages after the one Reichard proposes as "the" center of the manuscript. This second midpoint is the very same opening with which this chapter began: 81/85v+82/86r, which binds text and image, *Cleanness* and *Patience*, first and second (approximate) halves of the book.

17. Reichardt, "Counted," 124; and see further Barootes, "Number Symbolism in *Pearl*."
18. Crawford, "Architectonics of *Cleanness*."

Depending on how we look at it, then, the Pearl-Manuscript has at least two distinct, nearly overlapping codicological midpoints, both of which enhance the poems' resonance, though to slightly different effect. This kind of aesthetic expansion, or multiplication, complements chapter 2's reading of the last word of *Pearl*, line 616. There, the distillation of the literal into a single quantum letter (**ere*) metonymically represented the ever-expanding potential of the figurative, beyond singular or recoverable intentions. Here, that multiplicity operates through the material construction of the manuscript itself. The fact that the Pearl-Manuscript thus imitates or echoes its poems offers yet another instance of its generative interpenetration of codicological and literary form. Rarely if ever can we assign intention securely; but this uncertainty adds to the frisson such moments afford those who are open to them, even as it disqualifies them from certain forms of empiricist analysis.

These almost-overlapping midpoints also recall the Pearl-Manuscript's pattern of conspicuously wrought, slightly imperfect shapes, such as the 1211 lines and 101 stanzas of *Pearl*, or various forms of quatrain-syntax mismatch in *Cleanness*. Such textual examples (imperfectly) mirror comparable structural phenomena observable across the manuscript: for example, its last 145 lines' appearance on a much shorter quire, which breaks the suggestive symmetry of the quires-of-twelve to which it is appended. I earlier called this an aesthetics of anti-exactness, which in *Pearl*, especially, has persuasively been read as a structurally performed, homiletic modesty topos: the refusal to attempt a perfection that belongs to God alone.[19] Such potentially interpretable imperfections recall the many slight imprecisions across the visual echoes described earlier, which themselves reinforce the "almost-but-not-quite" aesthetic often at work in the poems themselves.

In proposing a resonant confluence of literary and codicological form in the Pearl-Manuscript, I do not deny that the crafting of books and pages was ordinarily far more instrumental than the crafting of poems. The recent counterturn against close reading (or toward distant reading) of the material page has shed important light on what medieval manuscripts normally looked like and what their scribes normally did, but that broader perspective should not preclude appreciation of the abnormal, the extraordinary. Daniel Wakelin, for example, rightly notes that "the defining feature of a bound codex, its division into a number of pages, is seldom perfectly formed to fit its textual contents."[20] There is an important difference, however, between

19. E.g., Spyra, *Epistemological Perspective*, 8–9; and Carlson, "*Pearl*'s Imperfections."
20. Wakelin, *Immaterial Texts*, 120.

that which seldom occurs and that which never occurs, or cannot occur. This obvious point is worth repeating for its necessary corollary: that at least a few norm-shattering objects do indeed exist, and we should be open to finding them. I suggest that the Pearl-Manuscript is one such object. For while its pages are not "perfectly formed to fit its textual contents," it conveys an impression of artful craftedness, frequently and in many dimensions, that defies pure coincidence, even as its imprecisions and uncertainties and many unknown makers mean that we will never truly pin it down. Its allure, like that of its poems, is bound up in its imperfections and in our own: recall Elaine Scarry's account of beauty inspiring a sense of "being in error."[21]

The foregoing suggests that an affirmatively speculative lens may shed light on unusual features of the Pearl-Manuscript. Our next such irregularity occurs with the opening lines of *Patience* on folio 83/87r (fig. 5.4), opposite the image of Nineveh. The poem opens with a large, blue-and-red decorated initial ***P***, which at eight lines is the same height as the first letter of *Cleanness*. There, however, cropping of folio 57/61r has just shaved the top of its decorated **C**; here, by contrast, the six-line gap at the top of the page creates the first such poem-initial white space in the manuscript. The first six lines are ruled, but the decoration in the left margin has foliated outward into the ruling, making this blank space seem both incipiently textual and not-textual. In that sense, it offers a mirror image of the last page of *Pearl* (55/59v; fig. 3.1): there, we saw lineated blank space below a poem's final two stanzas; here, we see lineated blank space above a poem's opening words. (*Cleanness*, appropriately, is enclosed within.) Chapter 3 argued for the aesthetic significance of 55/59v's blank space, but the empty lines above *Patience* are hard if not impossible to interpret, for "ruling is neither 'linguistic' nor 'pictorial' and so does not readily convey meaning."[22]

Ruling is both numerical and visual, however, two dimensions that greatly interest the Pearl-Manuscript and its poems. So, while a first-time reader might not linger upon or even notice the white space above *Patience*, this anomaly gains potential, retroactive interest when we turn the page. For at the top of the verso, we find the catalog of allegorical ladies (see fig. 5.6) who personify the eight Beatitudes listed on the recto—emphasized by an unusually large, display form of ***D*** quite different from the *D* one line below (which itself looks quite sprightly).

21. Scarry, *On Beauty and Being Just*, 28. See further Nolan, "Beauty."
22. Wakelin, *Immaterial Texts*, 73.

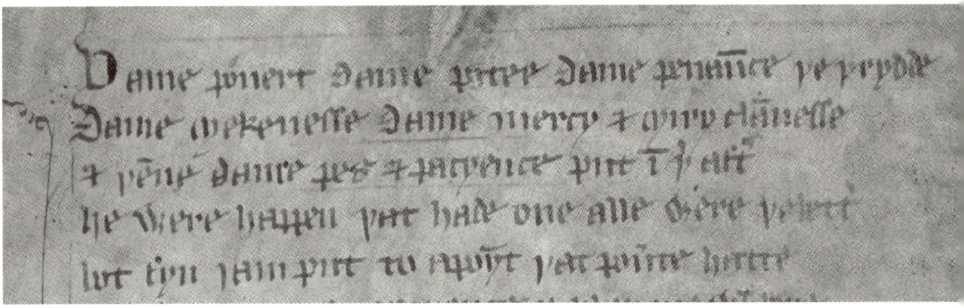

FIGURE 5.6. Folio 83/87v of Cotton Nero A.x/2. Close-up of lines 31–35 of *Patience*. Photograph © 2024 by The British Library Board.

Dame Pouert, Dame Pitee, Dame Penaunce þe þrydde,
Dame Mekenesse, Dame Mercy, and **miry Clannesse**,
⸿ and þenne Dame Pes, and Pacyence put in þerafter. [33]
He were happen þat hade one—alle were þe better!
Bot syn I am put to a poynt þat Pouerte hatte,
I schal me poruay Pacyence and play me with boþe.
⸿ For in þe tyxte þere þyse two arn in teme layde, [37]
hit arn fettled in on **forme**, þe **forme** and þe **laste**,
and by quest of her quoyntyse enquylen on mede,
and als in myn vpynyoun hit arn of on **kynde**.[23]

Chapter 6 will explore this important passage in more depth; here I draw attention to how the boldfaced words above echo beginnings and endings of the previous two poems in the manuscript. As chapter 3 showed, *forme* and *kynde* are central to the first quatrain of *Cleanness*, whose opening word line 32's "miry Clannesse" obviously repeats here; "Dame Penaunce *þe þrydde*" also recalls *Cleanness*'s emphasis on the number three.

More subtly, the wordplay on *forme* in line 38, where it designates both

23. "Dame Poverty, Dame Pity, Dame Penance the third, Dame Meekness, Dame Mercy, and merry Cleanness, and then Dame Peace, and Patience added thereafter. Whoever has one is lucky—all were the better! But since I am put in the position [*poynt*] of having Poverty, I will provide for myself with Patience and play with them both. For in the text where these two are laid in place, they are settled in one formula [*forme*], the first [*forme*] and the last, and the search for their wonders [*quest of her quoyntyse*] attains the same reward. And thus, in my opinion, they are of one nature [*kynde*]" (lines 31–40).

verbal expression and firstness, recalls the word's two different meanings across the transition from *Pearl* to *Cleanness*: the "forme of bred and wyn" elevated by the priest at Mass ("the form of bread and wine," *Pearl*, line 1209), followed by the "faire formeȝ" of *Cleanness*, line 3. The phrase "þe forme and þe laste" ("the first and the last") also recalls *Pearl*'s narration of the parable of the vineyard, where the equal reward of both first- and last-arriving laborers so provoked the Dreamer. Collectively, these textual echoes continue what I have argued is these four pages' (82/86r–83/87v) larger project of binding the two halves of the Pearl-Manuscript into a generatively imperfect whole. That the top of 83/87r does so by echoing beginnings and endings ("þe forme and þe laste") of the previous two poems also suggests a larger-scale version, across poems, of the *Pearl*-like, quasi-concatenating lexical echoes that chapter 3 traced across the turn from *Pearl* to *Cleanness*.

These textually significant lines gain visual prominence by appearing at the top of 83/87v—but only because the previous page had just thirty instead of the usual thirty-six lines of text, a feature made conspicuous by the curious blank space above the poem's opening lines.[24] This is precisely the kind of unusual codicological feature, which offers to highlight or deepen a literary effect, that empiricist scholarship has long tended to dismiss.[25] The quirk in ruling on 83/87r may not signify anything in itself, but it has the effect of highlighting a significant moment in the poem, which the display form of ***D*** at the top of the following page suggests the scribe understood as significant. As earlier chapters have demonstrated, this is not the first time that a scribal or decorative peculiarity has highlighted moments of literary significance: consider the manicule drawing attention to the second anomalous instance of *makeleȝ* at line 757 of *Pearl* (fig. 2.1), or its extra decorated initial at line 961; or the paraphs and decorated initials that more pervasively, if ambiguously, shaped our apprehension of *Cleanness*.

The gap at the top of 83/87r initiates a series of textual emphases and

24. Along these lines, Reichardt notes that "the appearance of the opening line of Daniel's commentary on the three mysterious words written on Belshazzar's wall . . . as the first line of folio 81r is largely the result of a unique variance in the manuscript's habits of script apportionment on the two pages immediately preceding the conjugate sides which lie at the center of its quiring structure" ("Counted," 128). Specifically, the striking page-break from 80/84v to 81/85r is created by the fact that 79/83v and 80/84r both have thirty-seven lines of text, a number that occurs nowhere else in the manuscript.

25. E.g., "Scholarship cannot often say with confidence that a quirk in ruling signifies something, or that a set of paraphs had a provable effect on readers" (Sawyer, *Reading English Verse*, 8).

visual page-shapes that the following chapter will trace more fully. But it also looks forward even further, to the first page of *Sir Gawain and the Green Knight* (91/95r), whose still more dramatically anomalous layout will emphatically reward speculation. Thus 83/87r proleptically links the Pearl-Manuscript's shortest poem with its longest, despite their many obvious differences in form and content. This is one way the second half of the Pearl-Manuscript gains literary coherence, complementing its poems' shared interest in *poynts*: the "nobel poynt" of *Patience*, whose five decorated initials will bloom into Gawain's five-lined, five-pointed pentangle, celebrated in a poem approximately five times as long (531 vs. 2530 lines).

Like the chiastic, cross-poem illustrative pattern considered earlier, such connections emerge only retrospectively; and as with constellations, whether in the sky or on the page, we must elect to perceive them.[26] Because the Pearl-Manuscript encourages reflective rereading, such evolving, participatory acts of perception become central to its effects, if not its demonstrably recoverable purpose. What I have called its aesthetics of anti-exactness creates so many patterns that are incontrovertibly present—empirically, mathematically, on the page and in the book—that it encourages us to test the limits of our perception, and from there to stretch our understanding. The fact that some see coincidence where others see pattern, or error instead of art, reminds us that there is no secure way (here on earth) to distinguish noise from signal. This is what I mean in calling the Pearl-Manuscript a pedagogical compilation in the art of speculation: its gradually increasing perceptual challenges can be contemplated but never fully solved. The manuscript's surprisingly elusive third poem will next distill this constellation into a single point.

26. See further Anderson, "Medieval Star-Gazing."

SIX

TOUCHING *PATIENCE*

If *Cleanness* is the Pearl-Manuscript's least loved poem, then *Patience* seems like its least substantial. At 531 lines, it is less than half the length of the next shortest poem, *Pearl*. Unlike *Cleanness*, *Patience* narrates a single book of the Bible, that of Jonah, which is itself remarkably short. Its opening line is even a complete sentence, anticipating the poem's own compactness: "Pacience is a poynt, þaȝ hit displease ofte."[1] Yet the meaning of that short, almost prosaic statement multiplies dramatically thanks to the many meanings of Middle English *poynt*: a topic for discussion or preaching (probably closest to its primary meaning here);[2] a brief moment in time; a constituent part; a puncture or pricking; the tiniest amount; a condition or quality; a punctuation mark; the nondimensional basis of all Euclidian shapes; and more.[3] Such polysemy recalls the "more and more" lexical and aesthetic landscape of *Pearl*: one of many ways in which *Patience* echoes the previous two poems, though often with an element of distortion or even reversal. Like *Cleanness*, for example, *Patience* draws on the Beatitudes in its opening lines, but its emphasis on aurality and a vivid narrative persona creates a more intimate, "I-thou" relationship that reinforces its central homiletic message: to be low is to be loved.[4]

The poem's pages often invite us to think and feel with other senses, too: not just the visual (always at work in this manuscript) but also the tactile. I found that touching *Patience* reinforces the Pearl-Manuscript's status as imperfect skin of an abjected animal, complete with variable texture, occasional holes and tears, and frequently prominent hair follicles. I will argue

1. "Patience is a *poynt*, though it is often displeasing" (line 1). On the unlikelihood that *poynt* most naturally means "virtue" here (its gloss in several modern editions), see Eldredge, "Late Medieval Discussions," and McGillivray, *Patience*.

2. Here I follow McGillivray's gloss from his edition for the Cotton Nero A.x Project.

3. The *Middle English Dictionary* lists fifteen main meanings and fifty-two total meanings for "pointe, n." (accessed August 31, 2023, https://quod.lib.umich.edu/m/middle-english-dictionary/dictionary/MED33862).

4. Buber, *I and Thou*.

that these phenomena amplify the poem's themes of sufferance, abasement, and repentance. These themes flashed into prominence thanks to another of the Pearl-Manuscript's resonant exceptions to the rule: here, the Rule of Gregory by which quires of parchment should have the smoother, flesh-side of the skin facing outward.[5] All but one of the manuscript's nine quires follow this rule; the exception (folios 87/91–98/102) means unexpectedly encountering adjacent, especially hairy hair-side rectos. The decorated initial that appears on this inversion of the rule governing inside (flesh) and outside (hair) also narrates Jonah's prayer for deliverance (outside) from the whale (inside). Feeling unexpected hair follicles as we turn the page helps us feel, however slightly, Jonah's visceral shock at his own divinely authored, pedagogical, animal inversion.

Patience thus adds touch to the senses with which it invites us to speculate, amplifying the speculative challenges that the Pearl-Manuscript poses. The animal continues to resonate through the end of the poem, both textually and materially: most obviously, in the warty growths that punctuate the margin of its penultimate page.[6] These material imperfections signify multiply, I argue. They offer visceral reminders of the animal whose flesh we are reading, reinforcing the poem's themes yet also interrupting the visual symmetry of its final material opening, which foregrounds suffering and the need for patience. In addressing textual cruces near the end of *Patience*, modern editors use punctuation to reduce ambiguity; yet if patience is a *poynt*, such points cater to *impatience*. Materially and thematically, *Patience* subtly suggests unpunctuating such cruces to embrace its insistence on epistemic humility when seeing, hearing, or touching *per speculum in aenigmate*.

PATIENCE AS ECHO

As chapter 5 showed, *Patience* opens with visual and textual echoes of *Pearl* and *Cleanness*, thereby suggesting such echoes as one key to its meaning within the Pearl-Manuscript. Here I focus on how its depiction of the Beatitudes echoes *Cleanness* in ways that foreground the tension between written and aural apprehension, thereby anticipating the poem's core narrative.

5. Gregory, "Quires in Greek Manuscripts." Clemens and Graham note that "normal practice in Western Europe throughout the Middle Ages . . . was to arrange the sheets so that, wherever the finished manuscript was opened, like sides would face one another across the opening" (*Introduction to Manuscript Studies*, 14). The Pearl-Manuscript's anomalous quire violates that "normal practice."

6. Thanks to Gillespie and Wakelin for pointing out both the warty growths on 89/93 and the earlier exception to the Rule of Gregory; see further introduction, n. 3.

As A. C. Spearing has noted, *Patience* also evokes *Pearl* in its construction of a personally inflected narrative persona.[7] Yet whereas *Pearl* and *Cleanness* famously open with words like *plesaunte* and *faire*, *Patience* begins by acknowledging that it often displeases ("hit displese ofte"). This contrast suggests that *Patience* may distort or reverse its echoes from the first half of the manuscript, priming us to read carefully from the poem's very first, semantically open-ended line.

Like *Cleanness*, *Patience* begins with a generalized frame of reference and gnomic tone appropriate to its homiletic content.[8] The second quatrain of *Patience*, however, concludes with a sudden shift into the personal: "Þen is better to abyde þe bur vmbestoundes / þen ay þrow forth *my* þro, þaȝ *me* þynk ylle."[9] Nothing in line 7 prepares us for the following repeated reference to the narrative persona's unfortunate emotional position. The final half-line, "þaȝ me þynk ylle," evokes the second half-line of line 1 ("þaȝ hit displease ofte") and thus suggests that one challenge of this poem will be to translate abstract homiletic truths like those of lines 1–7 into the lived experience of particular individuals, like the "me" of the poem's narrator or Jonah—and, by extension, the reader. Moreover, by evoking the end of the first line at the end of the second quatrain, line 8 performs a version of the echoic circularity that will become an important theme in *Patience*—additionally if only retrospectively reinforced by the fact that *Patience* itself cycles back to this narrative "me" twice in its last four lines (lines 528–29).

As chapter 3 showed, lines 1–12 of *Cleanness* displayed a comparably echoic circularity, so the echo across *Patience* lines 1–8 further recalls the previous poem. But just as *Cleanness*'s early echoes of *Pearl* also presaged important contrasts between the two poems, so too with *Patience*'s echoes of *Cleanness*. These echoes intensify immediately after line 8's unexpectedly intimate turn, when the narrator's reference to the Beatitudes recalls a closely parallel passage early in *Cleanness*:

> ℭ *I herde* on a halyday at a hyȝe masse
> *how Mathew melede* þat his Mayster his meyny con teche.
> Aȝt happes he hem hyȝt and vcheon a mede,
> sunderlupes for hit dissert vpon a ser wyse . . .

7. Spearing, *Gawain-Poet*, 75–76.

8. See, e.g., their use of the word "whoso" to universalize their claims: "Clannesse ***whoso*** kindly cowþe comende" (*Cleanness* line 1, emphasis added) and "for ***quoso*** suffer cowþe syt, sele wolde folȝe" (*Patience* line 5, emphasis added).

9. "Then it's better to sometimes suffer the blow than always to throw forth my anger—though I don't like it very much [þaȝ me þynk ylle]" (lines 7–8, emphasis added).

Kryst kydde hit hymself in a carp oneȝ,
þer as he heuened aȝt happeȝ and hyȝt hem her medeȝ.
⁋ *Me myneȝ* on one amonge oþer, *as Maþew recordeȝ*,
þat þus of clannesse vncloseȝ a ful cler speche . . .[10]

These echoes ultimately reinforce how much more fully individuated, even autobiographical, the narrative persona of *Patience* seems than that of *Cleanness*.[11] There, personal pronouns are used infrequently, and when they are (e.g., lines 25 and 193), they sound conventional and largely divorced from the narrative drive of the poem itself. In *Patience*, by contrast, they introduce an element of rueful humor as the narrator explains the constrained nature of his decision to praise patience: "Thus Pouerte and Pacyence arn nedes playferes. / Syþen I am sette with hem samen, suffer me byhoues; / þenne is me lyȝtloker hit lyke and her lotes prayse."[12] Indeed, humor is central to *Patience*, as Piotr Spyra, A. C. Spearing, and others have shown—and thus another point of contrast with *Cleanness*.[13]

The wry tone of those lines also reinforces how conversational *Patience* can be, a tone set early by the depiction of the Beatitudes as an aural, communally celebrated experience: "herde on a halyday at a hyȝe masse" ("heard on a holy day at a High Mass," line 9). As Ad Putter has noted, this gesture "effectively abolishes the distance that separates the sermon from its hearers," an "identification with his audience [that] characterizes the narrator throughout *Patience*."[14] This emphasis on aurality is further suggested by the different verbs given to Matthew in the accounts quoted above: in *Cleanness*, "as Maþew recordeȝ" ("as Matthew records," line 25), which can suggest both written and aural dimensions, and here probably the former;[15] but in

10. "I heard on a holy day, at a High Mass, how Matthew said that his Master taught his company. Eight blessings he taught them and each a reward, severally, according to its merit, in various ways" (*Patience*, lines 9–12, emphasis added). "Christ himself made it known in a speech once, when he exalted eight blessings and promised them their rewards. I recall one among the others, as Matthew records, who discloses a very clear speech about cleanness thus . . ." (*Cleanness*, lines 23–26, emphasis added).

11. See further Molstad, "Adaptation."

12. "Thus Patience and Poverty are necessarily companions. Since I am set/beset with them both, it behooves me to suffer; so it's better to like it and praise their words" (*Patience*, lines 45–47).

13. Spyra, *Epistemological Perspective*, 35–40; Spearing, *Gawain-Poet*, 79–90.

14. Putter, *Introduction to the Gawain-Poet*, 104.

15. *Middle English Dictionary* (accessed August 31, 2023, https://quod.lib.umich.edu/m/middle-english-dictionary/dictionary/MED36224), s.v. "recorden, v.," meanings 5 and 6

Patience "how Mathew melede" ("how Matthew said," line 10), which has a much narrower, more conversational range of meaning.[16]

This and other aural emphases in *Patience* make striking its use of a word with strongly written connotations, *tyxte*, to emphasize the ordering of the "aȝt happes" ("eight blessings") of Jesus's sermon:

> ¶ For in þe **tyxte** þere þyse two arn in teme layde, [37]
> hit arn fettled in on **forme**, þe **forme** and þe **laste**,
> and by quest of her quoyntyse enquylen on mede,
> and als, in myn vpynyoun, hit arn of on **kynde**.[17]

As chapter 5 noted, the boldface words above echo the beginning and end of *Cleanness*, as well as the end of *Pearl* and its parable of the vineyard. Line 38's self-conscious punning on two meanings of the word *forme*—one literary-formal, the other spatial-temporal—also suggests, with typically playful economy of expression, the interrelatedness of those two dimensions in the poem whose main body is yet to come. Circularity and near-circularity have been integral to this manuscript, and even at this early point in *Patience*, the poet has twice evoked this circularity at the ends of quatrains, first in line 8's relatively subtle evocation of line 1, considered above ("þaȝ me þynk ylle" vs. "þaȝ hit displease ofte"), then with the precise quotation of the first Beatitude in the last one ("For hores is þe heuen-ryche, to holde for euer" vs. "For hores is þe heuen-ryche, as I er sayde," lines 14 and 29), thus performing the poem's insistence on the theological significance of "þe forme and þe laste" ("the first and the last," line 38). These accurately prefigure the poem's plot and homiletic thrust.

Lines 37–40 also shift away from the initial depiction of the Beatitudes as an aural phenomenon, characterized by the verbs of hearing and speaking that we saw in lines 9–10, to one in which they are a text (*tyxte*, 37). This word has appeared only one other time in the manuscript thus far:

---

respectively. Line 25 of *Cleanness* is cited as an instance of meaning 5a, "of writers, books, etc., to recount in writing," and I concur with that reading.

16. *Middle English Dictionary* (accessed August 31, 2023, https://quod.lib.umich.edu/m/middle-english-dictionary/dictionary/MED27246), s.v. "mēlen, v.," with just one main meaning ("to speak, talk, say") in contrast with seven different meanings of *recorden*.

17. "For in the text where these two are laid out as a theme [*in teme layde*], they are fixed in one formula [*forme*], the first [*forme*] and the last, and the search for their wonders [*quest of her quoyntyse*] receives the same reward. And thus, in my opinion, they are of one nature [*kynde*]" (lines 37–40, emphasis added).

when Belshazzar tremblingly begs Daniel to "telle me þe tyxte of þe tede lettres" ("tell me the text of the tied letters," line 1634), written into the wall by an angry God.[18] As Seamus Dwyer has shown, this reference evokes the scribe's own textura ("woven") hand, a particularly embellished form of which appears at the top of this page (see fig. 5.6); so *tyxte*'s recurrence here reinforces the written-ness of the eight Beatitudes, each individual proposition having been manually *layde* in place by the scribe.[19] By presenting the Beatitudes first as an aural, historically discrete experience ("herde on a halyday"), then as a visually apprehended and physically embodied *tyxte* that can be read and reread, the poet emphasizes two different ways of receiving God's Word: one an immediate and not fully replicable sensory experience, the other a more extended and reflective process that can be supplemented by material textuality. It thereby suggests that *Patience* expects us to be open to both of these modes in reading.

It is therefore worth reexamining the page where this *tyxte* is laid (see fig. 6.1). The decoration of this page is neither lavish nor atypical of the manuscript, but nevertheless suggests a sense of the page as an aesthetic whole. As we saw in chapter 5, the display form of ***D*** gives the top line unusual prominence, reinforcing the importance of the allegorical *Dames* that represent the Beatitudes. The decorated capital ***H*** near the bottom of the page introduces the main narrative of Jonah ("Hit bitydde sumtyme . . ."), but it also extends decorative foliation up and down the page, with the topmost tendrils subtly highlighting the catalog of *Dames* whose significance we have already considered. Even as the decorated ***H*** marks an important textual transition that encourages us to read on, it also shapes and lends integrity to the contours of the page as a whole.

Yet its blue-and-red decoration also acts like an echo of the poem's much larger initial ***P***, whose comparable decorative motifs show through clearly from the recto, drawing the eye up and to the right: we are seeing double,

18. The word *tyxte*'s only other three appearances, according to Kottler and Markman's *Concordance*, are *Cleanness*, line 1634 (noted above), and *Sir Gawain and the Green Knight*, lines 1515 and 1541.

19. Dwyer, "Reading the Tied Letters."

FIGURE 6.1. Folio 83/87v of Cotton Nero A.x/2. Photograph © 2024 by The British Library Board.

Dame pouert dame pitee dame penaunce þe þrydde
Dame mekenesse dame mercy & miry clannesse
& þenne dame pes & pacyence put in þer after
He were happen þat hade one alle were þe better
Bot syn I am put to a poynt þat pouerte hatte
I schal me poruay pacyence & play me wyth boþe
For in þe tyxte þere þyse two arn in teme layde
Hit arn fettled in on forme þe forme & þe laste
& by quest of her quoyntyse enquylen on mede
& als in myn vpynyoun hit arn of on kynde
For þer as pouert hir proferes ho nyl be put vtter
Bot lenge wheresoeuer hir lyst lyke oþer greme
& þere as pouert enpresses þaȝ mon pyne þynk
Much maugre his mun he mot nede suffer
Thus pouert & pacyence arn nedes playferes
Syþen I am sette wyth hem samen suffer me byhoues
Þenne is me lyȝtloker hit lyke & her lotes prayse
Þenne wyþer wyth & be wroth & þe wers haue
If me be dyȝt a destyne due to haue
What dowes me þe dedayn oþer dispit make
Oþer ȝif my lege lorde lyst on lyue me to bidde
Oþer to ryde oþer to renne to rome in his ernde
What grayþed me þe grychchyng bot grame more seche
Much ȝif he me ne made maugref my chekes
& þenne þrat moste I þole & vnþonk to mede
Þe had bowed to his bode bongre my hyre
Did not Jonas in Jude suche jape sumwhyle
To sette hym to sewrte vnsounde he hym feches
Wyl ȝe tary a lyttel tyne & tent me a whyle
I schal wysse yow þer wyth as holy wryt telles

Hit bitydde sumtyme in þe termes of Jude
Jonas joyned watz þerinne jentyle prophete
Goddes glam to hym glod þat hym vnglad made
With a roghlych rurd rowned in his ere
Rys radly he says & rayke forth euen
Nym þe way to Nynyue wyþouten oþer speche

an imperfect mirroring from lower left to upper right, through the alabaster translucence of parchment. The fact that we read six full lines on the verso before hitting the reflection of the opening ***P*** recalls the six blank lines at the top of the recto, analyzed in chapter 5. Those six lines are echoed, in a way, by the last six lines of 83/87v that start the main story of Jonah (lines 61–66), initiated by the decorated ***H***. The prologue to *Patience* thus emerges as a sixty-line unit divided into equal halves by the two sides of its first folio: the six blank lines before the prologue mirror the six lines at the bottom of 83/87r, which introduce Jonah and so pull the reader along to the next recto. The many complex shapes of the page on which line 37's *tyxte* has been *layde* thus subtly reinforce the importance of these lines and propose folio 83/87, another near-midpoint in the manuscript, as a fit object for speculation. For while nothing obliges the reader to linger here, this folio performs a visual and spatial version of the mirror- or echo-effect that *Patience* has already started to create verbally with its predecessors in the manuscript. Here, these effects take shape across and through a single page—appropriately, for a poem that valorizes the singular.

The folio's two decorated initials also recall the complex numerical patterning created by the initials of *Cleanness*. At first glance, *Patience* presents nothing so complex; on the contrary, the subdivisions created by its five decorated initials are coherent enough that several modern editions reproduce them: prologue (1–60); introduction of Jonah and his flight (61–244); Jonah thrown overboard and swallowed by the whale (245–304); his prayer from the whale, reprieve, and preaching to Nineveh (305–408); his resentment at Nineveh's reprieve and God's response (409–531).[20] These moments in the poem highlight Jonah's comic anti-exemplarity, which is central to his role as a foil or mirroring of Daniel in the preceding *Cleanness* as well as *Patience*'s comparable role more generally.[21] The number five, meanwhile, anticipates the many fives of *Sir Gawain and the Green Knight*, next and final poem in the manuscript—particularly since it is about five times as long (531 vs. 2530 lines as traditionally reckoned), as if Gawain's pentangle were blooming out of the five decorated initials through which *Patience* praised its single "nobel poynt."

Yet these five initials also resonate beyond their obvious function of highlighting particular points in the narrative or of obliquely anticipating *Sir*

20. E.g., Putter and Stokes, *Works of the Gawain Poet*; Anderson, *Patience*.

21. See, e.g., Hatt, *God and the Gawain-Poet*; Spyra, *Epistemological Perspective*; Spearing, "Subtext of Patience."

Gawain. We have seen already how the first two decorated initials visually anchor a complex constellation of page-shapes on folio 83/87. In so doing, the first folio of a poem so concerned with aurality invites us to hold the material *tyxte* in mind as well—another challenge the Pearl-Manuscript places upon our speculative faculties. The next two initials foreground another of the five senses: touch, and in particular the difference in feel between outside and inside. That is because the third and fourth initials of *Patience* appear on especially hairy hair-sides of the parchment, reinforcing the manuscript's status as animal skin: three-dimensional, often rough and leathery, complete with hair follicles, frequent discoloration, and occasional warty growths, as we will see.[22]

INSIDE OUT

It is poetic that the animal should thus materially flash into prominence around the middle of *Patience* (lines 245–305 of 531), for these lines see Jonah swallowed by an animal: an inversion of the "natural" hierarchy that prompts Jonah to his prayer of repentance from inside the whale, marked by the fourth initial. That initial appears on a hair-side of the manuscript (87/91r) thanks to yet another of the Pearl-Manuscript's exceptions to the rule: here, the so-called Rule of Gregory by which quires should have the smoother, flesh-side of the parchment facing out.[23] The only one of the manuscript's nine quires to present hair-side outermost, 87/91r contravenes this rule. This exception is concretized in large hair follicles, clearly visible and quite sensible to the touch, that are especially prominent at the edges, where one naturally turns the page. They thereby highlight the anomalous outside of one animal at the very moment Jonah prays for deliverance from the inside of another.

The potential power of that fourth initial and anomalous quire is prepared, in part, by the third initial on the previous folio (86/90), which concludes the previous quire. This leaf's abundant discoloration and large hair follicles also reinforce the fact that we are handling animal, adding resonance to its capital ***N***'s marking of Jonah's judgment: to be cast out of humanity and into the animal, as depicted in the illustration of 82/86r (fig. 5.1). There,

22. On parchment and the animal, see in particular Holsinger, "Of Pigs and Parchment," and Kay, *Animal Skins*.

23. Gregory, "Quires in Greek Manuscripts." See further Clemens and Graham, *Introduction to Manuscript Studies*, 14–15.

we saw the whale rise menacingly from the lower left of the page—much the same position, in fact, as the capital here, just two lines from the bottom of the page (see fig. 6.2). This is the only one of the manuscript's forty-eight decorated initials that appears so far down on the page,[24] and although this is just two lines lower than the decorated *H* considered earlier, it contributes to the sharply different effect of the two pages overall. Tendrils extending up from the decorated *H* near the bottom of 83/87v highlight decorative elements at the top, lending the page visual balance and creating the complex shapes discussed earlier. By contrast, the foliation of 86/90r's *N* extends just six lines upward, confining the decoration to a much smaller portion of the page; the capital itself is dwarfed, almost swallowed, by the resolutely unadorned text-block.

That is appropriate, for just four folios earlier, we saw the whale rise up from the same extreme lower left of the page to swallow Jonah as he is thrown overboard—the very narrative point emphasized by the decorated *N*:

> Now is Jonas þe jwe jugged to drowne.
> Of þat schended schyp men schowued hym sone.
> A wylde walterande whal, as wyrde þen schaped,
> þat watȝ beten fro þe abyme, bi þat bot flotte. . . .
> Þe folk ȝet haldande his fete, þe fysch hym tyd hentes—
> withouten towche of any tothe he tult in his þrote.[25]

This vivid description, of the whale rising up to engulf Jonah even as the sailors clutch at his feet, is precisely what the first illustration of the poem depicted on 82/86r. The text of the poem thus recalls the earlier image, and

24. This is thanks largely to the fact that the first page of *Patience* contains thirty lines rather than the usual thirty-six lines, which means the poem's quatrains consistently begin two lines lower on the page than they did in *Cleanness*. See further chap. 5.

25. "Now Jonah the Jew is condemned to drown. The men swiftly shoved him off that damaged ship. As fate shaped it then, a wild roiling whale that had been sent from the depths was swimming by the boat. . . . The folk still holding his feet, the fish seizes him swiftly—without touching the teeth, he fell in its throat" (lines 245–48, 251–52).

FIGURE 6.2. Folio 86/90r of Cotton Nero A.x/2.
Photograph © 2024 by The British Library Board.

Forþy berez me to þe borde & baþes me þeroute
Er gete ȝe no happe I hope forsoþe
He ossed hym by vnnynges þat þay vndernomen
Þat he watz flawen fro þe face of frelych dryȝtyn
Þenne such a ferde on hem fel & flayed hem withinne
Þat þay ruyt hym to rowwe & letten þe rynk one
Haþeles hyȝed in haste wyth ores ful longe
Syn her sayl watz hem aslypped on sydez to rowe
Hef & hale vpon hyȝt to helpen hymseluen
Bot al watz nedles note þat nolde not bityde
In bluber of þe blo flod bursten her ores
Þenne hade þay noȝt in her honde þat hem help myȝt
Þenne nas no coumfort to keuer ne counsel non oþer
Bot Ionas into his iuis iugge bylyue
Fyrst þay prayen to þe prynce þat prophetes seruen
Þat he gef hem þe grace to greuen hym neuer
Þat þay in balelez blod þer blenden her handez
Þaȝ þat haþel wer his þat þay here quelled
Tyd by top & bi to þay token hym synne
Into þat lodlych loȝe þay luche hym sone
He watz no tytter outtulde þat tempest ne sessed
Þe se saȝtled þerwith as sone as ho moȝt
Þenne þaȝ her takel were torne þat totered on yþes
Styffe stremes & streȝt hem strayned a whyle
Þat drof hem dryȝlych adoun þe depe to serue
Tyl a swetter ful swyþe hem sweyed to bonk
Þer watz louyng on lofte when þay þe londe wonnen
To oure mercyable god on moyses wyse
With sacrafyse vpset & solempne vowes
& graunted hym on to be god & graythly non oþer
Þaȝ þay be iolef for ioye Ionas ȝet dredes
Þaȝ he nolde suffer no sore his seele is on anter
For what so worþed of þat wyȝe fro he in water dipped
Hit were a wonder to wene ȝif holy wryt nere
Now is Ionas þe Iwe iugged to drowne
Of þat schended schyp men schowued hym sone

the decorated **N** highlights the extreme lower left of the page—the very spot from which the whale rises "fro þe abyme" ("from the depths," line 248). That may prompt us to leaf back to the earlier image; if we then flip quickly back from image (82/86r; fig. 5.1) to text (86/90r; fig. 6.2), we get a subtle version of the "jump-cut" effect described by Eric Flanders of the illustrations of *Pearl*.[26] Here, it is almost as if the whale swallows the **N** across the pages, shades of the great Old English Exeter Book riddle for bookworm ("a moth ate words . . .").[27]

In fact, the Pearl-Manuscript features several wormholes and other comparable imperfections: tears or holes in the parchment, some repaired but many not. In most cases the scribe simply worked around the problem: skipping over a large hole after writing *gre-* to add the final *-t* of *gret* (43/47v); writing around a tear, subsequently repaired on folio 76/80v. Another tear on folio 69/73 was so bad that it had to be stitched together—a number of holes (more points) run visibly up the right side of the tear, which the scribe has doggedly written across, with multiple words jumping the gap. This practice seems consistent with Daniel Wakelin's conclusion that many late medieval English scribes believed in an ideal, "immaterial text" that they tried to reproduce: the material can be written around, or ignored when convenient, because the text is the point.[28] The decision to use even damaged parchment may speak to the modest means of the patron; it may also suggest a more ethically grounded determination to use the whole animal, a refusal of waste consonant with the manuscript's devotional aesthetics and echoed in the brittling scenes of *Sir Gawain and the Green Knight*.[29]

At certain points, however, the Pearl-Manuscript's materiality becomes so messy as to preclude the reader's apprehension of an immaterial text, whatever effect the scribe may have wished or tried to create. Such at least was my own experience when I handled the manuscript; I was surprised by how obtrusive 87/91's exception to the Rule of Gregory felt, especially compared to what could be seen on the screen. The page itself looks much less discolored than the preceding 86/90, just considered. Even its prominent hair follicles along the sides of the page don't look like much in the facsimile

26. See chap. 1 here and Flanders, "Resetting *Pearl*," 20.

27. "Moððe word fræt . . . Stalgiest ne wæs / wihte þy gleawra þe he þam wordum swealg" ("A moth ate words. . . . The thieving guest was not one whit the wiser for having eaten those words," lines 1, 5–6).

28. Wakelin, *Immaterial Texts*. We see comparable deference to the text in the Pearl-Manuscript's long stretches of regular, unadorned verse.

29. On the theological dimension of waste, see Johnson, *Waste and the Wasters*.

(see fig. 6.3). In themselves—and like so many remarkable features of this manuscript, approached singly—such things look like nothing, a mere mote (stain/spot) like Jonah himself as he is "þrwe in at hit þrote withouten þret more / as mote in at a munster dor so mukel wern his chawleȝ" ("thrown in at its throat without any more difficulty than a speck [*mote*] at the cathedral door, so great were his [the whale's] jaws," lines 267–68).

But *Patience* insists that we take motes and points seriously, and 87/91r's codicological inversion of flesh-side and hair-side, in and out, resonates powerfully with the text it presents, which I quote from the decorated initial ***L*** to the bottom of the page:

(☾) "Lorde, to þe haf I cleped **in** careȝ ful stronge. [305]
Out of þe hole þou me herde of hellen wombe!
I calde and þou knew myn vncler steuen.
Þou dipteȝ me of þe depe se **into** þe dymme hert.
☾ Þe grete flem of þy flod folded me vmbe, [309]
alle þe goteȝ of þy guferes and groundeleȝ powleȝ,
and þy strynande stremeȝ of stryndeȝ so mony
in on daschande dam dryueȝ me ouer;
☾ and ȝet I sayde as I seet **in** þe se boþem: [313]
'Careful am I kest **out** fro þy cler yȝen
and deseuered fro þy syȝt, ȝet surely I hope
efte to trede **on** þy temple and teme to þyseluen.'
☾ I am wrapped **in** water to my wo stoundeȝ; [317]
þe abyme byndes þe body þat I byde **inne**. . . ."[30] [bottom of folio 87/91r]

This intimate address is replete with the language of inside and outside, whose dialectics Sarah Stanbury has demonstrated are foundational to

30. "Lord, to you have I called ***in*** very strong sorrows. ***Out*** of the hole of the womb of Hell you heard me. I called and you knew my unclear voice. You dipped me ***into*** the dim heart of the deep sea. The great flow of your flood folded me around, all the watercourses of your depths and bottomless pools, and your straining streams of so many currents, drives over me in a rushing tsunami; and yet I said as I sat ***in*** the bottom of the sea: 'I am sorrowful, cast ***out*** from your clear eyes and severed from your sight, yet surely I hope once more to step ***in*** your temple and cleave to you.' I am wrapped ***in*** water to the point of times [*stoundeȝ*] of woe; the abyss binds the body that I bide ***in***" (lines 305–18). The phrase "to my wo stoundeȝ" in line 317 is difficult, interpreted differently by each of McGillivray, Putter and Stokes, Andrew and Waldron, and Anderson. My understanding is closest to Putter and Stokes's.

FIGURE 6.3. Folio 87/91r of Cotton Nero A.x/2. Close-up of hair follicles on the bottom right of the folio. Photograph © 2024 by The British Library Board.

Patience.[31] From within dire straits (305), the dim heart and bottom of the sea (308, 313), and a body bound to the abyss (318), Jonah prays to be delivered out from all of these and back into God's sight (another subtle echo of *Cleanness*). The page ends midquatrain thanks to 83/87r's anomalous lineation (see chap. 5), but line 318 concludes a clause, allowing us to pause and appreciate that *in* is the last word on the page—recalling the decorated line 305 ("**in** careȝ ful stronge") and thence the next line's contrasting "**Out** of þe hole" (306), which help establish the dialectic traced by Stanbury. The

31. Stanbury, *Seeing the Gawain-Poet*, 71–95.

power of this dialectic is enhanced, I suggest, by its shaping on 87/91r and its visible, tangible inversion of the codicological rules of inside and outside.

Intertextual echoes and art-historical convention enhance this dialectic, for the prayer that the decorated ***L*** initiates (lines 305–36, a close translation of Jon. 2:3–10) echoes a number of psalms, including Psalm 129/130 ("Out of the depths I have called to thee, Lord") in its very opening lines.[32] Jonah's situation also evokes that of Psalm 68/69 ("Save me, O God, for the waters are come in even unto my soul"), which fourteenth-century English psalters often depicted with an image of Jonah, whether emerging out of the whale or being thrown into the sea—or both.[33] Both scenes, in and out, appear within the top and bottom chambers of the historiated **S** of *Salvum* in several significant psalters, including the somewhat earlier (ca. 1310–20) Queen Mary Psalter (British Library Royal MS 2 B VII, fol. 168v) and Morgan Library MS G.53 (fol. 59r). Those points in the narrative are the two scenes highlighted by the third and fourth initials of *Patience*, whose connection is subtly amplified by their appearance on adjacent hair-side rectos: the last of one quire and first of the next.

Folio 87/91's anomalous reversal of inside and outside thus reinforces the manuscript's own status as animal, on the very pages that narrate Jonah's unnatural but divinely ordained envelopment by an animal. We can only speculate as to what any particular medieval reader might have made of this thematically resonant juxtaposition of text and matter. But the Pearl-Manuscript's many other artful imperfections suggest ways of finding meaning and beauty in its creative fusion of textual, visual, and material form. The speculative ladder that it offers, together with the manuscript's evidence of considerable use (dirt in the gutter), suggests that some (re)readers of the manuscript might feel and appreciate the exception to the rule (of Gregory) that these follicles represent. That is especially so since the catchphrase at the bottom of the facing page appears to be decorated, like several others in the manuscript, further reinforcing both quire divisions and the artfulness of the codex as a whole.[34]

These reflections emerged from handling the Pearl-Manuscript, and in particular from my surprise at how striking its single violation of the Rule of Gregory proved to be in the flesh. Sarah Kay's analysis of the physicality of medieval bestiaries is apposite here; so too is the animal agency that Myra

32. See further Putter and Stokes, *Works of the Gawain Poet*, 589–92.

33. See Andrew and Waldron, *Poems*, 198; Pierson Prior, *Fayre Formez*, 85–91; and Staley Johnson, *Voice of the Gawain-Poet*, 241n12.

34. E.g., 50/54v, on which see further chap. 3, pages 98–100.

Seaman has found at work in Ashmole 61.[35] I entered the British Library with quite a different plan for this chapter, which my encounter with the Pearl-Manuscript—experiencing it as animal—upended. I knew about the exception to the Rule of Gregory going in but had no plan to write about it; I was looking for other things. By the time I got to *Patience*, however, I had settled down slightly from the first rush of excitement and was better able to let the manuscript guide me toward a version of the *suffraunce* ("sufferance, suffering, patience") that the poem itself proposes: to submit to external contingency and sometimes, at least, to be object rather than subject ("this creature," in Margery Kempe's memorable phrase).[36] That is one effect, on one handler, of 87/91r's exception to the Rule of Gregory, which seems consonant with the homiletic purpose of *Patience* as a whole. I conclude by proposing that reading with a multisensory spirit (seeing, touching, hearing) should lead us to unpunctuate several cruces at the end of *Patience* and to embrace the manuscript's ambiguities.

UNPUNCTUATING *PATIENCE*

I begin with two cases in which Malcolm Andrew and Ronald Waldron's fifth edition of the poems revises their earlier punctuation, changing who is speaking (the poet/narrator becomes God in lines 524–27) or who is being referred to (the "he" of line 407 refers to God in earlier editions, but to the king of Nineveh in the fifth). The latter case is especially interesting since it recalls the question raised disquietingly at the end of *Cleanness*: Is God's judgment irrevocable, or is repentance possible? As we saw in chapter 4, Belshazzar was given no time to repent like his father, and Jonah clearly expects that history to repeat itself when he preaches to Nineveh: swift, final judgment. *Patience* has already amply demonstrated its interest in both resembling and inverting *Cleanness*, so this episode fits a larger pattern by which *Patience* comically or reparatively reverses elements of the previous poem.

After exhorting his whole city to repent—"boþe burnes and bestes, burdeȝ and childer" ("both men and beasts, women and children," line 388)—the king concludes by speculating upon divine mercy with words that will be echoed in the poem's conclusion:

35. Kay, *Animal Skins*; Seaman, *Objects of Affection*. The whale of *Patience* is both like and unlike the cheerfully grinning (but unnervingly toothy) fish of Ashmole 61.

36. *The Book of Margery Kempe*, passim.

☾ "Who **wote** oþer **wyte may** ȝif þe Wyȝe lykes, [397]
þat is hende in þe hyȝt of his gentryse?
I **wot his** myȝt is so much, þaȝ **he** be myssepayed,
þat in **his** mylde amesyng **he** mercy **may fynde**,
☾ and if we leuen þe layk of oure layth synnes, [401]
and stylle steppen in þe **styȝe** he styȝtleȝ hymseluen,
he wyl wende of **his** wodschip and **his** wrath leue,
and forgif vus þis gult, ȝif we **hym** God leuen."
☾ Þenne al leued on his lawe and laften her synnes, [405]
parformed alle þe penaunce þat þe prynce radde,
and God þurȝ **his** godnesse forgef as **he** sayde—
þaȝ **he** oþer bihyȝt, withhelde **his** vengeaunce.[37]

Several elements of this complex twelve-line passage are worth noting, and they heighten the stakes of an ambiguous pronoun in the final quatrain. The king's curiously periphrastic assertion of divine unknowability—"Who knows or may know if it pleases the Lord?"—sets up the contrast that concludes the quatrain: "I know . . . he [God] may find mercy." The theological paradoxes thus intimated are beyond the scope of my argument here,[38] but it will resonate at the end of the poem that the king uses a word that can mean ladder (*styȝe*, line 401) to describe the path of repentance.

The problem of mercy and divine knowability recurs in the third quatrain, which adds the phrase "as he sayde" (line 407) to its biblical source.[39] These lines feature a profusion of "he/him" pronouns: four instances in the last two lines of all three quatrains, twelve in all. The only one that does not clearly refer to God is that of the added "as he sayde," near the end of the passage.

37. "'Who knows, or may know, if it pleases the Lord, who is gracious in his delight in liberality [*gentryse*]? I know his might is so great that he may find mercy in his mild moderation, though he is displeased, and if we leave off the enjoyment of our foul sins, and step onto the path/ladder [*styȝe*] that he ordains himself, he will turn from his fury and leave his wrath and forgive us this guilt, if we believe in him as God.' Then all believed in his law and left their sins, performed all the penance that the prince counseled, and God through his goodness forgave as he said—though he promised otherwise, withheld his vengeance" (lines 397–408). See *Middle English Dictionary* (accessed August 30, 2023, https://quod.lib.umich.edu/m/middle-english-dictionary/dictionary/MED42909), s.v. "styȝe," meanings 1, 2.

38. Much has been written about divine knowability in the Pearl-Poems. See, e.g., Clopper, "God of the 'Gawain-Poet'"; Hatt, *God and the Gawain-Poet*; Raschko, *Politics of Middle English Parables*; and Spyra, *Epistemological Perspective*.

39. "And God saw their works, that they turned from their evil way; and God repented of the evil [*malitiam*], that he had said that he would do unto them; and he did it not" (Jon. 3:10).

Having just heard so many such pronouns referring to God, the cumulative, almost spillover effect—particularly without the guidance of modern punctuation—is to hear its *he* as referring to God, too: "and God in His goodness forgave (them), as He said He would; though He promised otherwise, He withheld His vengeance," as Andrew and Waldron translate in a footnote to their first through fourth editions of the poems.[40] This reading has fallen from favor: Andrew and Waldron's fifth edition silently revises their earlier "as He said He would" to "as he (i.e. the king) said He would," and both Murray McGillivray and Ad Putter and Myra Stokes understand the line similarly. Either way, McGillivray's practice of not capitalizing pronouns of God (shared with the Pearl-Manuscript and University of Chicago Press) retains a momentary ambiguity in line 407 that reverential capitalization eliminates.

This ambiguity forces us to slow down, which in turn invites us to contemplate the significance of the poem's addition to its biblical source: highlighting the unnamed king of Nineveh, who emerges as a positive antitype for Belshazzar in *Cleanness* and for Jonah himself in *Patience*. Whereas Jonah promised destruction and proves peevishly disappointed at Nineveh's reprieve, the king's prayerful repentance causes God to change his mind—in fact, to follow through on his promise in the previous poem, to send a "warnyng . . . er harme hem he wolde in haste of his yre" ("warning . . . before he would harm them in haste of his ire," *Cleanness* lines 1503–4). The king of Nineveh thus reparatively mirrors two figures in two poems, and although the poem is careful not to give the king causality—the reprieve happens "as" he said, not "because" he said—its approving addition suggests value in his periphrastic, ambiguous expressions of knowing.

Andrew and Waldron make another interpretively resonant revision to their punctuation at the end of the poem; the crux concerns where we should hear God's final speech to Jonah as ending. Below are the poem's final twelve lines, as punctuated by them but without quotation marks:

Wer I as hastif as þou heere, were harme lumpen;
⸿ Couþe I not þole bot as þou, þer þryued ful fewe. [521]
I may not be so malicious and mylde be halden,
For malyse is noȝt to mayntyne boute mercy withinne.
Be noȝt so gryndel, godman, bot go forth þy wayes;
⸿ Be preue and be pacient in payne and in joye; [525]
For he þat is to rakel to renden his cloþez

40. Andrew and Waldron, *Poems* (1st–4th eds., 1978, 1987, 1996, 2002), 201.

Mot efte sitte with more vnsounde to sewe hem togeder.
Forþy when pouerté me enprecez and paynez innoȝe
℃ Ful softly with suffraunce saȝttel me bihouez; [529]
Forþy penaunce and payne topreue hit in syȝt
Þat pacience is a nobel poynt, þaȝ hit displease ofte. Amen[41]

Clearly the first-person pronouns in the first three lines of this passage are in God's voice: here, making explicit what has long been clear from reading, namely that Jonah, despite his usual typological association with Jesus, has been a frequently humorous countermodel for the reader of this particular poem. By the same token, the first-person evocation of poverty and suffering in lines 528–29 is clearly spoken by the poet-narrator, marking a return to the theme and characterization developed at lines 45–56. Editors therefore use quotation marks to designate the end of God's speech somewhere in between, usually either at the end of line 523 (as Andrew and Waldron did in earlier editions) or at the end of line 527 (as they do in their 2008 edition, the most recent as of this writing).

Significantly, their revision retains much of their earlier language to describe the competing claims on which the decision could be based: "Both are legitimate interpretations. It can be argued on the one side that 524 sounds more like the tone of God speaking to Jonah than the narrator addressing his audience, and on the other side that the exhortation to patience in 525 picks up the concerns of the 'prologue,' and is thus more appropriate to the narrator than to God. A definitive argument either way is difficult to envisage. . . . [T]he precise point at which the speaker changes remains elusive."[42] This language is followed, in 2008, by a "tentative" explanation of why they changed their minds, but the similarity of their overall logic suggests the potentially irresolvable status of the question. Indeed,

41. If I were as hasty as you here [Jonah], harm would befall. If I could suffer no better than you, very few would thrive. I may not be so cruel [*malicious*] and be considered mild, for harshness [*malyse*] is not to be maintained without mercy within. Be not so angry, good man, but go forth on your ways; be resolute and patient in pain and in joy; for whoever too swiftly rends his clothes must then sit more woefully to sew them together. Therefore when poverty presses me, and numerous pains, it behooves me to settle down, very softly, with sufferance; therefore penance and pain together prove visibly [*in syȝt*] that patience is a noble *poynt* though it is often displeasing. Amen (lines 520–31).

42. Andrew and Waldron, *Poems*, 5th ed. (2007) and 2nd ed. (1987), 206. In the passages that I omitted, they use very slightly different language to describe the rhetorical effect of the passage in question, but in both cases write that "[t]he passage (524–7) functions as a bridge" between the voice of God and that of the poet.

McGillivray quotes and reinforces their revised conclusion, noting that the manuscript's absence of quotation marks "allows for such ambiguities, perhaps intentional here," although he ultimately adopts their revised placement after line 527.[43]

I propose rather that we take the logical next step and simply not place the final quotation mark, leaving that absence for the reader to process (though perhaps with an explanatory footnote). Modern editorial punctuation understandably tends to reduce ambiguity in the pursuit of a clear, straightforward text, but "clarity" and "straightforwardness" are not essential characteristics of the literary. The swift reading that clarity enables also works against one homiletic goal of the poem, which is to make us slow down; *Patience* suggests that patient reading is one thing that makes us an ethical subject. Contemplating when God stops speaking is thus analogous, at an appropriately micro level, to the difficult, larger search for the "fayre formeȝ" of *Cleanness*. Unpunctuating the end of *Patience* would concretize one challenge that it poses, by frustrating our expectation that speech will have clearly circumscribed contours. God's speech often does not, as Thomas Hill and others have shown.[44] The poem's own understanding of divine aurality is therefore consonant with such a creative approach to (un)punctuation.

Comparable embrace of uncertainty enhances a crux in the immediately preceding lines, still part of God's speech to Jonah. Specifically, I propose accepting lines 510–15 as written in the manuscript, warts and all; most editors try to massage these lines into a more pleasing shape. McGillivray summarizes the situation and previous editorial treatments as follows:

> That there is a textual problem here is suggested by the *failure of the scheme of marked quatrains* probably due to a missing line somewhere between 509 and 520 (*though scribal marking of the quatrains continues to be regular, it is out of step with the sense*), and by apparent duplication of content between 512 and 514–15. Gollancz (1913, 1924) suggested that lines 513–15 represented text cancelled by the author to be replaced with the current 510–12, and therefore square-brackets lines 513–15 but prints them, a tack also followed by Anderson (1969), Moorman (1977), and Putter and Stokes (2014). Andrew and Waldron (1978+) achieve reasonable sense by instead exchanging 510–12 and 513–15.

43. McGillivray, *Patience*, 79. Putter and Stokes do the same (*Works of the Gawain Poet*). See further Molstad, "Adaptation," 11–12. Stanley Fish's analysis of irresolvable ambiguity in Milton is apposite here (*Is There a Text*, 154–58).

44. Hill, "God's 'Inquits.'"

> Like Vantuono (1984), I think that adequate sense can be achieved by punctuation here, though I do not follow his particular choices.[45]

McGillivray's closing appeal to "punctuation" is worth noting, given the poem's own investment in points and its final lines' quantum quotation marks, considered earlier.

A version of the syntax-quatrain mismatch described by McGillivray (italicized in the quotation above) occurs to aesthetic effect near the end of *Cleanness*, so its recurrence at the end of *Patience* clearly merits investigation. Yet one challenge of *Patience* is that its much smaller size makes it harder to interpret patterns that take time to emerge—like syntax-quatrain mismatch, some degree of which can be simple variation. Below, I print McGillivray's version of these lines and punctuation, but with paraphs as marked in the manuscript, and with the previous, uncomplicated quatrain (lines 505–8) as initiating context:

¶ And if I my trauayl schulde tyne of termes so longe [505]
and type doun ȝonder toun when hit turned were
þe sor of such a swete place burde synk to my hert,
so mony malicious mon as mournez þerinne.
¶ And of þat soumme ȝet arn summe, such sottez formadde [509]
(as lyttel barnez on barme þat neuer bale wroȝt
and wymmen vnwytte), þat wale ne couþe
þat on hande fro þat oþer, for alle þis hyȝe worlde,
¶ bitwene þe stele and þe stayre disserne noȝt cunen, [513]
what rule renes in roun bitwene þe ryȝt hande
and his lyfte, þaȝ his lyf schulde lost be þerfor—
and als þer ben doumbe besteȝ in þe burȝ mony,
¶ þat may not synne in no syt hemseluen to greue. [517]
Why schulde I wrath wyth hem, syþen wyȝez wyl torne,
and cum and cnawe me for kyng and my carpe leue?[46]

45. McGillivray, *Patience*, 77–78 (emphasis added).

46. "And if I should lose my labor of such long duration [*of termes so longe*], and throw down yonder town when it had repented [*turned*], the sorrow/pain for such a sweet place should sink into my heart, so many wicked men as repent therein. And of that number [*soumme*], yet there are some [*summe*], such foolish sots (like little children in the lap that never did wrong, and foolish women), that cannot pick one hand from the other, for all this high world; cannot distinguish between the upright and step of a ladder, or what rule runs in secret between the right hand and the left, though his life should be lost for this reason—and

The opening quatrain reinforces the human dimensions God displays in *Patience*, specifically that he laments the loss of his labor (*trauayl*) in terms of time spent ("of termes so longe")—despite normatively existing outside of time.[47] This tension may help make sense of the loosely associative logic by which the subsequent lines proceed.

I agree with McGillivray that the overall thrust of these lines as written in the manuscript (and punctuated by him) is clear enough, although they depict a rather chatty, digressive God. Whether divine logic proves significantly clearer as reordered by Andrew and Waldron I leave to the reader to assess:

> And if I should lose My work of such long duration, and overthrow yonder town when it had repented, the pain of such a sweet place ought to sink into My heart [there being] so many wicked men who are repentant there. And of that number yet are some, so utterly without reason, that [they] cannot distinguish between the upright of a ladder and the rung, nor [can they see] what rule inscrutably applies to the right hand and what to the [*lit.* its] left, though they might lose their lives thereby; like little children at the breast who never did harm, and ignorant women who could not distinguish one hand from the other, for all this great world. And also there are many dumb beasts in the city, that may not commit any sin to harm themselves. Why should I be angry with them, since [i.e., if] people will repent, and come and acknowledge Me as King and believe My speech?[48]

As the frequent clarifying brackets above attest, these lines are challenging even when reordered. Strangest is the sequence of three kinds of ignorance attributed to "some" fools within the sinful but repentant city: how to tell one hand from the other, or two parts of a ladder, or "what rule runs secretly [*in roun*]" between right and left hands. The first two sound easy to distinguish, and the third repeats the first—but adds the phrase "in roun," which upends this straightforwardness by embedding mysterious secrecy (primary associations of Middle English *roun*) within the passage's second

also there are many dumb beasts that cannot sin so as to grieve themselves with misfortune. Why should I be angry with them, since creatures will turn/repent [*torne*] and come and know me for king and believe my speech?" (lines 505–19).

47. For example, Molstad writes that "God is a character that suffers emotions of compassion and . . . affection" ("Adaptation," 9), and Putter describes the God of *Patience* as "embodied and impassioned" (*Introduction to the Gawain-Poet*, 140).

48. Andrew and Waldron, *Poems*, Folio Society facsimile of the manuscript (2015), 285.

(doubled, mirrored) reference to hands. Editors have tended to read this duplication as evidence of inauthenticity.[49] Given the importance of hands to these poems, elegantly demonstrated by Robert J. Blanch and Julian N. Wasserman,[50] I regard this doubling rather as supereffable, for the second instance is the same but different: the same two hands, but with a secret rule running between them.

By suggesting that hidden rules may inform apparently straightforward phenomena, this line invites readers to speculate upon the Pearl-Manuscript's own multiform dialectics of rule and exception. The phrase also echoes God's "runish" writing upon the wall in *Cleanness* (lines 1545, 1724). It thus connotes literal runes and divine writing even as God speaks far more gently, at the end of a poem that has reparatively rewritten other textual precedents as well. Gentler tone and human-seeming expression cannot overwrite divine unknowability, however, which is one important connotation of the phrase "in roun," namely the potential for radical epistemological alterity even in commonsensical distinctions like right and left—much as we saw in the paradoxes of *Pearl*.[51] The word *rune* also invites us to attend to the visual and material, however, much as the repeated reference to hands reinforces the manuscript's tactility, itself already heightened by this quire's violation of the Rule of Gregory.

The unexpected emergence of the animal that violation caused on 87/91r, described earlier, reemerges on folio 89/93 as a constellation of warty growths in the margin (see fig. 6.4). Appearing here as circular or ovular depressions, they offer an opportunity to heed Bruce Holsinger's advice that we shed our "fear of the seasoned paleographer's disdain for the neophyte's awe (and even, on some level, revulsion) at what medieval manuscripts actually *are*."[52] I have described heeding this advice involuntarily on reaching this quire's inversion of the Rule of Gregory. Here, near the middle of the quire, we encounter a different instance of the animal: a marginal metagrotesque, unintended by beast and (presumably) scribe alike.

These warty growths signify multiply. The poem's concluding emphasis on

49. E.g., Putter and Stokes's note that lines 513–15 "represent canceled or displaced material" (*Works of the Gawain Poet*, 234). Even McGillivray (*Patience*, 77–78), who accepts their authenticity and ordering, gives these lines a stanza of their own so as to restore the quatrain-syntax matchup in lines 528–31. (He hypothesizes a lost line, a point to which to which we will return.)

50. Blanch and Wasserman, *From Pearl to Gawain*, 65–110.

51. I draw inspiration here from Staples, "Poynts and Spots."

52. Holsinger, "Of Pigs and Parchment," 619.

"suffraunce" suggests empathy with animals consonant with the narration of the Flood in *Cleanness*. We might therefore see in the Pearl-Manuscript's use of damaged, low-grade parchment, an ethical statement against waste: a determination to use the whole animal.[53] It might also, or instead, signify no more than the limited means of the patron, or an ascetic temperament for which Maidie Hilmo finds evidence in some illustrations.[54] These growths also signify more abstractly, as a series of shapes that enhance the page's three-dimensionality. They are both points (in their Barthesian interruption of the reader's experience) and not-points (in their multidimensionality); they mean something(s) and nothing and are thus true contradictions as described by Laura Ashe.[55] They invite us, as Holsinger proposes, to reconnect with the vibrant materiality of the manuscript page even as they insist upon the limits of our knowledge about how medieval readers "really" experienced such anomalous pages in their books.

As they exist in folio 89/93, these growths have some of the meanings described above. They also mar the mirror image created by the offset of the text from 90/94r, and in that sense their disfiguration multiplies, expanding across the opening (see fig. 6.5). Here, some of the recto's ink has transferred to the verso opposite, creating a distorted mirroring across the book's spine. The two text-blocks even seem to touch in the lower left of figure 6.5, as the ends of lines 493–94 (ending in *ryȝt* and *noldeȝ*) almost blur into the reversed, offset ink from the final three lines of the poem, clearly visible on the preceding verso.

This strangely beautiful mirror-effect is both punctuated and distorted by the warty growths in the margin of the verso (fig. 6.4); they thereby anticipate the following poem, as (pre)disfigurations of the skin akin to Sir Gawain's own ultimately nicked neck. In that sense, they evoke both human and animal participants in the poem's hunts, which will see Sir Gawain and Reynard the fox alike outwitted by the forces of Castle Hautdesert. More locally,

53. See further Johnson, *Waste and the Wasters.*

54. E.g., Hilmo, "Creating a Visual Narrative."

55. See Ashe, "How to Read Both."

FIGURE 6.4. Folio 89/93v of Cotton Nero A.x/2. Warty growths on the interior margin of the folio. Photograph © 2024 by The British Library Board.

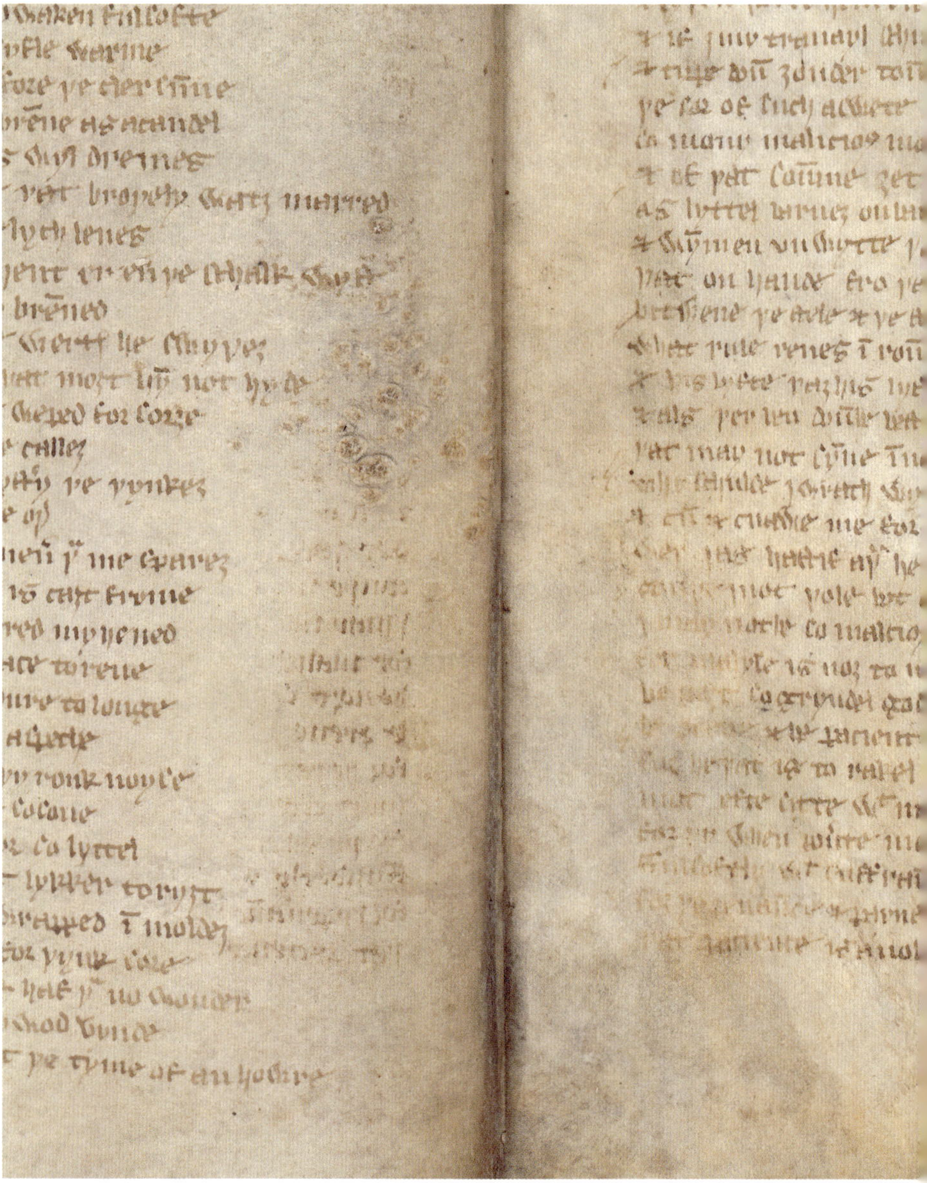

FIGURE 6.5. Folios 93v/94r of Cotton Nero A.x/2.
Photograph © 2024 by The British Library Board.

however, these disfigurations argue for accepting things as they come, which itself is an argument for accepting the poem's conclusion as transcribed: with anomalous quatrains and strange, doubled reference to hands; and without positing a missing line (thus rounding up to a notional 532) or potential cancellation of lines 513–15, whose phrase "in roun" (514) proves central to the poem's concluding insistence on epistemic humility.

Moreover, Janet Gilligan has found several affirmative forms of meaning in the number 531, among them as the sum of the first four perfect numbers (1, 6, 28, 496), in whose lines she likewise finds particular meaning.[56] I find the thrust of her argument persuasive, especially since the line she is least sure of seems to me the most apposite, for it touches on divine rather than human patience: "if I wolde help my hondewerk, haf no wonder" ("do not marvel if I should desire to help my handwork," line 496). This line distills into a point the theme of God's concluding address to Jonah and of *Patience* as a whole. For these reasons and more, I propose accepting, and at times unpunctuating, the end of *Patience*.

56. Gilligan notes that "the number one is not strictly a perfect number, [but] it is traditionally included in [medieval] discussions of the perfect numbers" ("Numerical Composition," 7).

BRITISH
MUSEUM

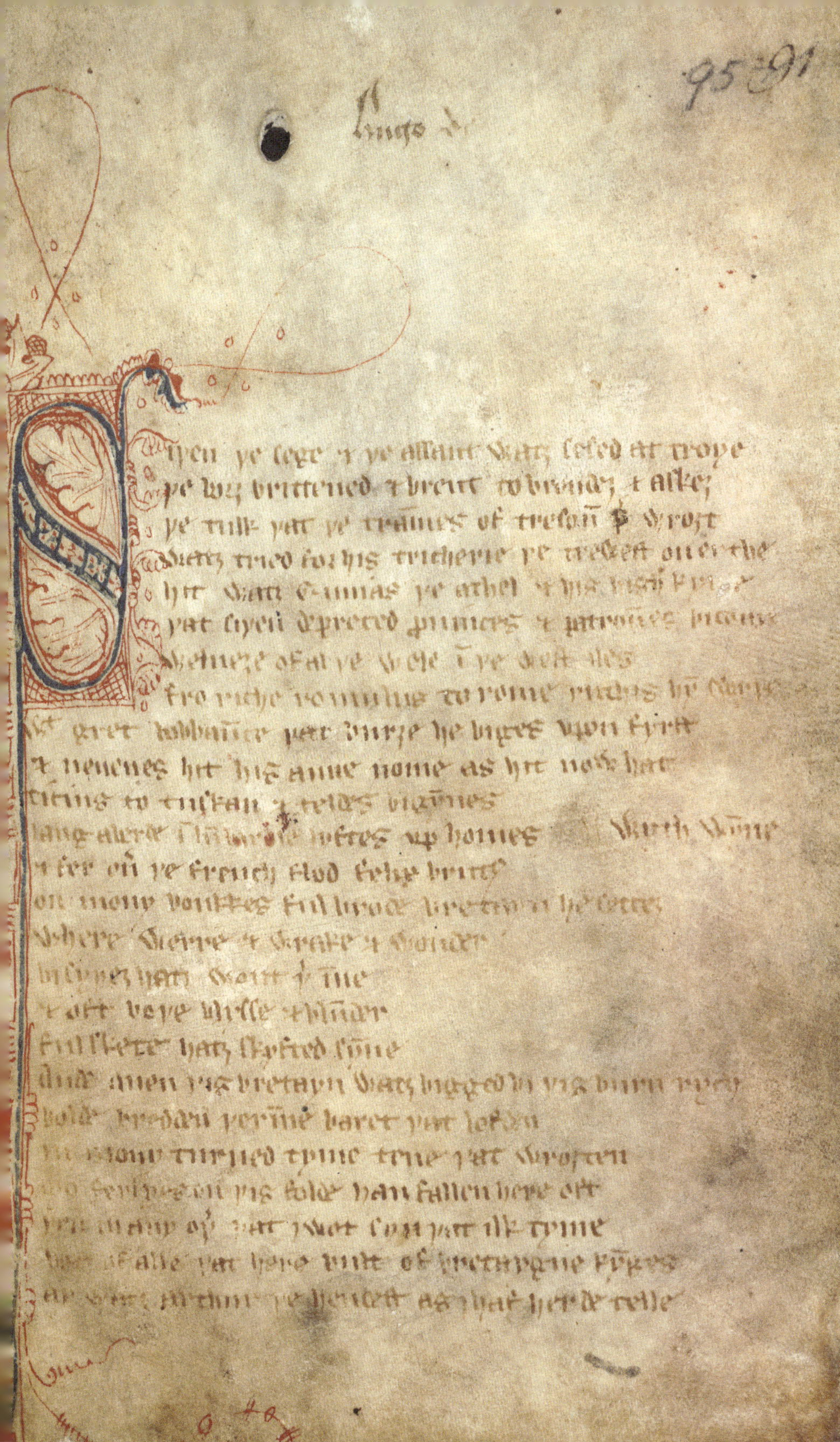
95 91

Hugo de

Siþen þe sege & þe assaut watz sesed at troye
þe borȝ brittened & brent to brondez & askez
þe tulk þat þe trammes of treson þ wroȝt
watz tried for his tricherie þe trewest on erthe
hit watz ennias þe athel & his highe kynde
þat siþen depreced prouinces & patrounes bicome
welneȝe of al þe wele in þe west iles
fro riche romulus to rome ricchis hym swyþe
wt gret bobbaunce þat burȝe he biges vpon fyrst
& neuenes hit his aune nome as hit now hat
ticius to tuskan & teldes bigynnes
langaberde in lumbardie lyftes vp homes
& fer ouer þe french flod felix brutus
on mony bonkkes ful brode bretayn he settez wyth wynne
where werre & wrake & wonder
bi syþez hatz wont þ inne
& oft boþe blysse & blunder
ful skete hatz skyfted synne
ande quen þis bretayn watz bigged bi þis burn rych
bolde bredden þ inne baret þat lofden
in mony turned tyme tene þat wroȝten
mo ferlyes on þis folde han fallen here oft
þen in any oþer þat I wot syn þat ilk tyme
bot of alle þat here bult of bretaygne kynges
ay watz arthur þe hendest as I haf herde telle

SEVEN

SPECULATIVE GEOMETRY

The transition from *Patience* to *Sir Gawain and the Green Knight* is perhaps the most dramatic textual juncture in the Pearl-Manuscript. For the first and only time, we must turn the page (folio 90/94) to see a poem's opening illustration, which enhances the inherent drama of what it depicts: a royal feasting table evocative of Belshazzar's Feast, as it appeared opposite the first page of *Cleanness*—but with a severed head prominently displayed as if part of the dinner service. This gory addition, and the page's greater visual complexity overall, nicely anticipates one role of *Sir Gawain and the Green Knight* in its material context: to offer a delightful final trial of our speculative capacities as shaped by the manuscript thus far. Readers' eagerness to take up this challenge is amply attested by the voluminous scholarship the poem has attracted, to say nothing of translations and adaptations. For many, *Sir Gawain* itself is the ultimate, eternal quarry, and its first opening, 90/94v+91/95r (figs. 7.1, 7.2), is an appropriately challenging introduction to the quests it proposes.

In describing the *punctum*, Barthes writes of "that accident which pricks me," and Middle English *poynt* can also mean puncture or pricking.[1] It is therefore striking that weapons and wounds feature so prominently on folio 90/94v, which depicts the Green Knight's entry, challenge, and beheading in a single complex tableau. As this chapter will show, these weapons are more

1. Barthes, *Camera Lucida*, 27; *Middle English Dictionary* (accessed August 31, 2023, https://quod.lib.umich.edu/m/middle-english-dictionary/dictionary/MED33862), s.v. "pointe n. (1)," meaning 1b.

Preceding spread: FIGURE 7.1. Folio 90/94v of Cotton Nero A.x/2. Photograph FIGURE 7.2. Folio 91/95r of Cotton Nero A.x/2. Photograph

than thematic; they also suggest a set of embedded triangles whose angles and sight lines preview the poem to come, and whose geometric complexity visually anticipates Gawain's famously intricate pentangle. The first illustration thus primes us to read the poem itself for page-shape. This is significant because the shape of its facing page, folio 91/95r, is like none other in the manuscript: a large, eleven-line gap at the top, followed by a twenty-five-line text-block that combines alliterative long-lines with much shorter, roughly iambic rhymed stanzas. Its conjunction of the two literary textures we have seen in the Pearl-Manuscript thus far rightly suggests that this poem may synthesize elements of what has come before, while its visual strangeness invites speculation in its own right. Although not representationally illustrative like its facing page, the anomalous layout of 91/95r previews and in that sense illustrates some of the perceptual challenges that the poem will afford. Read closely, the speculative geometries of its first two pages offer interpretive tools with which to chase the endless, Gordian knot of *Sir Gawain*.

SEEING DOUBLE

In distinct though overlapping ways, both 90/94v and 91/95r encourage versions of the double perspective that *Sir Gawain* thematizes and tests with its many resonant, often concealed pairings (among them Green Knight/Bertilak, "loathly lady"/Morgan the goddess, and Camelot/Hautdesert). Such narrative doubling is prefigured by the visual doubling of Gawain, where he appears both in the upper left of the page, saluting King Arthur with his left hand as he takes up the Green Knight's ax in his right; and again below, facing the opposite way and now gripping the ax firmly in both hands, as if steadying himself from the shock of what has just happened. Reading the image as a whole, these Gawains clearly represent our protagonist just before and just after making the dramatic cut.[2] The gory aftermath of that cut, with the Green Knight's trunk and head radiating blood from their prominent neck-bones, appears on the feasting table that divides the two moments in time—and the two Gawains.

This scene is striking for its doublings and symmetries, and for the lines those resemblances suggest. The Green Knight's severed head divides the two Gawains, as noted above; but it also links them along a line sloping

2. As Jennifer Lee points out in a foundational study of the manuscript's images, this illustration "can be 'read' from top to bottom, the scene behind the table leading to the scene in front" ("Illuminating Critic," 22).

downward at what looks very close to a 45-degree angle. (I will call the upper-left figure G1, for "Gawain at time-1," and the one gripping the ax in both hands G2, for "Gawain at time-2.") This line starts at the top of G1's ax (Point A) and proceeds down through his head, barely grazing the top of the Green Knight's severed head before ending around G2's neck (Point A1; see fig. 7.3). This trajectory is fitting since Gawain's neck is ultimately nicked by the very ax he holds here. Line A–A1 also passes through Arthur's sword and G2's ax, further emphasizing the illustration's conspicuous cleaving imagery. Though not part of this line, the top-right figure holds yet another blade above and just slightly to the right of G2's head, almost like a guillotine, whetting our appetite for the poem to come.

This diagonal contrasts with the strong verticality of G2's ax, which is nearly parallel to the two knights' bodies and suggests a line extending up through the table and Guinevere's crowned head—less than one degree shy of a straight line (180.36 degrees). The diagonal of G1's ax, meanwhile, extends down into the feasting table, and is related by rotation to the ax of G2: specifically, rotating the near-vertical created by G2's ax (the G2 axis) yields a line that extends through the Green Knight's leg into and through G1's ax (see fig. 7.4; the G1 axis). These lines emerge from the doubling of Gawain across the Green Knight's severed head, and are strengthened by how neatly the Green Knight's body continues or complements the lines created by his axes: his erect torso roughly parallel with the G2 axis, but the diagonal of his leg continuing through the G1 axis. Although held here by (the) Gawain(s), these axes belong to the Green Knight, who will ultimately repay the cut this page depicts. In that sense, these lines offer a preview of the complex games (hunt, tease, bluff, requite) that the two men play in the poem.

G2's ax also prompts greater attention to Guinevere than she typically receives. On the one hand, she helps create the horizontal of four faces above the feasting table, and in that sense, her look across to G1 combines with the two axes discussed above to create a (nearly) right triangle. Guinevere's connection to G1 highlights the fact that they both seem to be looking slightly downward, quite unlike King Arthur, whose intervening head appears to look outward horizontally. The Green Knight's severed head is angled upward so as to look at the queen; the line of their gaze is created by rotating the G1 axis 45 degrees from its midpoint (just where the Green Knight sits on his

Facing page: FIGURE 7.3. Folio 90/94v of Cotton Nero A.x/2. Photograph © 2024 by The British Library Board.

A
A1
BRITISH MUSEUM

23.8° rotation
G1
G2

horse), adding to the symmetry of the scene (see fig. 7.5). The green line of figure 7.5 anticipates the Green Knight's dramatic revelation, near the end of the poem, that the whole grisly spectacle was organized by Morgan Le Fay in hopes of frightening Guinevere to death. This geometric emergence of the female is further strengthened by Guinevere's green dress: not just for the connection to the Green Knight, but also for its contrast with the earlier depiction of Belshazzar's queen, as we will see.[3]

Earlier versions of this chapter speculated more venturesomely, finding additional triangles and patterns embedded within these three lines and the page's strong horizontals: the line of faces above the table, plus the table's own lines. Those shapes proved more persuasive in person than in writing (hence their absence from this version), which I find illustrative of my larger point: that in addition to previewing the poem by linking key figures, another important effect of 90/94v's composition is to encourage speculative shape-making. When I showed the shapes of this page to friends, they often responded by noticing or suggesting other shapes: wondering how the upper-right figure holding his sword like a guillotine might fit in, for example. And it was my research assistant Kelsey Glover who found the 45-degree angle of rotation depicted in figure 7.5, which underpins the sight lines described above and reinforces Guinevere's connection with G1 in the upper left.

Such participatory shape-making, or rather shape-finding, is exactly how the poet frames his encounter with a more famous literary polygon, namely the pentangle of Gawain's shield:

> Now alle þese fyue syþeȝ forsoþe were fetled on þis knyȝt [Gawain]
> and vchone halched in oþer, **þat non ende hade**,
> and fyched vpon fyue poynteȝ þat fayld neuer,
> ne samned neuer in no syde, ne sundred nouþer,
> **withouten ende** at any noke **I oquere fynde**,

3. On the importance of connections across the Pearl-Manuscript's illustrations of women, see Hilmo, "Re-Conceptualizing," 409–15.

Facing page: FIGURE 7.4. Folio 90/94v of Cotton Nero A.x/2.
Photograph © 2024 by The British Library Board.

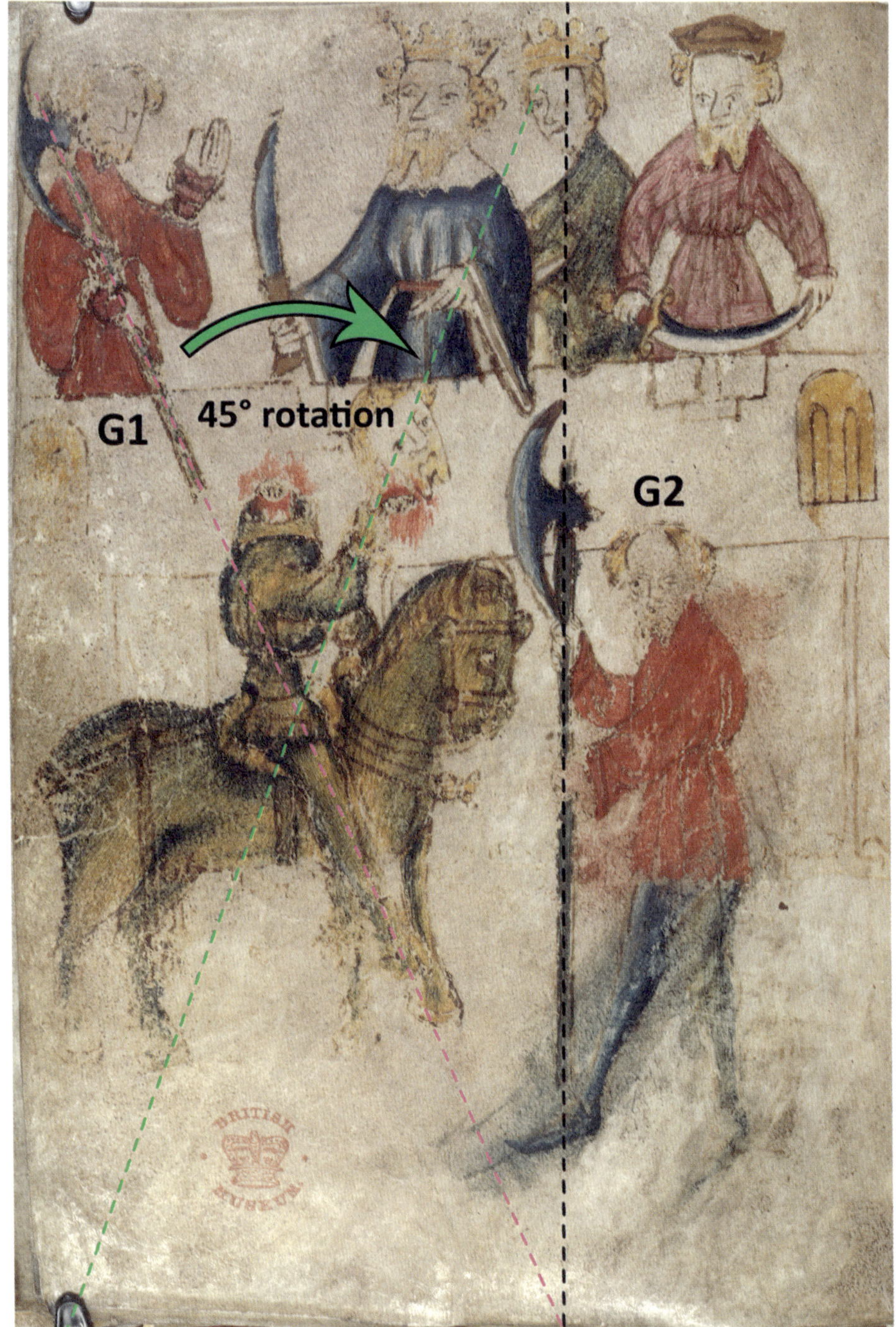
45° rotation
G1
G2
BRITISH MUSEUM

whereeuer þe **gomen** bygan or **glod to an ende**.
Þerfore on his schene schelde schapen watȝ þe *knot*.[4]

The poet personalizes this account, turning the description of Gawain's pentangle into a game (*gomen*) of finding ("I oquere fynde"), the same verb used of the "fair forms" of *Cleanness* (line 3). Those forms were described as easy for the rightly intentioned poet to find, and by extension to give textual shape; but as we saw in chapter 4, many of *Cleanness*'s patterns required a compass to craft and active speculation to find. Here, the poet tries and fails to find a fault, a clustering or sundering or even an "end" to the shape earlier described as "þe endeles knot" (line 630). He then describes this entire process as a game that begins and ends.

The contrast between ending and endlessness in the passage above recalls the manuscript's only other use of the word *endeles*, in the Maiden's description of the Pearl of Price set within her transfigured clothing: "for hit is wemeleȝ, clene and clere, / and **endeleȝ rounde** . . ." ("for it is flawless, clean and clear, and endless round . . ." [lines 737–38]). This lexical parallel between pentangle ("endeles knot") and pearl ("endeleȝ rounde") suggests reading their geometry similarly, as ideals that no mortal can fully embody on earth. In describing the pentangle, the poet speaks of a "game" that begins and ends; but these are fleeting, imperfect (because human) impositions upon a shape whose endless geometry can symbolize chivalric perfection because it reflects and embodies divine order, like the Pearl of Price.[5]

In this way, 90/94v anticipates *Sir Gawain*'s rich explorations of the complexity of shapes, previewed above. It also creates suggestive mirrorings with two other images that appear at nearly the same distance in the manuscript,

4. "Now all five of these groups of five [virtues] were fixed on this knight, and each one interwove with the other, **so that they had no end**, and were established upon five points that never failed, neither clustered at any side nor sundered either, ***without end*** at any nook ***that* I can find anywhere**, wherever the **game began or came to an end**. Therefore the knot was shaped on his bright shield" (lines 656–62).

5. For a beautiful meditation upon the geometric-theological aesthetic of *Pearl*, which has shaped my reading of the entire manuscript, see Marie Borroff, "*Pearl*'s 'Maynful Mone.'"

✣

Facing page: FIGURE 7.5. Folio 90/94v of Cotton Nero A.x/2.
Photograph © 2024 by The British Library Board.

forward and backward: 56/60v (34 folios earlier; fig. 3.7), the portrayal of Belshazzar's Feast opposite *Cleanness*; and 125/129v (35 folios later; fig. 8.4), which depicts the hero's mounted approach to the Green Chapel, with the Green Knight impassively grasping his ax. Maidie Hilmo has shown that the figures of Gawain and the Green Knight on 125/129v evoke those of 90/94v in ways that suggest "a kind of mysterious identification of the two in person as well as in the roles they play in the beheading game."[6] Building on that suggestion, it will be significant for my argument in chapter 8 that the mounted Gawain on 125/129v holds his lance at a similar though slightly less vertical angle to the G1 axis of 90/94v; and, further, that the Green Knight holds his ax at almost exactly the same angle as the earlier G2 axis.

The image of Belshazzar's Feast also bears striking, though very different, similarities to 90/94v's beheading scene. In each, a king and queen gesture in amazement at a supernatural event that interrupts a celebratory royal gathering. A long feasting table with decorative elements divides both pages horizontally about a third of the way down, and in the lower left, a figure in green sits, or rides, in judgment of the proud court above. Indeed, Daniel and the Green Knight look improbably similar, with bearded blond faces looking up to the right at the queen, past the king nominally in charge of the proceedings. Such resemblances make other obvious contrasts between the images interpretively interesting: whereas Arthur wears the same royal blue as Belshazzar in the structurally parallel illustration on 56/60v, for example, Guinevere's green on this page contrasts with the red of Belshazzar's queen, further highlighting her connection to the Green Knight through the green line of figure 7.5.

More dramatically, whereas the lower-right quadrant of 56/60v is conspicuously vacant, G2 takes up much of that visual energy on 90/94v. Does this suggest Camelot's greater ability to respond to external judgment, or do the many other similarities between the scenes outweigh this contrast and make the two pages' resemblances more cautionary? Given the earlier depiction of a sacrilegious feast, might this severed head at a royal feast recall that of John the Baptist, as Maidie Hilmo has proposed?[7] The visual echoes that prompt such questions highlight the moral and spiritual dimensions of *Sir Gawain* and suggest that we should attend to its textual echoes of *Cleanness*, in particular. I take up some of these, such as a shared interest in paper and polishing, in chapter 8.

Moreover, while most other illustrations in the Pearl-Manuscript depict a

6. Hilmo, "Did the Scribe Draw," 125.

7. Hilmo, "Re-Conceptualizing," 406–7.

single *poynt* in time (to use yet another of that complex word's many Middle English meanings),[8] 56/60v and 90/94v are more temporally complex. As we saw in chapter 3, 56/60v collapses multiple moments into a single tableau: God writes, Belshazzar trembles, the queen intervenes, and Daniel reads, all within the same visual space—and all with gestures that suggest simultaneity, even though each of those actions occurs sequentially in biblical and poetic accounts alike. This visual multitemporality intimates the Boethian metaphor, that God perceives history like a vista seen from above: all at once rather than linearly. Elsewhere, the illustrator conspicuously reminds us of our limited perspective: for example, by failing to depict the full circuit of either the Heavenly Jerusalem or Nineveh on 38/42v (fig. 1.4) and 82/86v (fig. 5.3), respectively. Yet on 56/60v (fig. 3.7), which depicts the very act of textual interpretation, he associates both holy writing and right reading with a multitemporality fundamentally at odds with the human experience of time as linear.

The first illustration of *Sir Gawain* is also multitemporal, but in a different and almost opposite way. Whereas 56/60v collapses discrete points of time into a single frame, suggesting the immediacy of divine judgment and the atemporality of divine perspective, 90/94v uses its doubled Gawain(s) to depict time as sequential, and in that sense linear: it moves from top to bottom and left to right, like the English text visible on the opposite page. This abstract notion of linearity is concretized, or enacted, by the geometry of 90/94v, which anticipates the poem's depiction of Gawain's pentangle in terms of lines and points; it also invites close reading of the dimensions of its facing page, to which I now turn.

OF BOBS AND NUMBERS

My argument here is that 91/95r's unusual page-shape (see fig. 7.2) invites us to read its words as an artfully constructed whole. Doing so requires reading synesthetically and across time, for the placement of *Sir Gawain*'s opening bob—a tiny, often seemingly superfluous verbal phrase—is such that we encounter it twice (fig. 7.6): when it first appears in the manuscript, to the right of line 12, and again when we hear its final syllable as the *a*-rhyme of the quatrain, or wheel, that starts three lines below and rhymes *baba*.[9]

8. *Middle English Dictionary* (accessed August 31, 2023, https://quod.lib.umich.edu/m/middle-english-dictionary/dictionary/MED33862), s.v. "pointe n. (1)", meaning 4.

9. The question of the bob's placement in manuscripts generally, and the Pearl-Manuscript specifically, has been the subject of considerable recent scholarly interest. Important studies include Solberg, "Imagining the Bob and Wheel"; Kerby-Fulton, Olson, and Hilmo,

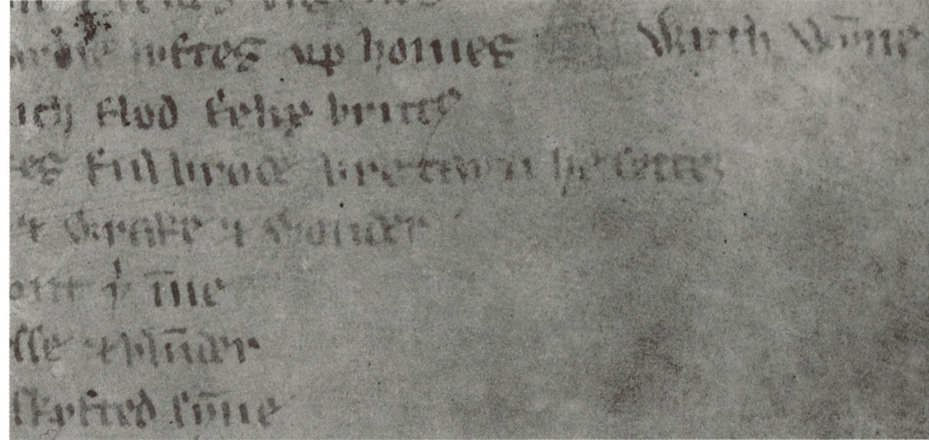

FIGURE 7.6. Folio 91/95r of Cotton Nero A.x/2. Ending of lines 12–18 of *Sir Gawain and the Green Knight*, with first bob in upper right. Photograph © 2024 by The British Library Board.

This temporal and sensory doubling, by which we see the bob before we hear it, echoes other forms of doubling visible in the illustration opposite and in the manuscript more broadly.

As we will see, this and other aspects of 91/95r's page-shape also recall the more-and-more, "supereffable" nature of *Pearl*'s aesthetic and interpretive landscape.[10] Such echoes reinforce that *Sir Gawain* is integral to the Pearl-Manuscript despite its obvious contrasts with the previous three, explicitly religious poems.[11] The recurrence of structurally essential rhyme for the first time since the end of *Pearl* links it to *Sir Gawain* across the middle two poems,[12] anticipating a deeper structural correspondence that can be

Opening up Medieval Manuscripts, 56–63; Kerby-Fulton and Klein, "Rhymed Alliterative Verse"; Putter, "Adventures in the Bob-and-Wheel Tradition"; and Warner, "Notes on *Sir Gawain and the Green Knight*." Chickering has sensitively and persuasively described the bobs' literary effects in "Stanzaic Closure and Linkage." Weiskott offers a helpful reexamination of the issue in "Stanza-Linking."

10. On "supereffability," see Cervone, *Poetics of the Incarnation*, 5.

11. Recent monographs emphasizing *Sir Gawain*'s theological commitments include Campbell, *Gawain-Poet*; Hatt, *God and the Gawain-Poet*; and Spyra, *Epistemological Perspective*.

12. *Sir Gawain*'s opening lines on 91/95r appear thirty-six folios after the end of *Pearl* (55/59v), and thirty-six has its own significance to the Pearl-Manuscript: as the typical number

appreciated only retrospectively: both poems have 101 stanzas and a total number of lines (as traditionally reckoned, 1212 and 2530) that resonate thematically. Yet those who find meaning in such numerical shaping—and I am among them—must account for some countervailing material realities: our only copy of *Pearl* has 1211 lines, and the bobs of *Sir Gawain* never receive their own line in the manuscript, "a fact that not all advocates of number symbolism in the poem are disposed to discuss," as A. S. G. Edwards rightly notes.[13] In chapter 2, I presented an affirmative reading of *Pearl*'s lack, its imagined "line 472," as spiritually and formally meaningful. Here I will argue that the bobs' sensory doubleness, described above, suggests reading them as both lines and not-lines, giving them a paradoxical, almost quantum existence that further links *Sir Gawain* to the supereffable *Pearl*.

Before going further, however, we should examine more closely the overall page-shape of 91/95r (fig. 7.2). Its eleven-line gap at the top of the page recalls the six-line gap at the top of *Patience*'s opening page but is considerably more dramatic. In the top middle, where we would expect the first line of the poem, appear the words "hugo de" in an angular, slightly larger display script.[14] From the initial capital, delicate red tracery extends up and out, toward the fragmentary name, drawing the blank space into the text-block; a hole in the parchment even evokes the tiny dot-like circles used to punctuate the tracery (fig. 7.7). A flower blooms out of the upper left of the decorated S of *Siþen*, and the red, foliated curlicues that run down the margin are the most exuberant of the entire manuscript, even crowding up against the text-block in places, the only time we see this effect (fig. 7.8). This integration of vegetal and floral decoration into the page-shape visually anticipates the poem's ecological interests.[15] Quick comparison confirms that in

of lines to a page, and as twelve (significant to *Pearl*) times three (significant to both *Cleanness* and Christianity).

13. Edwards, "The Manuscript," 202. Solberg nicely summarizes the chief angles of *Sir Gawain*'s numerical patterning that critics have found enticing: "Gawain's virtues are manifested in the magical number five: the five-sided red and gold pentangle on his shield, mirrored in the poem's five-line bob and wheel, its 2,530 (2,525 + 5) lines, and its 101 stanzas (2,530 divided by 101 equals twenty-five with a remainder of five)" ("Imagining the Bob and Wheel," 57).

14. As Brantley notes, this fragmentary name is "probably further obscure evidence of ownership" (*Medieval English Manuscripts*, 218). Unsurprisingly, this moment features prominently in debates about the poem's authorship and manuscript's ownership.

15. Recent ecocritical readings of *Sir Gawain* include Cohen, "Love of Life"; George, "Gawain's Struggle with Ecology"; Johnson, *Waste and the Wasters*, 126–49; Martinez, "Bertilak's Green Vision"; and Rudd, "Wilderness of Wirral."

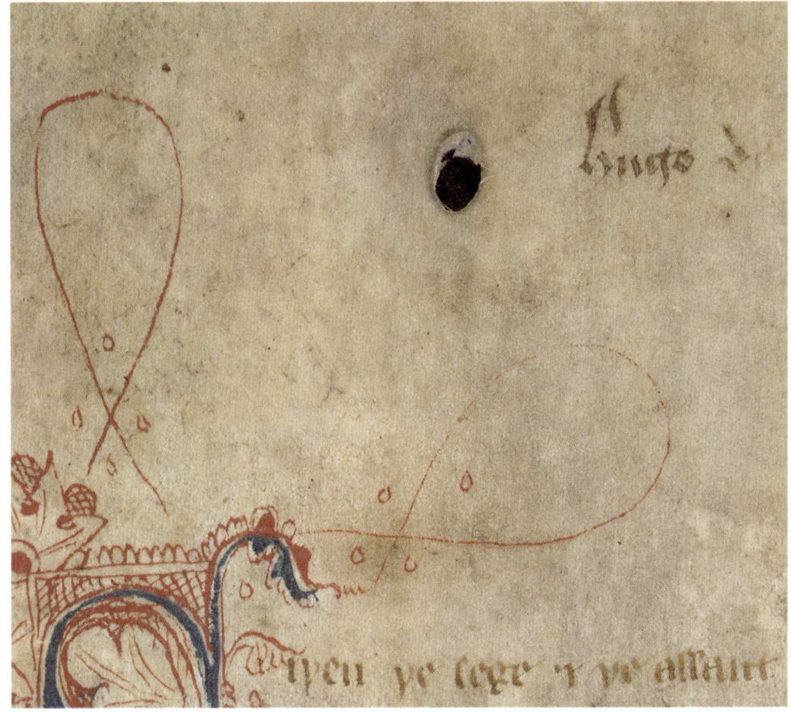

FIGURE 7.7. Folio 91/95r of Cotton Nero A.x/2. Decorative tracery and hole in parchment above the opening lines of *Sir Gawain and the Green Knight*. Photograph © 2024 by The British Library Board.

general terms and a host of particulars, the page-shapes and extratextual elements of 91/95r both recall and amplify the complexity of what we have seen on the first pages of the previous three poems.

This complexity prompts greater attention to the twenty-five lines that appear below the eleven-line gap, for they give this page a shape unlike any other in the manuscript: fourteen alliterative long-lines like those of *Cleanness* and *Patience*, followed by a much shorter rhyming quatrain, after which seven more long-lines appear. About halfway down this text-block, to the right of line 12, appear two words, *wyth wynne* ("with joy"); this so-called bob creates the *a*-rhyme answered by the quatrain (or "wheel") just below, which rhymes *baba*. *Sir Gawain* thus unites formal characteristics of the Pearl-Manuscript's previous three poems: syllabically irregular, alliterative long-lines (like *Cleanness* and *Patience*); and roughly iambic, alternately rhyming, generally alliterative stanzas (like *Pearl*). This basic rhythm of strophe, bob, and wheel,

FIGURE 7.8. Folio 91/95r of Cotton Nero A.x/2. Opening decorated initial of *Sir Gawain and the Green Knight*. Photograph © 2024 by The British Library Board.

persists through the poem, but with two additional complexities: the placement of the bob on the page shifts (Kerby-Fulton calls it a "floating bob"), though it always initiates the wheel's rhyme scheme;[16] and the length of the long-line strophe ranges from twelve to thirty-seven lines, though usually from fifteen to twenty-five. Each of these wrinkles further destabilizes us as readers, and in complementary ways: as Howell D. Chickering points out, "the poet can always surprise us with the bob, since the strophe length is irregular," so for the material placement of the bob itself to shift from stanza to stanza adds another dimension to the surprise.[17]

The narrowing of the text-block at the wheel draws attention to that part of the page, whose lines especially repay detailed attention. I reproduce the bob both where it appears in the manuscript (to the right of line 12, complete with double arrow) and where modern editors have universally placed it (as its own line 15):

> . . . Langaberde in Lumbardie lyftes vp homes, << wyth wynne
> **and** fer ouer þe French flod, Felix **Brutus**
> on mony bonkkes ful brode **Bretyan** he settez
> wyth wynne,
> where *werre* and wrake and wonder
> bi syþez hatz wont þerinne,
> ande oft boþe blysse and blunder
> ful skete hatz *skyfted* synne.
>
> **Ande** quen þis **Bretayn** watz bigged bi þis burn rych
> bolde bredden þerinne, *baret* þat lofden,
> in mony *turned* tyme tene þat wrozten.[18]

16. Usually (as here: seventy-four times), the bob appears one or more lines above the last long-line of the strophe; less frequently (twenty-four times) at the same line; and thrice just below, opposite the wheel. See further Kerby-Fulton, Olson, and Hilmo, *Opening up Middle English Manuscripts*, 59–63.

17. Chickering, "Stanzaic Closure and Linkage," 3. Putter also draws attention to this "element of surprise" in "Adventures in the Bob-and-Wheel Tradition."

18. ". . . Langaberde lifts up homes in Lombardy [with joy], and far over the French flood, Felix Brutus sets Britain along many broad banks with joy, where war and vengeance and wonder have often dwelled by turns, and often both bliss and strife have swiftly alternated since. And when this Britain was built by this noble man, bold men flourished therein, who loved battle and wrought harm at many a pivotal [*turned*] time" (lines 12–22). The verb *turnen* is almost endlessly polysemous in Middle English, with twenty-eight principal meanings and

Layout and text alike invite us to read these lines in multiple ways, and the sui generis nature of *Sir Gawain*'s form—no other extant poem combines alliterative long-lines, bobs, and rhymed verse—makes it additionally plausible that different readers might have experienced these lines differently.[19] As Kathryn Kerby-Fulton has noted, the meaning of this particular bob could conceivably "apply to several of the stanza's final lines at once," so it might initially be construed as concluding line 12.[20] Alternately or additionally, the bob might suggest a structural boundary between the twelve preceding and thirteen succeeding lines on the page, like a lexical version of the paraph mark that appears after the twelfth line of *Cleanness*. The fact that twelve has been such a richly resonant number throughout the Pearl-Manuscript strengthens such hints; given the manuscript's fascination with midpoints, so does the bob's appearance at nearly the midpoint of the page's text-block.

Yet the significant gap and faint double arrow between line 12 and the bob, along with the fact that the long-line is metrically complete as written, suggests that "wyth wynne" does not belong solely or even principally to line 12; and this is confirmed when we hear its *-ynne* sound answered by the wheel's *þerinne* and *synne*. Already distinguished by its shorter line-length and rhyme, the wheel is also bracketed by nearly parallel "And . . . Britain" formulations in the long-lines just before and after, boldfaced in the quotation above. These echoes further enclose the bob-and-wheel in the strophes that surround it, an effect that recalls *Pearl*'s use of *pyȝt* ("set, placed," with suggestions of both fastening and decoration) as its fourth concatenating word; the wheel's much shorter lines even visually echo *Pearl*.

Such associations with *Pearl* are reinforced by the sheer poetic bravura of this opening wheel, whose first line stands out for especially thick alliteration and assonance. It alliterates with the bob on *w-* (*wynne, werre, wonder*), further reinforcing the formal integrity of bob-and-wheel. Meanwhile its thick cluster of *w-*/*wr-*/*-r*(*re*) sounds creates a growliness in the mouth that pleasurably extends our engagement and retards the strong forward narrative drive of the earlier long-lines. Its initial sequence of three nouns ("werre and wrake and wonder") works in tension with the wheel's dyads ("boþe blysse and blunder," and its syntactically parallel first two and last two

many submeanings given in the *Middle English Dictionary*. It recalls *skyfted* ("shifted") three lines earlier and also conveys a physicality that is complemented by *wroȝten* ("wrought") at the end of the line.

19. On the uniqueness of *Sir Gawain*'s form, see Chickering, "Stanzaic Closure and Linkage," 2; and Weiskott, "Stanza-Linking," 457.

20. Kerby-Fulton, Olson, and Hilmo, *Opening up Medieval Manuscripts*, 61.

lines), a bit like a run of triplets complicating the apprehension of 4/4 time in music. This aural and rhythmic complexity is complemented by a lexical and allusive sophistication that Chickering describes with admirable precision:

> '[W]ynne' has a contradictory double meaning: "joy, delight" if it is derived from OE 'wynn,' but 'strife, labor' if derived from OE 'gewinn.' Polysemous word-play is deeply ingrained in the poet's imagination . . . and when we let 'synne' become a pun as well [here it means 'since,' but it also can also mean 'sin'], this first series of *a*-rhymes suggests a sentence about the moral quality of Gawain's future actions: he takes 'wynne' in the Lady's company and in keeping the green girdle (see lines 1885–92), but 'þerinne' lies the 'synne' of breaking his pledge to Bertilak. In its two meanings, 'wynne' contains the 'blysse and blunder' that 'Ful skete' will shift back and forth for Gawain during the story.[21]

By looking both back to *Pearl* (via sonic lushness, "polysemous word-play," and alternating rhyme in short poetic lines) and forward into *Sir Gawain* (with hints of the drama to come), this bob-and-wheel presents a remarkable distillation of the poet's craft.

It seems aesthetically significant that this complex, jewel-like instance of verbal art should be further reinscribed, stitched, and *pyȝt* within the strophes that surround it on 91/95r, lexically and materially. As noted above, the bob is physically aligned with the first strophe, and the wheel's final word, *synne*, recalls the poem's very first word *siþen* (another form of the same primary meaning, "since"). But as the italicized pairs in the quotation above make clear, elements of the wheel also anticipate the following strophe: *werre* in line 16 the *baret* ("battle") of line 21, and line 19's *skyfted* ("shifted") the *turned* of line 22. Just as the bob was equipoised between strophe and wheel, so too this first bob-and-wheel as a whole looks forward and backward into the preceding and following strophes. As our first rhyming verse in the manuscript since *Pearl*, it also looks all the way back to that poem and prompts us to continue reading alive to echoes from earlier in the manuscript.

Such complex, multiply interlocking structures, which are typical of *Sir Gawain*, are further fixed in the reader's mind by the poem's next bob-and-wheel, which promises:

> I schal telle hit [the story] astit as I in toun herde
> with tonge:

21. Chickering, "Stanzaic Closure and Linkage," 16.

as hit is stad and stoken
in stori stif and stronge,
with lel lettres loken,
in londe so hatȝ ben longe.[22]

The last long-line's reference to orality, reinforced by the bob, echoes the beginning of *Patience* ("I herde on a halyday . . . ," line 9); but the wheel's lexicon of fastness and fixity (in words like *stad, stoken,* and *loken,* in particular) also evokes "the power of writing to fix the story in its present form," as Jason M. Herman has shown.[23] Together, these lines suggest a productive fusion of aural and written modes, a synthesis of the previous two poems in the manuscript (*Patience* more aural, *Cleanness* more written).

Whatever may once have been envisioned for it, the blank space at the top of 91/95r is arresting, both in itself and because it means that this page has only twenty-five lines of text, instead of the usual thirty-six. The number twenty-five is of great symbolic significance to *Sir Gawain,* much as twelve was to *Pearl,* which is another reason that the placement of this stanza's bob, next to line 12, is noteworthy. In addition to dividing the page's lines nearly in half, it divides the page into nearly equal thirds: eleven-line gap, twelve long-lines, a break (or Barthesian *punctum*: the bob), then thirteen metrically varied lines. The slight asymmetry of this 11-12-13 division of the page's typical thirty-six-line text-block (not 12-12-12) evokes other forms of anti-exactness, or exceptions to the rule, visible across the manuscript. Specifically, the initial gap also recalls the six-line gap at the top of *Patience*'s opening lines, which had the effect of highlighting the catalog of allegorical *Dames* at the top of the following verso and dividing the poem's sixty-line prologue into equal thirty-line halves, on either side of folio 83/87. We may therefore be more inclined to consider how this still more dramatic gap shapes the text of this page as a whole.

22. "I shall tell it right quick as I heard it in town with tongue: as it is stood and stuck in strong, unwavering story, fastened with loyal letters, as it has long been in the land" (lines 31–36).

23. Herman, "With Lel Lettres Loken," 313. Using the *Middle English Dictionary,* he translates these words as "fixed (in legend)," "retained, remembered," and "fastened, locked," respectively. He further notes that *loken* can mean "'set,' referring to a jewel" (311), another connection to *Pearl* though not noted by him. Dwyer likewise notes that the wheel's terms "evoke stable, material phenomena, not unstably variable speech" ("Reading the Tied Letters," 23). On the poem's complex use and invitation of metapoetic metaphors, see Solberg, "Imagining the Bob and Wheel," 57.

Doing so allows folio 91/95r to emerge with self-contained if complex literary coherence: after eleven lines of suspense, the first twelve lines take us from Troy's fall to the Italian peninsula, while the final thirteen ground us in the narrower confines of Britain, a shift that the bob marks visually, as noted above. This narrowing of focus continues, for the final lines of 91/95r conclude still more specifically by declaring that "of alle þat here bult, of Bretaygne kynges / ay watȝ Arthur þe hendest as I haf herde telle" ("of all the kings of Britain that built here, / Arthur was always the noblest as I have heard tell," lines 25–26). This third reference to Britain recalls lines 13–14, reinforcing the suggestion of an internal division at the end of line 12. Using a verb of construction like *bult* ("built," line 25) to describe the activities of kings of yore subtly recalls the artefactual nature of the book in which these activities are narrated, further inviting a material reading of this idiosyncratic page's verse.

The fact that the following page, 91/95v, starts with a rhetorical gesture of commencement ("Forþi an aunter in erde I attle to schawe" ["Therefore I intend to show a marvel on earth," line 27]), also retrospectively implies that the lines on the recto served as a self-contained prologue or stage-setting for the main event. The suggestiveness of its twenty-five total lines is clear, given that number's significance to *Sir Gawain* and the dramatic gap at the top of the page that completes the manuscript's usual thirty-six-line text-block. Its three references to Britain even appear at five-line intervals. All of this number play collapses if we award the bob its own line for purposes of reckoning, however, since by that lineation 91/95r contains lines 1–26 of the poem, rather than the symbolically significant twenty-five. And yet at least one enticing numerical shape of *Sir Gawain* depends upon the bobs being counted as their own lines: only thus does it contain 2,530 total lines, highlighted by its 101 stanzas (since 2,530 divided by 101 equals twenty-five with a remainder of five). Such tension is yet another way in which the bob pulls in two different, seemingly contradictory directions. Moreover, this form of tension is familiar, by now, from other moments in the manuscript, which we have seen in multiple media.

Counting the bobs toward numeration when it suits us (so that the poem has 2,530 lines) and not when it doesn't (so that 91/95r has twenty-five lines) sounds like having one's cake and eating it too, a noted mortal impossibility. But the supereffability of *Pearl* has invited reading in defiance of such earthly constraints, for "more and more" ways of finding beautiful shapes in the Pearl-Manuscript; and the character of the bobs offers one concrete, materially grounded way of doing so. My suggestion is therefore that together, the poem and the manuscript encourage us to read the bobs both where they are written in the manuscript, with all the complexity that creates; and as printed in editions, where they visually arrest the preceding long-lines and aurally initiate us into the wheel. The bobs' temporal and sensory doubleness invites us to read them as both lines and not-lines for the purposes of numerical shape-making, and the fact that they sometimes seem repetitive, even pointless, further endorses this way of reckoning them: they have complex shaping power even when narratively otiose.

Such "both-and" counting of bobs recalls Laura Ashe's account of "true contradictions" in medieval philosophy.[24] In this context, it is worth lingering on the fact that each of the Pearl-Manuscript's four poems has now featured at least one page whose anomalous layout enhances its text's literary potential: the last page of *Pearl* (55/59v), considered in chapter 3; the last page of *Cleanness* and first page of *Patience* (82/86r, 83/87r), considered in chapter 5; and the first page of *Sir Gawain* (91/95r), considered here. The invitation to perceive such page-shapes as meaningful emerges gradually and is shaped by the themes and forms of the poems. The supereffability of *Pearl* first encourages counterintuitive and paradoxical perspectives; then *Cleanness*'s emphasis on the moral significance of material craft generally, and of scribal craft specifically, further suggests that we attend closely to the manuscript's own complex shapes. *Patience*'s echoes of the first two poems confirm the rewards of reading the Pearl-Manuscript as a whole, while its inversion of the Rule of Gregory offers another way of finding resonance in the manuscript's materiality. Such gradually emerging perceptual challenges offer a ladder of speculative reading.

As such, *Sir Gawain and the Green Knight* becomes a kind of summa of the Pearl-Manuscript's art: its last, longest, and most complex poem. The following chapter will argue that *Sir Gawain*'s delights are inherently cumulative, in the sense that it gains meaning by echoing its precedents in the manuscript, even as tantalizing hints of its origins and reception invite us to speculate still more widely for clues to unlocking its courtly complexities. Yet its intertextuality and evocation of the "real world" also become the slipperiness by which *Sir Gawain* continues to elude our grasp. If *Pearl* was a (nearly) perfect sphere, then *Sir Gawain*'s fivefold facets give it a sharper and more angular character, one that resists singular interpretations—whether historicist, mathematical, or theological. Accordingly, rather than attempt a singular denouement, my final chapter will chase three distinct, occasionally overlapping threads of Sir Gawain's endless knot.

24. Ashe, "How to Read Both."

EIGHT

CHASING SIR GAWAIN'S ENDLESS KNOT

The last chapter proposed that the opening of *Sir Gawain and the Green Knight*, folios 90/94v+91/95r, especially rewards the deployment of our speculative faculties. Their multimodal shapes and temporalities anticipate *Sir Gawain*'s own poetic innovations, which constitute one important aspect of the Pearl-Manuscript's complex engagement with literary and bookish forms of newness. As we saw in the introduction, its decorative motifs look old-fashioned, even archaizing, and its scribe, "even if he was writing in the Ricardian period, was looking back," as Kathryn Kerby-Fulton has shown.[1] Yet two of its poems, *Sir Gawain* and *Pearl*, shape established literary tools and motifs into new, indeed unique, poetic forms. I will suggest that comparably resonant constellations of old and new emerge across two sets of cross-textual echoes: *Sir Gawain*'s of *Cleanness*, especially in their depiction of paper and parchment; and, more speculatively, the approving reference to "Gawayn, with his olde curteisye" in Chaucer's *Squire's Tale* (*Canterbury Tales*, 5.95).[2] This reference enhances the Squire's later repeated depiction of the quiddity, the point, of literary production as a *knotte* (5.401, 408): a very rare word in Chaucer but famously central to *Sir Gawain*. Its function in the *Squire's Tale* echoes the knot's comparably metaliterary quality in *Sir Gawain*, where it evolves from a chivalric symbol of geometric and moral perfection into the manipulable part of the (seemingly) contrasting Green Girdle—itself first a female undergarment, untied to seduce; then retied as a baldric, displayed to the world. As that by which the girdle continues be reshaped, literally and metaphorically, the knot becomes a figure for endless interpretability.[3]

Comparable endlessness-effects can be seen in how ambiguously, and

1. Kerby-Fulton, Olson, and Hilmo, *Opening up Middle English Manuscripts*, 57.

2. All Chaucer references are to the third edition of the *Riverside Chaucer*; parenthetical citations of the *Canterbury Tales* give fragment and line number as printed there.

3. On knots in medieval culture more broadly, see further Bernau, "Figuring with Knots."

multiply, *Sir Gawain* unspools across its final bob-and-wheel, the famous Order of the Garter motto just below, the little-remarked Middle English couplet at the top of the facing page, and three concluding illustrations—the only ones in the manuscript to follow, rather than precede, the poem they depict. Each of these additions creates new layers of interpretive potential around the end of the Pearl-Manuscript, an accretive development of aesthetic meaning reminiscent of *Pearl*, in particular. Likewise reminiscent of *Pearl* is this paradox: these add-ons, or outgrowths, mar the *Pearl*-like patterning of *Sir Gawain*'s final long-line (2525, which loops back to line 1, just like *Pearl* 1212/1211); yet by recalling earlier moments in the Pearl-Manuscript, they offer to loop us back still further, across and into the codex as a whole. Such complex, overlapping patterns give its final pages a paradoxically generative form of closure, whereby finishing the book invites the reader to leaf back through it, or open it once more.

MATERIAL DEVOTION

I begin with Gawain's shield, whose "endeles knot" we began to consider in chapter 7. That famous shape, the pentangle displayed to the world, contrasts notably with the image of the Virgin Mary, which is set within the shield itself as well as the larger narration of Gawain's five fivefold excellences, the fourth of which is his devotion to the five joys of the Virgin:

> his þro þoȝt watȝ in þat, þurȝ alle oþer þyngeȝ,
> þat alle his forsnes he fong at þe fyue joyeȝ
> þat þe hende Heuen-quene had of hir Chylde.
> At þis cause þe knyȝt comlyche hade
> in þe inore half of his schelde hir ymage depaynted,
> þat quen he blusched þerto his belde neuer payred.
> Þe fyft fyue þat I finde þat þe frek vsed. . . .[4]

Both images are "painted" (lines 620, 649), but whereas the pentangle takes shape impersonally, in the passive voice (lines 619–20 and 660), Gawain himself commissions the Virgin's image, as lines 648–49 above make clear.

4. "His earnest intent was that, through all other things, he should take [*fong*, lit. "seize, grasp"] all his courage from the five joys that the noble queen of Heaven had of her Child. For this reason, the knight graciously had her image painted in the inner half of his shield, so that when he looked upon it his courage never faltered. The fifth [set of] five that I find the man used . . ." (lines 645–51).

The next line reinforces this intimacy by emphasizing that visual contemplation ("quen he blusched þerto") strengthens his commitment to the chivalric perfection that his pentangle represents. As she does in Christianity more broadly, Mary mediates between human and ideal.[5]

Gawain's mode of apprehension, which is visual, anagogical, and devotional, shares elements of speculation as outlined in chapter 1, which the Pearl-Manuscript has invited at multiple points and in multiple media. The relationship that his shield suggests is also implicitly three-dimensional: from Gawain's eyes to the inward-facing image of the Virgin, and thence both back at him and, with her inspiration, outward to the pentangle seen by the rest of the world.[6] The lexicon of his devotion is also strikingly concrete: the Virgin's image helps him "grasp" (*fong*, line 646) her five joys, a verb that recalls Gawain's second fivefold excellence: "efte fayled neuer þe freke in his fyue fyngres" ("likewise the man never failed in his five fingers," line 641). This image of Gawain grasping or seizing at the Virgin's five joys—one of his pentangle's five, fivefold points—suggests a handhold from which his excellence can expand outward, through his fingers, to trace the shape on his shield. The fact that Gawain needs inspiration from the Virgin to do so emphasizes, at the moment of his ceremonial public association with abstract, geometric perfection, the protagonist's humanity—which is to say, from the poet's Christian perspective, his imperfection.

From Gawain's personalized devotion of lines 648–50, the poet resumes counting the knight's fivefold virtues with the first first-person pronoun in over twenty lines: "Þe fyft fyue þat I finde . . ." ("The fifth [set of] five that I find," line 651). This phrase of finding anticipates the poet's failure to find a fault in the figure of Gawain's perfection: "withouten ende at any noke *I oquere fynde*, / whereeuer þe gomen bygan or glod to an ende" ("without end at any nook *I find anywhere* / wherever the game began or came to an end," lines 660–61). Celebrating the pentangle's perfection in terms of a personalized, metapoetic admission of failure subtly prefigures Gawain's own failure to properly play the exchange-of-winnings game at Castle Hautdesert. Indeed, Paul F. Reichardt suggests that the decorator has inscribed skepticism

5. On Marian contexts for the poem, see Russell, "Sir Gawain and the White Monks."

6. On the optical theories that informed the poet's sources and near contemporaries, such as Jean de Meun, see Akbari, *Seeing through the Veil*; Biernoff, *Sight and Embodiment*; Denery, *Seeing and Being Seen*; Eberle, "The Lovers' Glass"; and Lindberg, *Theories of Vision*. The poet's evident learning suggests he may have been aware of the thirteenth-century Baconian synthesis of extramissive and intramissive theories of vision, by means of a theory known as "the multiplication of species."

FIGURE 8.1. Folio 99/103r of Cotton Nero A.x/2. Decorated initial next to lines 619–21 of *Sir Gawain and the Green Knight*. Photograph © 2024 by The British Library Board.

about Gawain's geometric perfection into the expression of the face inhabiting the initial where his pentangle is first mentioned (lines 619–21; see fig. 8.1[7]).

If the pentangle offers an ideal that no human can ever fully embody, then the image of the Virgin reminds us of the mercy with which she, and through her God, will respond to our inevitable failures. Metaphorically, divine mercy recognizes our three-dimensionality: our inability, as fallen mortals, to conform to the flat ideals of two-dimensional geometry. Here, the Virgin's protection is physical as well as spiritual, since the three-dimensionality provided by the backside of the shield, where she appears, is precisely what makes it a useful object. Shields must have depth, not just height and breadth, in order to offer protection; a two-dimensional shield is just a piece of paper.

In chapter 4, we saw paper associated with the empty pomp and sacrilege of Belshazzar's Feast, specifically its gaudy decorative elements.[8] The material's second and final appearance in the Pearl-Manuscript is more complex, for it describes Bertilak's Castle Hautdesert, which appears shortly

7. This is the fourth and last inhabited initial in the manuscript, and the first since lines 841–43 of *Pearl*. Reichardt notes that, compared with the previous three, it features "a slight elongation of the head, increased sloping of the eye lines, and a marked drooping of the mouth, a feature that produces a distinct expression of dismay or disapprobation." He further suggests that, "compared with the perfect purity of the Lamb [highlighted by the previous such face], the claims made for the pentangle could evoke a judicious measure of skepticism in the mind of a pious reader, and this skepticism may be mirrored in the dour features of the fourth ornamented capital face," though he acknowledges that more sympathetic assessments of its expression could also be advanced ("Paginal Eyes," 23, 28).

8. Orietta da Rold notes this association between sin (pride, especially) and castellated paper decorations for feasts in Chaucer's *Parson's Tale*, too, concluding that "paper decorations

after Gawain's earnest prayer to God and the Virgin for safe lodging (line 754), and scarcely a hundred lines after the description of her image in his shield. The nearly forty lines devoted to the castle's intricate construction conclude thus:

> chalk-whyt chymnees þer ches he innoȝe
> vpon bastel roueȝ þat blenked ful quyte—
> so mony pynakle payntet watȝ poudred ayquere
> among þe castel carneleȝ, clambred so þik,
> þat pared out of papure purely hit semed.[9]

Paper's association with pride and debauchery in *Cleanness* suggests a cautionary reading of Castle Hautdesert that will be validated, in some measure, by Gawain's failure to adhere strictly to the terms of its exchange-of-winnings game. Morally suspect excess may be further if lightly suggested by the phrase "clambred so þik" ("clustered so thickly," line 801), which contrasts with the evenness of Gawain's pentangle as previously described, whose five points "fayld neuer, / [n]e *samned neuer in no syde*, ne sundred nouþer" ("never failed, *neither gathered in any one side*, nor sundered either," lines 658–59).

Other elements of Hautdesert's construction, however, evoke *Cleanness*'s beautiful ekphrasis of Solomon's sacred vessels, for both passages delight in a technical lexicon of architectural decoration: *fylyolez*, *coprounes*, and *pynacles* describe both Bertilak's castle and Solomon's curiously castellated cups.[10] Orietta da Rold also notes this passage's "exquisite architectural details," and she persuasively suggests that the reference to chalk and paper quoted above "evokes the tools of architects and artists . . . [since they] painted with chalk and shaped forms with paper."[11] She regards these architectural associations as largely superseding paper's earlier association with sinful extravagance, but I wonder whether both sets of associations might not uneasily coexist,

are indeed considered by Chaucer and the *Gawain* poet as extravagant and redundant luxuries in their pious texts" (*Paper in Medieval England*, 193). See also Stanbury, *Seeing the Gawain-Poet*, 64–66.

9. "Chalk-white chimneys he saw plenty of there, which glistened quite dazzlingly above the roofs of towers, so many painted pinnacles sprinkled all about among the castle battlements, clustered so thickly, that it seemed entirely cut out of paper" (lines 798–802).

10. *Cleanness* 1462 and *Sir Gawain* 796; *Cleanness* 1461 and *Sir Gawain* 797; and *Cleanness* 1463 and *Sir Gawain* 800, respectively. *Cop(er)roun* and *fylyoles* appear nowhere else in the manuscript, further linking the two passages.

11. Da Rold, *Paper in Medieval England*, 195.

depending on when and how we read.[12] She rightly notes that "there is no worry, hesitation or fear when Gawain approaches the castle," which must appear welcoming and innocent enough for him to let down his guard—he is formally disarmed at lines 861–63. But as she also notes, "if the critic . . . knows about the magical nature of the castle by hindsight, then she might interpret the comparison to paper as a symbol of the castle's worldliness and insubstantiality."[13] This (re)reading is persuasive on its own terms and also nicely enacts the evolving nature of literary apprehension: multiple perspectives shift in and out of view, much as Castle Hautdesert seems to when Gawain first sees it: "as hit schemered and schon þurȝ þe schyre okeȝ" ("as if shimmering and shining through the bright oaks," line 772).

The fundamental ambivalence of Hautdesert and its household is thus suggested by the competing associations of its material appearance: its elaborate architectural ornamentation recalls *Cleanness*'s earlier depiction of holy craftedness in Solomon's vessels, but the reference to paper may also recall the prideful pomp of Belshazzar's Feast, where those very vessels are desecrated. Paper's greater complexity, as a figure, in *Sir Gawain* compared to *Cleanness* is an example of what I mean in calling the former a delightful "final trial" of our speculative capacities, two of which are reflection and retrospection. If, like Gawain, we are taken in by Hautdesert's (or the poem's) enticing surfaces on a first reading, then intertextual echoes like those considered here offer a concrete invitation to reflect later on whether we could, or should, have seen it coming. I agree with da Rold that, even if we ultimately (re)read textual echoes like "pared out of papure" as cautionary, the passage includes enough counterindications, like the echoes of Solomon's "cleanly wrought" vessels, that it resists secure interpretation the first time we encounter it. This debatability is part of the point, I believe, for the intertextuality created by such echoic diction is one way in which the Pearl-Manuscript proposes itself as a fit object for repeated reading and study. Here, we should recall Sara Ritchey's account of the *Speculum virginum*, whose multiple and

12. Da Rold writes: "Paper is the object which conveys forms and reality, rather than an agent of magic or deception" (*Paper in Medieval England*, 198), and while I agree with the first set of associations, I do not find those mutually exclusive with the second. For as she earlier acknowledges, "[t]he arrogance of Morgan and her strong feelings against Guinevere and Arthur's court might have inspired the *Gawain* poet to juxtapose paper, food decoration, and pride, creating an explicit intertextual link with his other work and possibly wider cultural references" (*Paper in Medieval England*, 194). I suggest this is indeed one way that the Pearl-Manuscript's references to paper could act, then and now.

13. Da Rold, *Paper in Medieval England*, 194.

shifting referents train pious readers to see more clearly the beauty of God's Creation.[14] *Sir Gawain*'s placement within the Pearl-Manuscript enables it to function comparably for different audiences, using the *materia* of courtly romance and the potential of compilational interlace to stimulate both delight and self-reflection.

Such self-reflection is required for confession, whose importance to *Sir Gawain* can be seen in the periodically buzzing scholarly conversation about Gawain's confession just after accepting Lady Bertilak's girdle.[15] Hautdesert's apparently paper construction may therefore recall a contrasting moment in *Cleanness*: the Pearl-Manuscript's only reference to parchment, an older material with very different affordances and associations. It appears in a passage about the importance of confession and penance:

¶ So if folk be defowled by vnfre chaunce, [1129]
þat he be sulped in sawle, seche to schryfte,
and he may **polyce** hym at þe prest by **penaunce** taken,
wel bryʒter þen þe beryl oþer browden perles.
¶ Bot war þe wel, if þou be waschen wyth water of schryfte, [1133]
and **polysed** als playn **as parchmen schauen,**
sulp no more þenne in synne þy saule þerafter,
for þenne þou Dryʒten dyspleses with dedes ful sore,
¶ and entyses hym to tene more trayþly þen euer, [1137]
and wel hatter to hate þen hade þou nat waschen. . . . [16]

These lines' references to polishing link the sacrament of penance to parchment-scraping, a metaphor worth noting given parchment's contrast with paper in this regard.[17] Scraping allowed scribes to correct mistakes by "shaving" the surface of the parchment, which could then be polished and

14. Ritchey, *Holy Matter*, 24–54. See further chap. 1, page 36.

15. E.g., Wasserman and Purdon, "Sir Guido and the Green Light"; and Outhwaite, "Sir Gawain's Penitential Development."

16. "So if someone is befouled by ignoble circumstance, such that his soul is polluted, he may seek confession and **polish** himself at the priest, by receiving **penance**, much brighter than the beryl or embroidered pearls. But be well aware [or "beware"], if you are washed with the water of confession, and **polished** as smooth as **scraped parchment**, do not pollute your soul in sin afterwards, for then you displease the Lord very grievously with your deeds, and provoke him to anger more grievously than ever, and to hate more fiercely than if you had not washed" (lines 1129–38, emphasis added).

17. As Andrew and Waldron point out, an extended version of this simile also appears in a twelfth-century sermon "designed to appeal to illuminators of manuscripts" (*Poems*, 159; Olsen's edition also notes this analogue).

rewritten upon.[18] Paper did not admit of such erasure nearly so readily, however, because its greater porosity allowed ink to seep in more deeply.[19] As a result, those working with paper relied more on strike-throughs and other forms of correction that left the original error visible.

I believe this context should inform our assessment of the Green Knight's own assessment of Gawain's fault, which echoes the passages considered above:

> "I halde hit hardily hole, þe harme þat I hade.
> Þou art confessed so **clene**, beknowen of þy mysses,
> and hatȝ þe **penaunce** apert of þe poynt of myn egge,
> I halde þe **polysed** of þat plyȝt and pured as **clene**
> as þou hadeȝ neuer forfeted syþen þou watȝ fyrst borne."[20]

The first use of *clene* in line 2391 prepares us for the other echoes of *Cleanness* above, which are sealed by the repetition of *clene* two lines later, thereby enclosing the textual echo and presenting it to readers as an interpretive opportunity. I suggest that its sacramental echo helps the later scene serve as a moment of metajudgment by inviting us to assess for ourselves: Is the Green Knight a fitting confessor, and do we, or should we, hold Gawain in comparably high esteem? Such questions have long inspired readers, as the many fine interpretations of *Sir Gawain*'s denouement attest; the contrasting affordances of paper and parchment may offer a useful lens for considering these scenes afresh.

Recognizing that paper encouraged strike-through as a method of correction, rather than the scraping and erasure commonly used with parchment, suggests that we attend closely to the varying accounts of Gawain's nicked neck, the site of his "penaunce apert" ("clear/open penance"). As we have just seen, the Green Knight uses language of polishing and wholeness to emphasize the fullness of Gawain's satisfaction; but although the poet, describing Gawain's return to Camelot, is unambiguous that "þe hurt watȝ hole þat he

18. See further Wakelin, *Scribal Correction*, 102–9.

19. See da Rold, *Paper in Medieval England*, 114–16, and 198–208 (on paper's porosity). Wakelin also notes the rarity of correction-by-erasure in paper manuscripts (*Scribal Correction*, 104).

20. "I consider it entirely whole, the harm that I had [i.e., Gawain's failure to adhere to the terms of the Green Knight's game]. You have confessed so fully [*clene*], acknowledged your misdeeds, and received clear **penance** from the point of my blade, such that I hold you **polished** of that guilt, and purified as completely [*clene*] as if you had never transgressed since you were first born" (lines 2390–94).

hade hent in his nek" ("the hurt that he had received in his neck was whole," line 2484; note the repetition of the word *hole* from the Green Knight's earlier speech), Gawain himself is equally emphatic, later, that his neck remains marked: "'Lo, lorde,' coþe þe leude, and þe lace hondeled, / 'Þis is þe bende of þis blame I bere in my nek'" ("'Lo, lord,' said the man, as he handled the fabric, 'This [baldric] is the band/binding of this blame that I bear in my neck,'" lines 2505–6). Gawain's use of the present tense ("this blame that *I bear*") suggests that the wound has become a scar—which, indeed, is how Andrew and Waldron gloss *blame* in their edition of the poem.[21] Like paper, whose porosity made it resistant to erasure, Gawain remains marked by his fault: his scar, like a strike-through, becomes an ugly but necessary testament to human frailty.[22]

Gawain's inability to accept this ultimately superficial imperfection may therefore suggest a failure to recognize that our souls are less porous than paper, as *Cleanness*'s simile makes clear: Christ's sacrifice means that our sins really can be scraped and polished away. *Cleanness*'s association of penance with "browden perles" ("embroidered pearls," line 1132), as well as polishing and parchment, further links that passage to the Green Knight's reassurance of Gawain, who he later claims is "[a]s perle bi þe quite pese" ("like a pearl next to white peas," line 2364) when compared to other knights. But Gawain is not comparing himself to other knights, which is why he takes no comfort in either Bertilak's compliment or his comrades' jovial reassurance back at Camelot. Rather, he seems to be measuring himself against his pentangle, which suggests that his deeper flaw may be to have pridefully aspired to the kind of perfection that can inhere in geometry, but not in humans; to have believed the hype of those who shaped the knot on his shield—and forgotten the Virgin painted inside. Like the poet, who tried and failed to find a fault in the perfect pentangle thus ascribed to him, Gawain has failed to shape a perfect figure; and in that, at least, he is like all of us, as well.[23]

21. Andrew and Waldron, *Poems*, 299.

22. Indeed, da Rold suggests that this quality made paper attractive to the rapidly expanding bureaucratic and merchant class, which had an obvious interest in making it difficult to erase "any fraudulent interference with accounting, notarial and legal practices" (*Paper in Medieval England*, 115). The fact that later strike-throughs of the Pearl-Manuscript's initial foliation scheme are still visible on nearly every recto adds another degree of cross-temporal resonance to the thread I am tracing.

23. See further Bahr, "Compulsory Figures." We might also recall the story of Giotto's perfectly free-formed circle: his audition, supposedly, for a papal commission, and one that implied divine gifts since human beings are not compasses and should therefore not be able to produce such perfection. Thanks to Seth Lerer for this connection.

The echoes across this series of passages thus suggest complex, intertextual use of the different associations and affordances of paper and parchment, especially their typical methods of correction. These poetic references to scribal material refract intriguingly through the idiosyncratic materiality of the Pearl-Manuscript. Jane Roberts draws attention to its "simple pen-flourishing, usual from Romanesque book production onwards but by this time perhaps less fashionable," and Kathryn Kerby-Fulton notes the archaism of the scribe's *textualis rotunda media*, "a script that usually belongs to the thirteenth century, not the second half of the fourteenth century."[24] Archaism thus feels inscribed into the Pearl-Manuscript from its inception, despite its literary innovations and the strikingly avant-garde later addition of illustrations. Seamus Dwyer, meanwhile, reminds us that "in the fourteenth century, textualis's visually wrought aspect was most often used to clothe the most transcendent kinds of language: texts of scripture and of liturgy."[25]

Together, these associations suggest an evolving, slightly sacral archaism that I believe adds resonance to the Pearl-Manuscript's complex references to parchment and paper. Read through this lens, the poet's depiction of Gawain's form of spiritual misreading—supposing that his soul absorbs sin like paper, unable to be scraped, polished, and repurified like parchment—might look like oblique sympathy for the older and more monastic writing medium. As chapter 6's speculation into the warty growths of folio 89/93 made clear, moreover, the Pearl-Manuscript is emphatically parchment—animal skin, stretched and scraped—whose rough, often uneven construction would reinforce its difference from paper for those handling the book. Paper has many more associations in medieval England than novelty and extravagance, as da Rold expertly shows, so I do not propose a wholly cautionary reading of Hautdesert's paper-like appearance.[26] But the speculative opportunities it creates are enhanced by encountering this complex set of references to scribal craft in an idiosyncratic parchment book whose sympathetic conversance with monastic writing culture *Cleanness* has already made clear. In the following section, I will suggest that *Sir Gawain*'s paradoxically innovative archaism also resonates in a later poem explicitly concerned with novelty, literary and otherwise: Chaucer's *Squire's Tale*. The goal of this

24. Roberts, "Hand and Script," 2–3; Kerby-Fulton, Olson, and Hilmo, *Opening up Middle English Manuscripts*, 56.

25. Dwyer, "Reading the Tied Letters," 3.

26. Da Rold cites chromaticity, plasticity, porosity, and tensility as the chief ways in which paper captured the imagination of literary authors (*Paper in Medieval England*, 180–209).

outward turn is to illustrate the potential of speculative reading beyond the Pearl-Manuscript.

CHAUCER READS SIR GAWAIN

The *Squire's Tale* invites reading through the lens of *Sir Gawain and the Green Knight* in several distinct though ultimately overlapping ways: narratively, through shared plot points that include an initiating royal feasting scene interrupted by a mysterious knight; referentially, by the positive comparison of Chaucer's mystery-knight to "Gawayn, with his olde curteisye" (5.95, his only such reference); and lexically, through a later *occupatio* on literary value bookended by the word *knotte*, which is rare in Chaucer but obviously central to *Sir Gawain*.[27] The *Squire's Tale* has sometimes been read as suggesting Chaucer's disdain for Arthurian romance and the "native English" literary tradition more broadly, a reading that might seem reinforced by the *General Prologue*'s depiction of the pilgrim-Squire as young and poetically inclined, continentally affiliated and fashion-forward. Yet as Patricia Clare Ingham has shown, the *Squire's Tale* also makes newness "inherently paradoxical, a feature of creative production that can produce breakaway moments, even as it partakes of older, repetitive forms."[28] I believe *Sir Gawain and the Green Knight* does something similar, and I therefore hear in the Squire's echoes of *Sir Gawain* a respectful nod to the older poem, whose synthesis of old and new affords endlessly generative literary potential.[29] Such speculation about reading habits and authorial intention feels taboo, almost like fan fiction; I propose it rather as a thought experiment in reading for what we might find rather than only for what we can know.

I begin by returning to the knots of *Sir Gawain*. Many fine studies have explored the complexities of the Green Girdle, particularly the poem's shifting, conflicting accounts of what it does and means.[30] This labile quality contrasts sharply with Gawain's precisely and exhaustively symbolized

27. Besides the two instances in the *Squire's Tale* (5.401, 407), the word makes just one other appearance in the *Tales* (10.494). There is also one occurrence each in *Troilus* (3.1732), *Boece* (5.30), and the *Romaunt* (B.4698).

28. Ingham, *The Medieval New*, 138.

29. On revisionist arguments that the Pearl-Poems are Edwardian (ca. 1350s–70s) rather than Ricardian (1370s–90s), see introduction, n. 36. These arguments—many ongoing or unpublished at the time of this writing—have provisionally persuaded me that *Sir Gawain* was written perhaps a generation before Chaucer composed the *Squire's Tale*.

30. See in particular Hanna, "Unlocking What's Locked," and Heng, "Feminine Knots."

pentangle, the "endeles knot" with which he is first associated. It is therefore striking that the word "knot" should describe the girdle, too, in a climactic moment of self-denunciation:

> "Corsed worth cowarddyse and couetyse boþe!
> In yow is vylany and vyse, þat vertue disstryeȝ."
> Þenne he **kaȝt to þe knot** and þe kest lawseȝ,
> brayde broþely þe belt to þe burne seluen:
> "Lo þer þe fals þyng, foule mot hit falle!
> For care of þy knokke, cowardyse me taȝt
> to acorde me with couetyse, my kynde to forsake,
> þat is larges and lewte þat longeȝ to knyȝteȝ."[31]

The rough physicality with which Gawain catches at the knot recalls the comparably tactile language with which he earlier seized (*fong*, line 646) fortitude from the five joys of the Virgin, the image within his shield whose pentangle the word "knot" here vividly echoes. Having (temporarily) set aside his shield and accepted the Green Girdle at Hautdesert, Gawain is now (he claims) defined not by such virtue as "longeȝ to knyȝteȝ" and symbolized by the "endeles knot," but rather by the other, ignoble knot that he here unties and casts aside.

The girdle's physical manipulability reinforces its symbolic malleability, and, sure enough, this is not the poem's last word on the matter. Gawain ultimately reclaims and reshapes the girdle into (he says) an outwardly visible spur to humility:

> "Bot in syngne of my surfet **I schal se hit ofte** . . .
> And þus, quen pryde schal me pryk for prowes of armes,
> þe **loke** to þis luf-lace schal leþe my hert."[32]

31. "Cursed be both cowardice and covetousness! In you is villainy and vice, which destroy virtue." Then he **seized at the knot** and loosened the fastening, violently flung the belt to the man [the Green Knight] himself: "Lo, there is the false thing—may ill befall it! For fear of your stroke, cowardice taught me to accord with covetousness and forsake my nature, which is the generosity and loyalty that belong to knights" (lines 2374–81). Other editions read *falssyng* ("falsehood") in line 2378; for the reading "fals þyng" ("false thing"), adopted above, see McGillivray, *Sir Gawain and the Green Knight*, 324.

32. "But as a sign of my transgression/excess **I shall see it often. . . .** And thus, when pride in my martial prowess goads me, a **look** to this love-lace will humble my heart" (lines 2433, 2437–38). Gawain's use of the word *schal* ironically reinforces the pride he describes by presenting his future martial exploits as a matter of certainty.

This gesture contrasts sharply with Gawain's previous mode of finding inspiration: from an image of the Virgin visible only to him, within his shield, "quen he blusched þerto" ("when he looked upon it," line 650). Now he both contemplates and displays a very different icon, putatively to mortify his pride, but in highly performative fashion, such that his own "prowes of armes" and the amorous powers implied by "þis luf-lace" become the center of attention.

This is a striking change from his earlier specular practice, emphasized by his subsequent attempt to reshape the object itself, from feminine love-trinket into masculine baldric:

> and þe blykkande belt he bere þeraboute,
> abelef, **as a bauderyk, bounded** bi his syde,
> **loken** vnder his lyfte arme, þe **lace, with a knot,**
> in tokenyng he watȝ tane in tech of a faute.[33]

The reference to binding and locking suggests an attempt to impose interpretive mastery, sealed by the knot: what Gawain untied, he can retie, and redefine in so doing. But though bound as a baldric, it remains "the lace" in the following line, and these words' competing associations are tied together in the figure of the knot—which necessarily recalls his shield's pentangle (the "endeles knot"), as well. The knot thus begins to emerge as a metaphor for interpretability itself, and the challenge of locking literary meaning in place. It is this quality of the knot in *Sir Gawain* that I believe resonates in the *Squire's Tale*, to which I now turn.

One reason *Sir Gawain* offers a useful lens for the *Squire's Tale* is that it helps unite the latter's opening feasting scene (part 1) with its subsequent avian courtly-love drama (part 2). Early similarities in plot between the two poems prepare us to hear additional, subtler echoes such as the repeated use of *knotte* in part 2. I begin with a list of suggestive similarities:

1. Both poems open with scenes of feasting interrupted by a mysterious knight bearing strange gifts: magic devices in the *Squire's Tale*; in *Sir Gawain*, the offer of a Christmas game and the chance to prove the mettle of Arthur's court.
2. The knight's arrival in the *Squire's Tale* also prompts Chaucer's only mention of Gawain: the sudden visitor's excellence of speech and countenance is such

33. "And he bore the shining belt about himself, diagonally, as a baldric, **bound** by his side, the **lace locked** under his left arm **with a knot**, in tokening of his having been taken in the stain/sign of a fault" (lines 2485–88).

"that Gawayn, with his olde courteisie / Though he were comen ayeyn out of Fairye, / Ne koude hym nat amende with a word" (5.95–97).

3. From there both poems explore the erotics of "trawthe" and courtly-love speech: the bedroom scenes of *Sir Gawain*, and the seduction and betrayal of the female falcon by her smooth-talking avian lover in Chaucer's poem.
4. Both poems also take up the question of how meaning inheres in, or can be ascribed to, various talismans of the chivalric world: the brass steed, in particular, that excites such fevered speculation among onlookers in the *Squire's Tale*; Gawain's pentangle and then the Green Girdle that he brings back to Camelot, which is subject to frequent interpretive reshaping, as we have seen.

Such tangent points across the two poems encourage the kind of speculation that this book has proposed: reading for what can be seen, rather than what cannot. Here I propose reading the *Squire's Tale* as if an echo of *Sir Gawain and the Green Knight*.

Chaucer's mention of Gawain is significant because it cites him as a celebrated precedent to whom the mysterious knight favorably compares. The image of Gawain's old courtesy stepping out of Fairyland and into the Squire's more fashion-forward literary concoction is crystallized by a parallel figure in both poems: the mysterious knight with strange gifts to whom Gawain is compared explicitly (in the *Squire's Tale*) and implicitly (in *Sir Gawain*) by means of parallels between him and the Green Knight noted in chapter 7. Such parallels create an uncanny moment of mirroring across the two poems and their authors. Multiple forms of mirroring feature prominently in *Sir Gawain* and the Pearl-Manuscript as well, and cumulatively such tangent points invite us to juxtapose the two poems more venturesomely.

One thing we find in so doing is a shared interest in intertextuality and metaliterariness. The constellation of paper-and-parchment imagery considered in the previous section is a good example of what I mean by that, and a comparable though differently inflected version of this phenomenon can be heard in Chaucer's highly complex self-quotation within the female falcon's lament, a lyric set piece embedded within the *Squire's Tale*. That this tour de force is set within the self-described *knotte* of the Squire's performance offers an additional through-line to *Sir Gawain*, where the *endeles knot* of the pentangle-turned-girdle-turned-baldric became a figure, not for any particular shape (since it keeps changing), but rather for endless interpretability and in that sense for literariness itself. The cross-vocalizations and intertextuality of the falcon's lament create a comparable engine of interpretation, introduced as a *knotte*, and for Chaucer so to have described it helps suggest the appreciative echo of *Sir Gawain* I have proposed.

Having established some resonant parallels between the two poems, and thus hopefully supplied the necessary activation energy, let us dive more deeply into Chaucer's *knotte* so as to see what happens when we combine these two particular poetic reagents. I first consider the eight-line *occupatio* that twice uses the word *knotte* to describe the point or "why" of storytelling, thereby focusing the reader's attention on the narrative thus described.[34] The Squire cuts short his narration of Canacee's preparation for a garden walk as follows:

> The **knotte** why that every tale is toold,
> If it be taried til that lust be coold
> Of hem that han it after herkned yoore,
> The savour passeth ever lenger the moore,
> For fulsomnesse of his prolixitee;
> And by the same resoun, thynketh me,
> I sholde to the **knotte** condescende,
> And maken of hir walkyng soone an ende.[35]

This rhetorically sumptuous *occupatio* ("fulsomnesse of his prolixitee" is a fulsome phrase) highlights its metaliterary subject and thus prompts attention to the repetition of *knotte*, a rare word in Chaucer—these are two of just three appearances in the entire *Tales*—but one obviously central to *Sir Gawain*. Fainter echoes of *Sir Gawain* may be heard in 5.402's use of the word *tarrien* to describe narrative dilation; *Sir Gawain* used it thus at line 624, to excuse the poet's long excursus into the symbolism of the knight's pentangle—his endless knot. Such lexical tangents, or nodes, highlight the two poems' shared interest in literary structure: in how disparate narrative threads may be tied into a coherent knot or, conversely, fray wildly outward. In *Sir Gawain*, the knot becomes a figure for interpretation and, in that sense, literariness itself; in the *Squire's Tale*, it is the point that a storyteller mustn't lose sight of lest the audience lose interest. The question now becomes: How do we read, or hear, the *Squire's Tale*'s echo of a famous metaliterary metaphor from a poem, *Sir Gawain*, whose plot it has already several times evoked?

One way is to consider the narrative *knotte* to which the Squire's *occupatio*

34. See also Bernau, "Figuring with Knots," 24–25.

35. "The **knotte** of every tale's telling, if tarried over until desire has cooled in those who listened to it earlier—its savor fades ever longer the more [one keeps talking], for fulsomeness of one's prolixity; and for the same reason, it seems to me that I should get down to [*condescende*] the **knotte**, and quickly make an end of her walking" (*Squire's Tale* 5.401–8, emphasis added).

directs us, namely the female falcon whose love-lament consumes the bulk of part 2. Immediately after the *occupatio* just considered, we read:

Amydde a tree for drye as whit as chalk,
As Canacee was pleyying in hir walk,
Ther sat a faucon over hire heed ful hye,
That with a pitous voys so gan to crye
That all the wode resouned of hire cry.
Ybeten hadde she hirself so pitously
With bothe hir wynges til the rede blood
Ran endelong the tree ther-as she stood.[36]

This haunting image—a chalk-white tree, now blood-red and resounding with the falcon's piercing cry, echoed in adjacent *crye/cry* line-endings (this passage's central hinge)—contrasts strikingly with the Squire's preceding, comically amplified promise to "maken of hir [Canacee's] walkyng soone an ende" (408). Yet in their very different ways, and amplified by the tonal contrast between them, both eight-line passages argue that we should attend especially to the falcon's lament that follows. Doing so reveals a complex aesthetics of new and old that refracts kaleidoscopically across a host of textual echoes: both of *Sir Gawain*—the chalk-white tree above may recall the chalk-white chimneys of Hautdesert noted earlier, for example—and of other points in Chaucer's evolving *Tales* project.

In an important corrective to readings that emphasized the *Squire's Tale*'s supposedly disenchanted skepticism of earlier literary models and motifs, Ingham notes its ambivalent attitude toward novelty, whose attractions inspire both the tercel's treachery and Canacee's ability to understand and heal the abandoned falcon. She concludes:

> Chaucer demonstrates . . . that wonder in the new, precisely as something both unique and repeatable, can . . . create the conditions of possibility for new realizations, new relations, new poems . . . or it can converge in the same-old, same-old, inspiring the consolidating satisfactions of mere accumulation, of a deadening kind of hoarding.[37]

36. "In the middle of a tree as dry and white as chalk, as Canacee was enjoying her walk, there sat a falcon high above her head, that with piteous voice began to cry such that all the wood resounded with her cry. She had wounded herself so piteously with both her wings that the red blood ran down the tree in which she stood" (5.409–16).

37. Ingham, *The Medieval New*, 138.

Ingham's analysis of the falcon's lament establishes it as the generative version of literary newness described above; I supplement her account here by attending especially to its textual echoes, which both encapsulate and perform its complex dialectic of old and new. Specifically, its recycling of two memorable lines from the *Knight's Tale* invites speculation because of the pilgrim-tellers' relation as father and son. That relationship adds complexity to these echoes; so too does the fact that they are spoken by a female bird, whose voice Canacee is only newly able to understand, thanks to the strange knight's magic ring. The fact that Chaucer introduces this cross-generational dialectic of old and new as a *knotte* shapes the echo I am proposing.

In most manuscripts of the *Tales*, the substance of the falcon's opening line—"pitee renneth soone in gentil herte" ("pity flows swiftly in a noble heart," 5.479)—has already twice been heard, in the *Knight's Tale* (1.1761) and the *Merchant's Tale* (4.1986), and all three of these instances are highly gendered. As spoken by the pilgrim-Knight, the line accounts for Theseus's gracious acquiescence to his ladies' pleas not to execute Palamon and Arcite; as spoken by the pilgrim-Merchant, it sneers misogynistically at May's decision to show "pity" to Damyan by having sex with him and cuckolding her husband January. The queasy humor of the *Merchant's Tale* is nicely distilled by this spiteful recasting, which turns the Knight's idealistic praise of female empathy into a lascivious skewering of female virtue. Moreover, by showing how easy it is to recycle this memorable phrase's metrically perfect run of syllables into radically different contexts, the recurrence of "pitee renneth soone in gentil herte" in the *Merchant's Tale* gives it almost meme-like vitality, as we wait to hear how it will sound if and when it recurs.

We are therefore primed to note that this phrase initiates the falcon's lament, voiced by the pilgrim-Squire, whom the *General Prologue* describes as both a dashing, smooth-talking ladies' man and a dutiful son to his father the Knight. This figure quotes his father's general praise of female empathy in order to locate that praise specifically in Canacee's own "verray womanly benignytee," as manifest in fellow-feeling toward the female falcon (5.486). In most manuscripts of the *Tales*, moreover, the Squire does so after his father's formulation has been besmirched by the Merchant's lascivious recasting. We need not embrace old-school, "the pilgrims are people"-type analysis in order to appreciate the potential literary energy of such intertextual echoes: the Squire eagerly defending his father's rhetorical honor while also nodding to the ladies—all in accord with his portrait in the *General Prologue*.

Further adding to this complexity, Ingham has shown that, when read in the context of Chaucer's corpus as a whole, the "newfangledness" that the female falcon ends by decrying (5.610–19) seems—unusually—to be gendered male.[38] The falcon thus recalls the same word's application to a particular unfaithful man in Chaucer's earlier *Anelida and Arcite,* like the *Squire's Tale* an experimental, unfinished work:

> This fals Arcite, of his newfanglenesse,
> For she [Anelida] to him so lowly was and trewe,
> Tok lesse deynte of her stidfastnesse
> And saw another lady, proud and newe,
> And right anon he cladde him in her hewe—
> Wot I not whethir in white, rede, or grene—
> And falsed fair Anelida the queene.[39]

This stanza identifies "newfangledness" as a craving for newness in spite yet paradoxically also because of the desirable qualities of what already exists: it is the bad, hoarding appetite for novelty described by Ingham.

Anelida and Arcite is Chaucer's earliest attempt to make something new out of Boccaccio's *Teseida,* adapted in more complex and finished form in the *Knight's Tale.* The "fals Arcite" here defined by newfangledness thus anticipates, nominally if not psychologically, Palamon's rival for Emelye's love in the later poem.[40] That cross-textual connection adds complexity to other echoes of the *Knight's Tale* embedded in the falcon's lament: not just the recurrence of "pitee renneth soone in gentil herte," noted above, but also the falcon's later claim that, in finally acquiescing to the tercel's courtly-love pleading, she "made vertu of necessitee / And tok it wel, syn that it moste be" ("made virtue of necessity, and took it well since it must be so," 5.593–94). These lines precisely echo the words of Theseus near the end of the *Knight's Tale*:

> "Thanne is it wysdom, as it thynketh me,
> To *maken vertu of necessitee,*
> And *take it weel* that we may nat eschue."[41]

38. Ingham, *The Medieval New,* 119–32.

39. "This false Arcite, because of his newfangledness, and because she was so humble and true to him, took less account of her steadfastness, and saw another lady, proud and new, and right anon he clad himself in her hue—I don't know whether in white, red, or green—and betrayed fair Anelida the queen" (141–47).

40. See also David, "Recycling *Anelida and Arcite.*"

41. "'Then it is wisdom, as it seems to me, to *make a virtue out of necessity,* and *take well* what we cannot avoid'" (*Knight's Tale,* 1.3041–43, emphasis added).

Embedded within his famous First Mover speech, these lines preface Theseus's successful attempt to persuade (or compel) Emelye and Palamon to lay aside their grief for dead Arcite and to wed.

We may seem far afield from *Sir Gawain* and knots at this point, so I will briefly resketch the through-lines as I see them. The falcon's lament is the heart, the *knotte*, of part 2 of the *Squire's Tale*, whose echoes of *Sir Gawain* (in the unusual, repeated figure of the knot as well as earlier plot motifs) and the *Knight's Tale* create a Chaucerian, generationally inflected version of the ever-expanding interpretive landscape that we saw in the "endeles knot" of *Sir Gawain*. The falcon's lament performs a generative dialectic of old and new by taking an old theme (female love-lament, familiar from *Anelida and Arcite*, the *Legend of Good Women*, and classical antecedents), conventional language, and precise textual echoes; then reshaping them to novel effect by means of complex shifts in voice, generation, and gender (male Squire quoting father Knight in the voice of a lovesick female falcon) and the inherent interpretive dynamism of textual echoes. We have seen similar interpretive dynamism in textual echoes across the Pearl-Manuscript, such as those of *Cleanness* in *Sir Gawain*; a comparable dialectic of old and new also informs how *Sir Gawain* reshapes established poetic forms and motifs into something entirely unique. Thus, although the two poems are obviously different in form and content, the knot of the *Squire's Tale* echoes that of *Sir Gawain* by giving old literary forms new shape.

The value of such speculation lies neither in proof nor, I think, in objective likelihood of facticity ("Did Chaucer really read *Sir Gawain?*"), but rather in showing how looking at the *Squire's Tale* through the lens of *Sir Gawain* can make both more resonant pieces of literature, by expanding the range of networks in which they operate. To finish making this case, and with the *Squire's Tale*'s generative ambivalence about novelty now established, I return to the brass horse of part 1, whose unexplained mechanics excite such fevered speculation in its onlookers. In an important recent essay, Hannah Louise Bower shows that, in both the *Treatise on the Astrolabe* and the *Squire's Tale*, "Chaucer clearly recognized the potential interdependency of enigma and exposure, wonder and knowledge," and further, of the brass horse in particular, that "the spectators' cognitive dynamism and restless hypothesizing might be seen to perpetuate the marvels' mystery."[42] Already a literal machine, the brass horse becomes an interpretation-generating machine as well, whose

42. Bower, "Restless Rewritings," 38, 54. See also Karnes, "Wonder, Marvels, and Metaphor."

value is underwritten by the unknowability that enables it to continually inspire new theories, new readings.[43] In this it recalls both the intricate construction of *Sir Gawain* and that poem's metapoetic shape-making ability, beautifully described by Emma Maggie Solberg.[44]

Indeed, Ingham argues that readers have become so committed to the horse "as an interpretive enigma" that we ignore a simple explanation, earlier offered by Marijane Osborne: "that the steed of brass is, in fact, an astrolabe, one equipped with a governing horse's head, operated by the turning of a pin, at its top."[45] My interest lies less in the objectively true explanation for this marvel (if Chaucer even conceived one) than in the fact that he has created an object that replicates in us, as readers, the behavior of Chaucer's own swarm of people, murmuring and debating and "rehersynge of thise olde poetries" (5.206), as the Squire puts it. The brass horse thus becomes the engine of its own self-perpetuation by inspiring scholarly attention that reinscribes its centrality to the poem.

In that sense, it offers a miniature version of *Sir Gawain and the Green Knight*'s own generative interpretive power, reinforced by the Squire's respectful reference to Gawain as trusted arbiter of his own strange knight's excellence:

> That Gawayn, with his olde curteisye,
> Though he were comen ayeyn out of Fairye,
> Ne koude hym [the strange knight] nat amende with a word.[46]

The image of Gawain's old courtesy stepping "out of Fairye," to assess the strange knight and find him fitting, suggests a doubling, or mirroring, of the two figures. Comparable doubling across media is also central to *Sir Gawain* and its illustrations, as we have seen. Such tangent points between the poems subtly inflect our experience of the intertextual and polyvocal falcon's lament in part 2, the real *knotte* of the tale, an intertextual confection of old and new whose complexities expand further thanks to its embedded, multivocalic character (Chaucer writing Squire voicing lady-falcon echoing Knight-Dad).

43. Cf. Karnes's argument that the *Squire's Tale* shows "how misleading appearances enliven imagination much like literature itself . . . giv[ing] literature the power of startling objects" ("Wonder, Marvels, and Metaphor," 462).

44. Solberg, "Imagining the Bob and Wheel."

45. Ingham, *The Medieval New*, 136, summarizing Osborne, "The Squire's 'Steed of Brass.'"

46. "That Gawain, with his old courtesy, even if he were come again out of Fairyland, could not improve him [the strange knight] with a word" (5.95–97).

The generational character of this complexity is enhanced if we entertain recent arguments for an earlier (Edwardian rather than Ricardian) date for *Sir Gawain* than has long been supposed. Doing so would mean that by the 1390s, when Chaucer was probably writing the *Squire's Tale*, *Sir Gawain* would have been perhaps a generation old. That could prove a significant context for one speculative history of the *Squire's Tale* and its relation to the whole courtly, chivalric Tale-thread in which it participates.[47] Here, I have suggested that the echoic ventriloquism of the female falcon's lament rewards reading as a twofold appreciative nod to earlier generations: the Squire's to the Knight, by redeeming the Merchant's nasty reshaping of his father's idealistic "pitee renneth soone . . ." line; and Chaucer's to *Sir Gawain and the Green Knight*, by means of their multiple shared plot motifs, knotty metaphors, and generative synthesis of old and new.

I would note in closing that the metaliterary reflections of *Sir Gawain* and the *Squire's Tale* dwell especially on how poems end, and can often continue or expand beyond their endings. In many manuscripts, the Squire is interrupted shortly after embarking on a grandiloquent account of excitement to come (5.651–70), but his tale's codicologically contested aftermath (usually followed by the Franklin, but in Hengwrt and a few other manuscripts by the Merchant instead, to wildly different effect) performs materially and textually literature's tendency to evolve beyond its nominal last word.[48] So too does the poem's later revoicing by Spenser and others. In the generative messiness of its multiple endings, the *Squire's Tale* offers a distorted reflection of *Sir Gawain*, which likewise unspools ambiguously: intimating but also deferring closure, and creating additional "breakaway moments," as Ingham called them, that both envelop and look outward.

One such breakaway moment is the manuscript's anomalous final quire of just four leaves, folios 123/127–126–130, containing lines 2385–2530 of *Sir Gawain* and its final three illustrations. As we saw in chapter 5, this excrescence mars the symmetrical quires-of-twelve on which the manuscript's first 5,938 lines of verse appear. Why should the last 145 lines, just over 2 percent of the total, thus spill over into a new quire? Did the scribe forget, or never know, just how many lines *Sir Gawain* has? Perhaps likelier, and in keeping with the manuscript's often thrifty feel, especially its use of rough, pockmarked parchment: the scribe picked the smallest additional quire needed to finish the poem and leave room for a little more. I say "a little

47. See Bahr, *Fragments and Assemblages*, 168–207.

48. For a helpful summary, see Hanna's textual notes to the *Riverside Chaucer*, 1118–22.

more" because the last 145 lines of *Sir Gawain* actually fit neatly onto folios 123/127r–124/128v and could thus have been written onto a bifolium instead, saving some parchment. Literal, material openness to evolving endings is thus stitched into the end of the Pearl-Manuscript itself, further enhancing its kaleidoscopic force.

THE UNFOLDING ENDS OF *SIR GAWAIN AND THE GREEN KNIGHT*

My first text here is the last twelve lines of *Sir Gawain*, which I reproduce below as they appear in the manuscript and in the McGillivray edition (fig. 8.2)—using his numeration but placing the bob both where it appears in the manuscript and as we hear it initiate the alternating rhyme of the wheel.

For þat [the girdle] watȝ acorded þe renoun of þe Rounde Table,
and he honored þat hit hade euermore after,
as hit is breued in þe best boke of romaunce.
Þus in Arthurez day þis aunter bitidde;
þe Brutus bokeȝ þerof beres wyttenesse,
syþen Brutus, þe bolde burne, boȝed hider fyrst, << iwysse
after þe segge and þe asaute watȝ sesed at Troye,
iwysse.
Mony aunter ȝ herebiforne
haf fallen suche er þis.
Now þat bere þe croun of þorne,
he bring vus to his blysse! Amen.
Hony soyt qui mal pence.[49]

These lines suggest movement in several different directions: back into the Pearl-Manuscript, via textual echoes; onward, into one last, protruding-yet-perfect bob-and-wheel; and outside the book, into the "real world" of chivalric history suggested by the Order of the Garter motto, which has been

49. "For that [the girdle] was accorded the renown of the Round Table, and whoever had it was honored evermore after, as it is written in the best book of romance. Thus this adventure befell in Arthur's day; the books of Brutus [i.e., *Brut* chronicles] bear witness thereof, since Brutus, the bold fellow, first came here [<< *iwysse*], after the siege and the assault was ceased at Troy, indeed [*iwysse*]. Many such adventures have taken place before this. May he who bore the crown of thorns bring us to his bliss! Amen. 'Shame to whoever thinks ill'" (lines 2519–30).

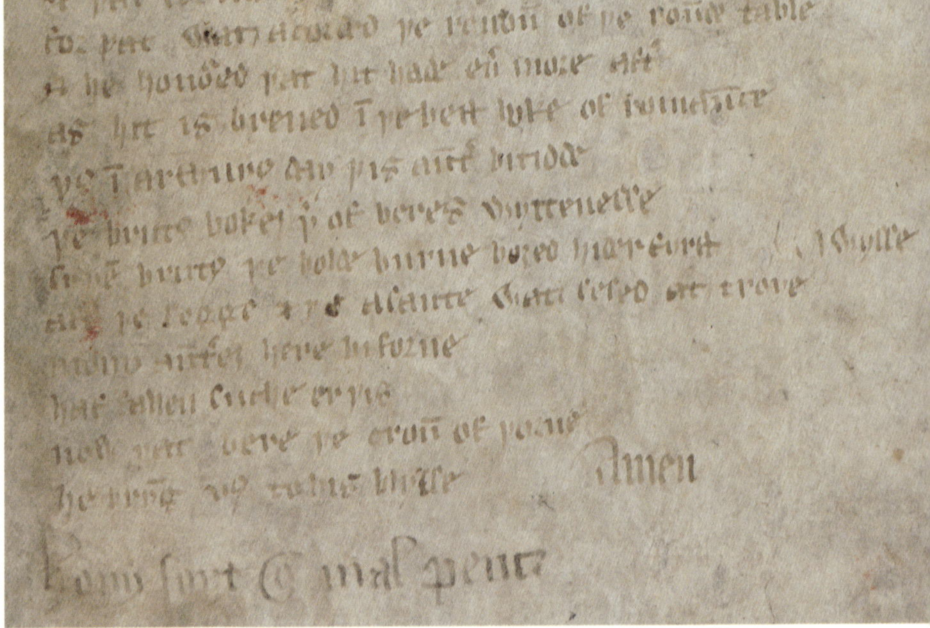

FIGURE 8.2. Folio 124/128v of Cotton Nero A.x/2. Lines 2519–31 of *Sir Gawain and the Green Knight*. Photograph © 2024 by The British Library Board.

✣

assumed into the poem's textual field (as above) by both scholarly editions and prominent translations.[50] Even the slight upward tilt of the lines, clearly visible in figure 8.2, conveys a restless sense of motion. Cumulatively, these movements shape the end of *Sir Gawain*, and of the Pearl-Manuscript itself, into a kaleidoscope of interpretive potential.

Famously, *Sir Gawain*'s final long-line (2525) loops back to its first, simply substituting *after* for the original, synonymous *siþen*. As Howell D. Chickering has noted, such echoes of the poem's opening multiply across these lines, with repeated references to books and adventures and King Arthur giving the end of *Sir Gawain* a comparable but more multiple form of circularity to that of *Pearl* and *Patience*, whose final lines also echo their first.[51]

50. Andrew and Waldron, McGillivray, and Putter and Stokes all conclude their editions with the Order of the Garter motto, as does Simon Armitage's translation.

51. Chickering, "Stanzaic Closure and Linkage," 25–28.

Sir Gawain's expanding circularity takes shape first poetically (that is, within the poem), then textually (Order motto and rhyming couplet), then pictorially (the three concluding illustrations). As we will see, each new layer loops back while also pulling the reader forward. The poem's celebrated resistance to interpretive closure is thus further performed materially across the Pearl-Manuscript's final pages.

Sir Gawain's echo of its opening line at line 2525 also loops the through-reader back to *Pearl* and *Patience*, for their final lines likewise echo their beginnings. There, circularity reinforced a fascination with first-and-last-ness (in *Pearl*, in the rewards of the parable of the vineyard; in *Patience*, with the prologue's explicit thematization of "þe forme and þe laste," "the first and the last," line 38). *Sir Gawain* offers an even more precise version of this pattern than *Pearl* and *Patience*, not even changing the meaning of its first-and-last (long-) line, merely substituting the synonym *After* for the poem's initiating *Sithen*. Our ears, therefore, might well hear line 2525 as the final line of the poem, which it perfectly well could be grammatically. The symbolism of the number 2525 to *Sir Gawain* is obvious, moreover, and would parallel the (notionally) 1212 lines of *Pearl*. Along multiple axes, therefore, we seem to have reached a moment of closure.

To a degree, this impression of finality is justified, for 2525 is indeed the poem's final long-line, and thus the manuscript's as well. *Sir Gawain* continues on from here, however, with a five-line excess analogous (from one perspective) to its protagonist's slight *surfet*, and comparable at smaller scale to the poem's "extruding," 101st stanza. *Pearl* also has 101 stanzas, of course, and its "perfect" 1212 lines are comparably imperfect, though by lack (since the absent "line 472" gives the poem just 1211 total lines) rather than excess (2530 lines instead of 2525). This excess creates a deeper or perhaps simply different unity, however, for it concludes the twelve-line passage quoted above (lines 2519–30), which begins and ends with circular images: the Round Table and the Crown of Thorns.

This repetition-with-a-difference—here, from secular to sacred modes of perfect roundness—across a symbolically resonant twelve lines (*Pearl*'s favorite number pervades this manuscript, as we have seen) recalls the artful transitions across poems discussed in chapters 3 and 5. Here, however, instead of linking to the next poem (for there is none), the Pearl-Manuscript's final poem loops back to its first.[52] *Sir Gawain*'s final word, *blysse*, organizes section 7 of *Pearl*, for example, while the image of the Crown of Thorns recalls the

52. See further Spyra, *Epistemological Perspective*, 67–76.

Dreamer's final commendation of the Maiden "in Krystez dere blessyng and myn, / Þat in þe forme of bred and wyn / þe preste vs schewez vch a daye" ("in Christ's dear blessing and mine, whom in the form of bread and wine, the priest shows us every day," lines 1208–10), the elevated Host answered and anticipated by *Sir Gawain*'s Crown of Thorns. As Solberg notes, this image also "circles back to the wheel of the first stanza, which describes that crown's typological mirror image, the wheel of fortune ([lines] 16–19)."[53] The poem's final bob-and-wheel thus offers multiple gestures toward embedded conclusiveness, even as it exceeds, just slightly, one version of the poem's proper contours. As noted above, moreover, these excrescences appear on an anomalous, shorter quire that disrupts the Pearl-Manuscript's symmetrical pattern of quires-of-twelve: a concluding "imperfection" that resonates materially with *Sir Gawain*'s own textual and pictorial outgrowths.

A large "Amen"—larger than those of the previous three poems, and in more of a display hand—might seem to impose closure, but it is immediately followed by the comparably embellished motto of the Order of the Garter, *Hony soyt qui mal pence* (as written, it lacks the referential *y* of the official Order motto—yet another of the manuscript's slight imperfections). These five words have spawned extraordinary acts of cultural shaping across centuries, as Stephanie Trigg's "vulgar history" of the Order elegantly demonstrates.[54] Among these acts of shaping is the generative force by which the motto has been assumed into *Sir Gawain*'s poetic field, despite not participating in *Sir Gawain* by any traditional sense of poetic wholeness. Thus presented, the Order motto becomes a talismanic tribute to the poem's participation in the "real world" of chivalric history that also, through its allusiveness, continues to generate scholarly and cultural activity: an engine of interpretation akin to the brass horse in the *Squire's Tale*. This generative force is reinscribed by the fact that the motto is not actually the last word in the manuscript. I wish to conclude by considering how textual and pictorial after-words to the Order motto invite retrospection upon both *Sir Gawain* and the Pearl-Manuscript as a whole.

I begin with the striking fact that, just after its attempt to lock the girdle's meaning within the martial, chivalric, male-dominated world of the Order of the Garter, the poem's facing page dramatically depicts female agency, both textually and visually. The depiction of a showily dressed Lady Bertilak trapping the stock-still, supposedly sleeping Gawain in bed—their physical

53. Solberg, "Imagining the Bob and Wheel," 62.

54. Trigg, *Shame and Honor*.

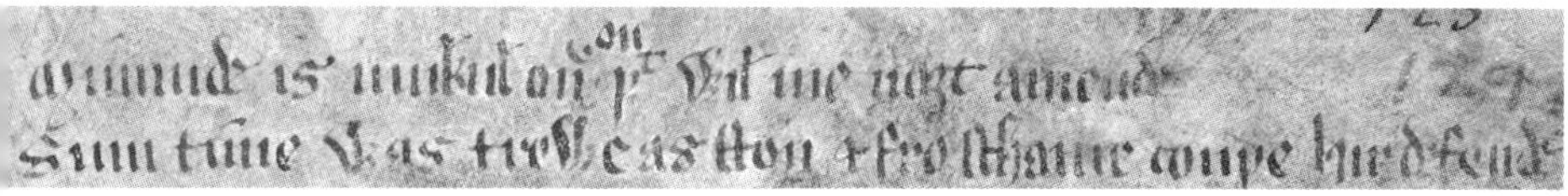

FIGURE 8.3. Folio 125/129r of Cotton Nero A.x/2. Close-up of couplet at the top of the folio. Photograph © 2024 by The British Library Board.

intimacy reinforced by the surrounding curtain—is among the manuscript's most famous and delightful images. It is therefore surprising that the curious couplet written just above, at the top of folio 125/129r, has been so little noticed (fig. 8.3):

> My minde is mukel on on þat wil me noȝt amende
> Sum time was trewe as ston & fro schame couþe hir defende.[55]

If the Order of the Garter motto is context that modern scholarship has shaped into text, this couplet seems like both text and context. On the one hand, it is indisputably text: a self-contained couplet marked by both end and medial rhyme, it receives its own entry (2262.5) in the *New Index of Middle English Verse*.[56] Yet it is so slight, and formally so unlike what has come before, that it is hard to imagine calling this the fifth poem in a five-text manuscript; in that sense, it seems more like context. I believe its significance to our apprehension of the Pearl-Manuscript lies partly in this shifting status: like the shimmering, paper-like outline of Castle Hautdesert, or the paraphs of *Cleanness*, or even the warty growths of *Patience*, it depends on how we look at it. In that sense, it is another speculative invitation created by the endlessly generative *Sir Gawain*.

As Jessica Brantley notes, the couplet suggests "themes of love-longing, betrayal, and shame familiar from the poem," and although the text can be mapped only imperfectly onto the image below it, such inexactness can be interpretively generative, as we have seen throughout the Pearl-Manuscript.[57] Here, we are invited to imagine the couplet's mystery-she,

55. "My mind is greatly on one who will not help/amend me, Who once was true as stone and could defend herself from shame."

56. Boffey and Edwards, *New Index of Middle English Verse*.

57. "[H]ere the (male?) narrator implies that a woman once true has fallen into disgrace. In *Gawain* itself it is the protagonist's fidelity that is under pressure, especially in the scene

once true and able to defend herself from shame, who now dominates the speaker's mind much as Lady Bertilak dominates the page. Her refusal to help or amend the speaker—but implied power to do so—refocuses the reader's mind on female agency, and from there perhaps back to the Green Knight's earlier explanation, to Gawain, that Morgan Le Fay orchestrated the whole beheading game in order to frighten Guinevere to death.

Critics have often been skeptical of this sudden revelation,[58] but as we saw in chapter 7, the construction of the beheading scene depicted on folio 90/94v subtly triangulated Guinevere, and perhaps this very plot point, into greater prominence. Moreover, the illustration means that a courtly, left-facing female figure appears near the middle of the *x*-axis of the pages that envelop *Sir Gawain*, opposite its opening and closing lines: first Guinevere, then Lady Bertilak. This resemblance visually encloses the poem, further suggesting finality, even as the strangely allusive, seemingly extra-authorial couplet radiates speculative potential outward. This potential takes additional shape when we turn the page, where two more illustrations await us: 125/129v+126/130r (figs. 8.4 and 8.5). Like the previous illustration, they loop us back in the manuscript: not just narratively, to the scenes they depict, but also, via visual echoes, all the way back to the 90/94v+91/95r opening with which the poem began.

In the left-hand image (fig. 8.4), a mounted Gawain approaches an ominous tumulus; between and above them, the Green Knight stands impassively, gripping his ax with both hands. As Maidie Hilmo has pointed out, the mirroring patterns of their figures across this illustration and that of 90/94v suggest a "mysterious identification of the two in person as well as in the roles they play in the beheading game."[59] Significantly, 125/129v depicts Gawain in full battle-dress, with lance, armor (slightly pinker than the red of his tunic in 90/94v), and curiously conical helmet.

pictured here. . . . There is not a perfect parallel between the couplet and the scene, in other words" (*Medieval English Manuscripts and Literary Forms*, 224).

58. E.g., "Morgan's role as adversary of Camelot, would-be seducer of its knights, and rival of Guinevere is so much a part of the literary tradition associated with the Matter of Britain that her belated invocation in *this* romance as *radix malorum* is all too convenient" (Kinney, "Best Book of Romance," 463).

59. "Further a shape-shifting relationship between Gawain and the Green Knight seems to be implied by their transposition in this miniature [90/94v] and that in which Gawain seeks the Green Chapel. In the first, the Green Knight is seated astride his horse while Gawain holds an axe; in the second, this configuration is reversed . . . imaging a kind of mysterious identification of the two in person as well as in the roles they play in the beheading game" (Hilmo, "Did the Scribe Draw," 125).

The significance of this depiction emerges on the right-hand page (fig. 8.5), for the awkwardly kneeling figure in front of Guinevere has similar armor to that of Gawain riding opposite: blue conical helmet, light red or pinkish chest, and blue legs with golden poleyns or *genouillères* at the knees. This resemblance helps establish the kneeling figure as Gawain; yet as Jennifer Lee points out, the upright figure standing with Arthur and Guinevere "greatly resembles in face and dress Sir Gawain of the first picture," both with comparable red tunic, blue hose, blond hair, cleft chin, and receding hairline. The only significant difference between them is that here, the upper-right Gawain has exchanged the great ax with which he beheaded the Green Knight in the first image for a more refined, knightly sword, held over his shoulder and signaling his reintegration into courtly life at Camelot. Lee therefore suggests, and I agree, that "we have again a repeated figure of Gawain back in court after the completion of his adventure."[60]

Shirley Kossick likewise argues that we are facing two different aspects of our protagonist:

> Gawain has returned to the court after his adventures and trial, and is seen standing alongside the king and queen as a representative member of the court. . . . But the artist also tries to reflect another aspect of the poem by presenting simultaneously with the reintegrated Gawain, the Gawain who bitterly refuses to accept his own imperfection . . . includ[ing] a kneeling and humbled representation of Gawain being raised to his feet by the king.[61]

The fact that the poem's first illustration on 90/94v also featured two representations of Gawain further supports this interpretation, as do continuities in color across the figures, noted above. Nevertheless, this final illustration poses more interpretive challenges than the first, for whereas 90/94v clearly presented two different time frames for its two Gawains—before and after

60. Lee, "Illuminating Critic," 26.

61. Kossick, "Illustrations of the *Gawain* Manuscript," 33.

Following spread: FIGURE 8.4. Folio 125/129v of Cotton Nero A.x/2. Photograph © 2024 by The British Library Board. FIGURE 8.5. Folio 126/130r of Cotton Nero A.x/2. Photograph © 2024 by The British Library Board.

the climactic beheading, helpfully divided by the horizontal feasting table—here the two Gawains nearly overlap, and an elaborate archway crowds them into the same frame, thereby suggesting a single action and moment in time. This adds to the obvious difficulty in construing both figures of 126/130r as Gawain: they do not actually resemble one another very much, quite unlike G1 and G2 of 90/94v. The tableau's full interpretive potential thus emerges only when we read across illustrations, which envelop the poem they depict—further adding to its accretive, *Pearl*-like layers.

And in one last paradox quite appropriate to the Pearl-Manuscript, folio 126/130r both is and is not the book's final image. Its verso is blank (fig. 8.6), but ink from the recto has bled through, leaving an image that looks like an arch or doorway. The recto's four human figures appear as indistinct blobs of vague color; far more striking is the outline of the pavilion at the top, and the somewhat fainter images of the pillars supporting it. This serendipitous and spectral doorway beckons us back into the book: to continue chasing Sir Gawain's endless knot and the comparably endless intricacies of the Pearl-Manuscript itself. The occasional imperfection of those intricacies is visually reinforced by the fact that its final page is not a placid reflective surface, despite the nominal blankness of the page. On the contrary, 126/130v features wormholes and traces of earlier ruling patterns, which combine with the fuzzy shapes described above to make this final page a generatively imperfect mirror. In that, it anticipates my final metaphor for the Pearl-Manuscript: the kaleidoscope.

FIGURE 8.6. Folio 126/130v of Cotton Nero A.x/2.
Photograph © 2024 by The British Library Board.

FINAL REFLECTIONS

The Pearl-Manuscript as Broken Kaleidoscope

Et bene Sacra Scriptura dicitur speculum, quia fracto speculo multe apparent ymagines, sicut Scripture multe sunt exposiciones, quia "pertransibunt plurimi et multiplex erit sciencia," Danielis xii.

*Holy Scripture is rightly called a mirror, because when a mirror is broken [*fracto speculo*] there appear many images, just as Holy Scripture has many explanations, for "many shall pass over, and knowledge shall be manifold [*multiplex erit sciencia*]," Daniel 12.*[1]

The Pearl-Manuscript is not Holy Scripture, but it is a devotional object that continues to inspire a large and diverse readership. It is therefore fitting that the richly evocative language above, from a widely read, roughly contemporaneous penitential manual, should suggest a more productive version of the mirror metaphor than the one that has animated so much fascination with the distant past, and with medieval manuscripts in particular. Unlike the passively reflective, one-to-one mirror of modernity, the *Summa virtutum*'s gloss on Daniel 12:4 proposes a generative model, by which the singular mirror, broken, creates many images, each of them illuminating. Thus, knowledge shall be *multiplex*. Lexicographers Charlton T. Lewis and Charles Short award three transferred meanings to this word, beyond its literal one of having many material folds: (1) "manifold, many, numerous, various" (this basic meaning gets the most citations); (2) "in implied comparisons, many times as great, far more"; and (3) that which "has many windings [*sic*] or concealed places."[2] In this last, rarest sense, *multiplex* describes the winding, tortuous home (*domus*) of the Minotaur in Ovid's *Metamorphoses* (8.158).

Fittingly, both *Pearl* and the Pearl-Manuscript embody all of these

1. *Summa virtutum de remediis anime*, 114–15.

2. Lewis and Short, *Latin Dictionary*, s.v. "multĭ-plex," accessed August 31, 2023, https://www.perseus.tufts.edu/hopper/text?doc=Perseus%3Atext%3A1999.04.0059%3Aentry%3Dmultiplex.

meanings. Indeed, if *Hony soyt qui mal pence* has become the motto of *Sir Gawain and the Green Knight*, then *multiplex erit sciencia* could serve as a motto for the Pearl-Manuscript as a whole. It is consonant with the Maiden's explication of grace as an infinitely generous wellspring, and with the manuscript's own "manifold" interpretive potential. For while all medieval books are literally "many folds" of parchment or paper, the Pearl-Manuscript's supereffable links between the poetic and the material make it much weirder than most manuscripts—as unique as its poems, in fact. As an exception to the rule that should expand our perspective on the possible, it offers "far more" of interest than most old books: more and more, like *Pearl*. I have proposed the Pearl-Manuscript as a *multiplex domus* for the manifold beauties of its poems; but its winding, "concealed" complexities are quite unlike the death-dealing home of Ovid's hybrid monstrosity. Rather, the Pearl-Manuscript's unique fusion of literary, visual, and material form offers meditative pathways toward self-knowledge, like the cathedral labyrinths of Chartres or Amiens.

Whereas those intricate figures on the floor present just one path, however, this book has shown that the Pearl-Manuscript reflects and refracts more multiply. We should therefore recall the *Summa virtutum*'s valorization of fracture: it is only *fracto speculo*, "when a mirror is broken," that we can see the many images which are then likened to the multiform plenitude of scriptural knowledge. This medieval metaphor—a broken mirror, whose shards somehow display more than they could as a unified whole—evokes the operation of a modern instrument: the kaleidoscope, whose beautiful patterns emerge from multiple mirrors arranged along the interior of a tube, with unsecured bits of colored glass or beads in an object chamber that we see when we look through the tube. Each of the several mirrors (most often three) within the tube reflects the colorful matter in the object chamber; these reflections bounce off the other mirrors to create a beautifully complex pattern, which shifts as the viewer rotates the tube and displaces the contents of the object chamber. The symmetry of the pattern we see is assured by the symmetrical arrangement of the mirrors within the tube.

The kaleidoscope is thus fragmentary, shifting, interactive, and aleatory, or subject to chance. As such, it offers a useful way of estranging our perspective on the mirror; for as Michael Camille has shown, "mirror" in modern English simply cannot convey, in our postphotographic and often disenchanted world, what *speculum* signified in the Middle Ages: a mirror, yes, but also more.[3] Fuller articulation of the kaleidoscope's potential to medieval

3. Camille, *Mirror in Parchment*, 15–48 and 309–50.

studies is matter for another project, but I would note briefly in closing its interactive and aleatory qualities, as well as its etymology. The word is a portmanteau of three Greek words: *kalos*, beautiful; *eidos*, form or shape; and *skopein*, to look at or examine. Its inventor, Sir David Brewster, thus calls it a "new Optical instrument, for creating and exhibiting beautiful forms."[4] This definition admirably suits the Pearl-Manuscript, for it was clearly made to exhibit the beautiful forms of its poems; and its own idiosyncratic, evolving construction creates ever-new ways of seeing and reading them. Using the self-consciously archaizing etymology of a nineteenth-century device to describe a fourteenth-century manuscript nicely reinforces how the Pearl-Manuscript and its poems expand our perspective on time as a straightforward, linear phenomenon.

The kaleidoscope is also interactive, unlike the passively reflective modern mirror—but like the medieval *speculum*, and indeed like speculation itself. By prompting us to do something in order to see its beautiful shapes, the kaleidoscope reinforces the interactive nature of our relationship with the world, which extends to our objects of study: as my own encounter with the anomalous quire of *Patience* vividly reinforced, we are changed by what we handle. The coimplication of reader with book, student with object, recalls the interactive dimension of medieval speculation, which is another reason I find that interpretive mode so powerful. The kaleidoscope's interactivity also makes it, and its images, subject to chance. Spinning the tube offers a beautiful new shape by rearranging the matter in the object panel, but viewers cannot control either the rearrangement of matter or the resulting pattern. The aleatory quality of what we see, *fracto speculo*, when we look at British Library MS Cotton Nero A.x/2, or any other medieval manuscript, is a useful spur to epistemic and methodological humility: just as close readers should resist overinterpreting the utilitarian and ordinary, so too others should resist underacknowledging the power of the unique and extraordinary to reshape the everyday.

I can offer no precise reconstruction of how the Pearl-Manuscript's complex symmetries emerged—none that would withstand scholarly scrutiny, anyway—so I keep my speculations on that front to myself for now. Rather than drive toward origins, I have tried to work kaleidoscopically, by focusing intensely on a single object in ways that I hope may open outward. But having proposed the kaleidoscope as a metaphor for the Pearl-Manuscript, I must note in closing one crucial dissimilarity. The marvel of the kaleidoscope is to

4. Brewster, *The Kaleidoscope*, 1.

produce unfailingly symmetrical images from the chaotically arranged matter in the object panel. We have seen, however, that the Pearl-Manuscript is almost never purely symmetrical; and yet its carefully cultivated aesthetic of anti-exactness, which resonates both poetically and materially, seems closely linked to its spiritual concerns. This anti-exactness continually reminds us of the limits of our knowledge, while encouraging us to stretch our perspective so as to see or comprehend more. Such tension is key to the Pearl-Manuscript's beauty: even its breakages make it more *multiplex*, more richly resonant, by simultaneously inspiring and resisting analysis. Speculation offers one way of finding more and more delight in these poems' ever-evolving shapes. In that spirit, I hope that this book helps others shape their own speculative histories: both for the readings they may find of *Pearl*, and for the pearls they may find elsewhere.

ACKNOWLEDGMENTS

Without the immense generosity of my family, friends, and colleagues, this book could never have been written. My deepest intellectual debts are to my advisers, Howell D. Chickering and Anne Middleton, tough and inspiring coaches whose examples I try to live up to. Randy Petilos has been an amazing editor, and the two anonymous reviewers for the University of Chicago Press offered much-needed perspective and valuable suggestions, for which I thank them. Thanks also to Beth Ina, Sue Olin, and Chicago's production and design teams for bringing this project to fruition. Jessica Brantley, Michelle Warren, and Nicholas Watson read a full draft of an early version of the book, and their generous feedback was crucial in helping me find its ultimate shape. Feedback from the working group Former has vitally informed this project: deep thanks to Seeta Chaganti, Rebecca Davis, Shannon Gayk, Eleanor Johnson, Marisa Libbon, Ingrid Nelson, Sarah Novacich, and Jennifer Sisk for their friendship and wisdom. Thanks to Anna Abramson, Eugenie Brinkema, Joel Burges, Seamus Dwyer, Marah Gubar, Diana Henderson, Bernardo Hinojosa, Michael Johnston, Julia Panko, Emily Richmond Pollock, Shankar Raman, James C. Staples, Kyle Stevens, Daniel Wakelin, and Eric Weiskott for reading individual chapters, which are sharper for their feedback. Richard Firth Green and Sarah McNamer generously took time to discuss their ongoing research on these poems. Alexandra Gillespie and Daniel Wakelin kindly shared their notes on the Pearl-Manuscript in advance of my visit, entertaining numerous questions along the way and afterward. At the British Library, Julian Harrison offered generous and learned hospitality.

Parts of this book were drafted at the Newhouse Center for the Humanities at Wellesley College: thanks to Carol Dougherty for her inspiring leadership, and to my fellow Fellows for their warmth and insights, especially Joel Burges, Brigid Cohen, Brenna Greer, and Lianne Habinek. This book was also shaped by rewarding conversations about the Pearl-Manuscript at Bard College, Bowdoin College, Concordia University, Hamilton College, Harvard University, Heinrich Heine Universität Düsseldorf, Indiana University,

New York University, Rutgers University, Université Sorbonne Nouvelle, University of Connecticut, University of Pennsylvania, University of Rochester, University of the South, University of Texas, University of Vermont, University of Washington, University of Wisconsin, Washington University in St. Louis, Wellesley College, and Yale University. Thanks to my hosts and audiences for their thoughtful questions and warm hospitality.

Working at the Massachusetts Institute of Technology has made this book weirder than it would have been otherwise, for which I am deeply grateful. Undergraduate research assistants Kelsey Glover and Madison Sneve did extraordinary work on the angles and paraphs of the Pearl-Manuscript, respectively, and Kelsey helped immensely in preparing the images and bibliography for publication. Boston-area medievalists have been unfailingly generous interlocutors, while my colleagues and students at MIT—in Literature, Ancient and Medieval Studies, and beyond—have offered profound support of many sorts. I also thank the current and recent chairs of the MIT faculty for their leadership and support: Mary Fuller, Lily Tsai, Rick Danheiser, Susan Silbey, and Krishna Rajagopal.

Training with Maren Kravitz has helped my mental and physical health immensely; TGUs and SLDLs give a way of doing compulsory figures once more, for which I thank her. Alex Rowland has been with me every step of the way, and all my sentiment will never fully express my gratitude: for Team Hot Mess, for making me embrace being bad at things, and more and more. My parents, Meredith and Will, and their spouses, Jon and Kathleen, have been unfailingly supportive: deep thanks and much love to you all. My sister Stephanie has shaped this book more than anyone, having read multiple drafts of every word multiple times; it is smarter and more generous for her interventions. Together, you all kept me sane and inspired me to keep going. I will always be grateful for that gift.

✣

An earlier version of chapter 2 appeared as "The Manifold Singularity of *Pearl*," in *ELH* 82, no. 3 (Fall 2015); earlier versions of portions of chapter 4 appeared in "Finding the Forms of *Cleanness*," in *Studies in Philology* 110, no. 3 (Summer 2013); and elements of chapters 7 and 8 draw on "Compulsory Figures," in *ELH* 84, no. 4 (Winter 2017). I thank the editors of both journals for allowing me to rehearse the ideas in this book first in their pages.

BIBLIOGRAPHY

PRIMARY TEXTS/FACSIMILES

Anderson, J. J. *Cleanness*. Old and Middle English Texts. Manchester: Manchester University Press; New York: Barnes and Noble Books, 1977.

———. *Patience*. Old and Middle English Texts. Manchester: Manchester University Press; New York: Barnes and Noble, 1969.

Andrew, Malcolm, and Ronald Waldron, eds. *The Poems of the Pearl Manuscript*. London: Folio Society, 2015. References to this facsimile are indicated as such in the notes.

———, eds. *The Poems of the Pearl Manuscript in Modern English Prose Translation: Pearl, Cleanness, Patience, Sir Gawain and the Green Knight*. Comprehensively rev. 5th ed. Exeter: Exeter Press, 2008; this is the edition used unless otherwise specified as the 1st (1978), 2nd (1987), 3rd (1996), or 4th (2002) edition.

Armitage, Simon, trans. *Pearl: A New Verse Translation*. New York: Liveright, 2017.

Augustine. *De trinitate*. Translated by Edmund Hill. New York: New City Press, 1991.

Bonaventure. *The Journey of the Mind to God*. Translated by Philotheus Boehner. Indianapolis: Hackett, 1993.

Chaucer, Geoffrey. *The Riverside Chaucer*. Edited by Larry Dean Benson. 3rd ed. Boston: Houghton Mifflin, 1987.

Gollancz, Israel, ed. *Facsimile Reproduction of Cotton Nero A.x: Pearl, Cleanness, Patience and Sir Gawain*. Early English Text Society, o.s. 162. London: Oxford University Press, 1923.

———, ed. and trans. *Pearl: An English Poem of the Fourteenth Century*. London: Nutt, 1891.

Gordon, E. V. *Pearl*. Oxford: Clarendon Press, 1953.

Kempe, Margery. *The Book of Margery Kempe*. Edited by Lynn Staley. 1st ed. Medieval Institute Publications, 1996. https://doi.org/10.2307/j.ctv16f6czq.

McGillivray, Murray, ed. *London, British Library MS Cotton Nero A.x. (Art. 3): A Digital Facsimile and Commented Transcription*. Publications of the Cotton Nero A.x, Project 3. Calgary: Cotton Nero A.x. Project, 2012.

———, ed. "Patience." In *London, British Library MS Cotton Nero A.x. (Art. 3): A Digital Facsimile and Commented Transcription*. Publications of the Cotton Nero A.x, Project 3. Calgary: Cotton Nero A.x. Project, 2017.

———, ed. "Sir Gawain and the Green Night." In *London, British Library MS Cotton Nero A.x (Art. 3): A Digital Fascimile and Commented Transcription*. Publications of the Cotton Nero A.x, Project 3. Calgary: Cotton Nero A.x Project, 2017.

McGillivray, Murray, and Jenna Stook, eds. "Pearl." In *Poems of London, British Library MS Cotton Nero A.x. (Part 3): A Critical Edition*, 2017.

Olsen, Kenna L., ed. "Cleanness." In *Poems of London, British Library MS Cotton Nero A.x. (Art. 3): A Critical Edition*. Publications of the Cotton Nero A.x., Project 4, 2019.

———. *Cleanness: A Diplomatic Edition with Textual, Codicological, and Paleographical Notes.* Publications of the Cotton Nero A.x., Project 1. Calgary: Cotton Nero A.x. Project, 2011.

Osgood, Charles G., ed. *The Pearl: A Middle English Poem.* Boston: Heath, 1906.

Putter, Ad, and Myra Stokes, eds. *The Works of the Gawain Poet: Pearl, Cleanness, Patience, Sir Gawain and the Green Knight.* Penguin Classics. London: Penguin, 2014.

Wenzel, Siegfried, ed. *Summa virtutum de remediis anime.* Chaucer Library. Athens: University of Georgia Press, 1984.

SCHOLARSHIP

Aers, David. "The Self Mourning: Reflections on Pearl." *Speculum* 68, no. 1 (January 1993): 54–73. https://doi.org/10.2307/2863834.

Ahern, John. "Binding the Book: Hermeneutics and Manuscript Production in *Paradiso* 33." *PMLA/Publications of the Modern Language Association of America* 97, no. 5 (October 1982): 800–809. https://doi.org/10.2307/462171.

Akbari, Suzanne Conklin. *Seeing through the Veil: Optical Theory and Medieval Allegory.* Toronto: University of Toronto Press, 2004.

Anderson, Sarah M. "Studies in Medieval Star-Gazing." *Arthuriana* 30, no. 3 (2020): 8–49. https://doi.org/10.1353/art.2020.0026.

Andrew, Malcolm. "Theories of Authorship." In *A Companion to the Gawain-Poet*, edited by Derek Brewer and Jonathan Gibson, 23–33. Arthurian Studies 38. Woodbridge, Suffolk, UK: D. S. Brewer, 1997.

Aranye Fradenburg, L. O. "Living Chaucer." *Studies in the Age of Chaucer* 33, no. 1 (2011): 41–64. https://doi.org/10.1353/sac.2011.0035.

Arnheim, Rudolf. *The Dynamics of Architectural Form.* Berkeley: University of California Press, 1977.

Ashe, Laura. "How to Read Both: The Logic of True Contradictions in Chaucer's World." *Studies in the Age of Chaucer* 42, no. 1 (2020): 111–46. https://doi.org/10.1353/sac.2020.0003.

Bahr, Arthur. "Compulsory Figures." *ELH* 84, no. 2 (2017): 295–314.

———. "Finding the Forms of *Cleanness*." *Studies in Philology* 110, no. 3 (2013): 459–81. https://doi.org/10.1353/sip.2013.0019.

———. *Fragments and Assemblages: Forming Compilations of Medieval London.* Chicago: University of Chicago Press, 2013.

———. "The Manifold Singularity of Pearl." *ELH* 82, no. 3 (2015): 729–58. https://doi.org/10.1353/elh.2015.0034.

Bahr, Arthur, and Alexandra Gillespie. "Medieval English Manuscripts: Form, Aesthetics, and the Literary Text." *Chaucer Review* 47, no. 4 (April 1, 2013): 346–60. https://doi.org/10.5325/chaucerrev.47.4.0346.

Barootes, B. S. W. "Number Symbolism in *Pearl*: Lines 720–721." *Studia Neophilologica* 89, no. 1 (January 2, 2017): 34–40. https://doi.org/10.1080/00393274.2016.1209426.

Barr, Helen. "Pearl—Or 'The Jeweller's Tale.'" *Medium Ævum* 69, no. 1 (2000): 59–79.

Barthes, Roland. *Camera Lucida: Reflections on Photography.* 1st ed. New York: Hill and Wang, 1981.

Benjamin, Walter. *The Arcades Project.* Edited by Howard Eiland and Kevin MacLaughlin. Cambridge, MA: Belknap Press of Harvard University Press, 2003.

———. "On the Concept of History." In *The Arcades Project*, edited by Howard Eiland and

Kevin MacLaughlin, 4:389–400. Cambridge, MA: Belknap Press of Harvard University Press, 2003.

———. "Paralipomena to 'On the Concept of History.'" In *The Arcades Project*, edited by Howard Eiland and Kevin MacLaughlin, 4:400–411. Cambridge, MA: Belknap Press of Harvard University Press, 2003.

Bennett, Michael J. *Community, Class, and Careerism: Cheshire and Lancashire Society in the Age of Sir Gawain and the Green Knight*. Cambridge: Cambridge University Press, 1983.

Benson, C. David. "The Impatient Reader of *Patience*." In *Text and Matter: New Critical Perspectives of the Pearl-Poet*, edited by Robert J. Blanch, Miriam Youngerman Miller, and Julian N. Wasserman, 147–61. Troy, NY: Whitston, 1991.

Bernau, Anke. "Figuring with Knots." *Digital Philology* 10, no. 1 (2021): 13–38. https://doi.org/10.1353/dph.2021.0000.

———. "Translating Form with *Patience*." In *The Medieval Literary: Beyond Form*, edited by Robert J. Meyer-Lee and Catherine Sanok, 161–83. Cambridge: Boydell and Brewer, 2018.

Biernoff, Suzannah. *Sight and Embodiment in the Middle Ages*. New Middle Ages. New York: Palgrave Macmillan, 2002.

Blanch, Robert J., Miriam Youngerman Miller, and Julian N. Wasserman. *Text and Matter: New Critical Perspectives of the "Pearl"-Poet*. Troy, NY: Whitston, 1991.

Blanch, Robert J., and Julian N. Wasserman. *From Pearl to Gawain: Forme to Fynisment*. Gainesville: University Press of Florida, 1995.

Boffey, Julia, and A. S. G. Edwards. *A New Index of Middle English Verse*. London: British Library, 2005.

Borroff, Marie. "Narrative Artistry in St. Erkenwald and the Gawain-Group: The Case for Common Authorship Reconsidered." *Studies in the Age of Chaucer* 28, no. 1 (2006): 41–76. https://doi.org/10.1353/sac.2006.0033.

———. "*Pearl*'s 'Maynful Mone.'" In *Traditions and Renewals: Chaucer, the "Gawain"-Poet, and Beyond*, 114–23. New Haven, CT: Yale University Press, 2003.

Bower, Hannah Louise. "Restless Rewritings: The Politics of Enigma and Exposure in the *Squire's Tale*." *Chaucer Review* 57, no. 1 (January 1, 2022): 32–67. https://doi.org/10.5325/chaucerrev.57.1.0032.

Bowers, John M. *An Introduction to the Gawain Poet*. Gainesville: University Press of Florida, 2012.

———. "The Politics of Pearl." *Exemplaria* 7, no. 2 (January 1995): 419–41. https://doi.org/10.1179/exm.1995.7.2.419.

———. *The Politics of Pearl: Court Poetry in the Age of Richard II*. Cambridge: D. S. Brewer, 2000.

Bradley, Ritamary. "Backgrounds of the Title Speculum in Mediaeval Literature." *Speculum* 29, no. 1 (January 1954): 100–115. https://doi.org/10.2307/2853870.

Brantley, Jessica. "Forms of the Hours in Late Medieval England." In *The Medieval Literary: Beyond Form*, edited by Robert J. Meyer-Lee and Catherine Sanok, 1st ed., 61–84. Boydell and Brewer, 2018. https://doi.org/10.1017/9781787442191.004.

———. "'In Things': The Rebus in Premodern Devotion." *Journal of Medieval and Early Modern Studies* 45, no. 2 (May 1, 2015): 287–321. https://doi.org/10.1215/10829636-2880899.

———. *Medieval English Manuscripts and Literary Forms*. 1st ed. Material Texts. Philadelphia: University of Pennsylvania Press, 2022.

———. *Reading in the Wilderness: Private Devotion and Public Performance in Late Medieval England*. Chicago: University of Chicago Press, 2007.

———. "Reading the Forms of *Sir Thopas*." *Chaucer Review* 47, no. 4 (April 1, 2013): 416–38. https://doi.org/10.5325/chaucerrev.47.4.0416.

Breeze, Andrew C. "A Celtic Etymology for *Glaverez* 'Deceives' at Pearl 688." *Notes and Queries* 42 (1995): 160–62.

Brewer, Derek, and Jonathan Gibson, eds. *A Companion to the Gawain-Poet*. Arthurian Studies 38. Woodbridge, Suffolk, UK: D. S. Brewer, 1997.

Brewster, David. *A Treatise on the Kaleidoscope*. Edinburgh: Archibald Constable, 1819.

Brown, Bill. "Thing Theory." *Critical Inquiry* 28, no. 1 (2001): 1–22.

Buber, Martin. *I and Thou*. Translated by Ronald Gregor Smith. New York: Scribner, 1957.

Butterfield, Ardis. *The Familiar Enemy: Chaucer, Language, and Nation in the Hundred Years War*. Oxford: Oxford University Press, 2009.

Bynum, Caroline. *Wonderful Blood: Theology and Practice in Late Medieval Northern Germany and Beyond*. Philadelphia: University of Pennsylvania Press, 2007.

Calabrese, Michael, and Eric Eliason. "The Rhetorics of Sexual Pleasure and Intolerance in the Middle English *Cleanness*." *Modern Language Quarterly* 56, no. 3 (September 1, 1995): 247–75. https://doi.org/10.1215/00267929-56-3-247.

Cameron, Sharon. *Choosing Not Choosing*. Chicago: University of Chicago Press, 1993.

Camille, Michael. *Mirror in Parchment: The Luttrell Psalter and the Making of Medieval England*. Chicago: University of Chicago Press, 1998.

Campbell, Ethan. *The Gawain-Poet and the Fourteenth-Century English Anticlerical Tradition*. Research in Medieval and Early Modern Culture. Kalamazoo: Medieval Institute Publications, Western Michigan University, 2018.

Cannon, Christopher. "Form." In *Middle English: Twenty-First Century Approaches to Literature*, edited by Paul Strohm, 177–90. Oxford: Oxford University Press, 2007.

Carlson, David. "*Pearl's* Imperfections." *Studia Neophilologica* 63, no. 1 (January 1991): 57–67. https://doi.org/10.1080/00393279108588061.

Carruthers, Mary. *The Experience of Beauty in the Middle Ages*. Oxford Warburg Studies. Oxford: Oxford University Press, 2013.

———. "Sweetness." *Speculum* 81, no. 4 (October 2006): 999–1013. https://doi.org/10.1017/S0038713400004267.

Cerquiglini, Bernard. *In Praise of the Variant: A Critical History of Philology*. Translated by Betsy Wing. Parallax. Baltimore: Johns Hopkins University Press, 1999.

Cervone, Cristina Maria. *Poetics of the Incarnation: Middle English Writing and the Leap of Love*. 1st ed. Middle Ages Series. Philadelphia: University of Pennsylvania Press, 2012.

Chaganti, Seeta. *The Medieval Poetics of the Reliquary: Enshrinement, Inscription, Performance*. New York: Palgrave Macmillan US, 2008. https://doi.org/10.1057/9780230615380.

Chickering, Howell D. "Stanzaic Closure and Linkage in 'Sir Gawain and the Green Knight.'" *Chaucer Review* 32, no. 1 (1997): 1–31.

———. "Unpunctuating Chaucer." *Chaucer Review* 25, no. 2 (1990): 96–109.

Chong, Kenneth. "'Bot a Quene!': Calculating Salvation in Pearl." *Studies in the Age of Chaucer* 40, no. 1 (2018): 217–55. https://doi.org/10.1353/sac.2018.0005.

Clemens, Raymond, and Timothy Graham. *Introduction to Manuscript Studies*. Ithaca, NY: Cornell University Press, 2007.

Clopper, Lawrence M. "The God of the 'Gawain-Poet.'" *Modern Philology* 94, no. 1 (1996): 1–18.

Cohen, Jeffrey J. "The Love of Life: Reading Sir Gawain and the Green Knight Close to Home." In *Premodern Ecologies in the Modern Literary Imagination*, edited by Vin Nardizzi and

Tiffany Jo Werth, 25–58. Toronto: University of Toronto Press, 2019. https://doi.org/10.3138/9781487519520-005.

Coleman, Joyce. *Public Reading and the Reading Public in Late Medieval England and France*. Cambridge Studies in Medieval Literature 26. Cambridge: Cambridge University Press, 2005.

———. "Translating Iconography: Gower, *Pearl*, Chaucer and the *Rose*." In *Chaucer: Visual Approaches*, edited by Susanna Fein and David B. Raybin, 177–94. University Park: Pennsylvania State University Press, 2016.

Coley, David K. *Death and the Pearl Maiden: Plague, Poetry, England*. Columbus: Ohio State University Press, 2023.

Condren, Edward I. *The Numerical Universe of the Gawain-Pearl Poet: Beyond Phi*. Gainesville: University Press of Florida, 2002.

Cooper, Helen. "Romance after 1400." In *The Cambridge History of Medieval English Literature*, edited by David Wallace, 690–719. Cambridge: Cambridge University Press, 1999.

Copeland, Rita, and Marjorie Woods. "Classroom and Confession." In *The Cambridge History of Medieval English Literature*, edited by David Wallace, 376–406. Cambridge: Cambridge University Press, 1999.

Cornelius, Ian. *Reconstructing Alliterative Verse: The Pursuit of a Medieval Meter*. Cambridge Studies in Medieval Literature 99. Cambridge: Cambridge University Press, 2017.

Cox, Catherine S. "*Pearl*'s 'Precios Pere': Gender, Language, and Difference." *Chaucer Review* 32, no. 4 (1998): 377–90.

Crawford, Donna. "The Architectonics of *Cleanness*." *Studies in Philology* 90, no. 1 (1993): 29–45.

Da Rold, Orietta. *Paper in Medieval England: From Pulp to Fictions*. 1st ed. Cambridge: Cambridge University Press, 2020. https://doi.org/10.1017/9781108886536.

Davenport, W. A. *The Art of the Gawain-Poet*. London: Athlone Press, 1978.

David, Alfred. "Recycling *Anelida and Arcite*: Chaucer as a Source for Chaucer." *Studies in the Age of Chaucer*, no. 1 (1984): 105–15. https://doi.org/10.1353/sac.1984.0037.

De Hamel, Christopher. "Books of Hours: Imaging the Word." In *The Bible as Book: The Manuscript Tradition*, edited by John L. Sharpe and Kimberly Van Kampen, 137–44. London: British Library; New Castle, DE: Oak Knoll Press, in association with The Scriptorium, Center for Christian Antiquities, 1998.

Deleuze, Gilles, and Félix Guattari. *A Thousand Plateaus: Capitalism and Schizophrenia*. Minneapolis: University of Minnesota Press, 1987.

Denery, Dallas G. *Seeing and Being Seen in the Later Medieval World: Optics, Theology and Religious Life*. 1st ed. Cambridge: Cambridge University Press, 2005. https://doi.org/10.1017/CBO9780511496462.

Derrida, Jacques. "Différance." In *Margins of Philosophy*, translated by Alan Bass, 3–27. Chicago: University of Chicago Press, 1982.

———. *Of Grammatology*. Translated by Gayatri Chakravorty Spivak. Baltimore: Johns Hopkins University Press, 1997.

Despres, Denise L. "Sacramentals and Ghostly Sights." *Religion and Literature* 42, no. 1/2 (2010): 101–10.

Dimock, Wai Chee. "A Theory of Resonance." *PMLA* 112, no. 5 (October 1997): 1060–71. https://doi.org/10.2307/463483.

Dinshaw, Carolyn. "All Kinds of Time." *Studies in the Age of Chaucer* 35, no. 1 (2013): 3–25. https://doi.org/10.1353/sac.2013.0025.

———. *How Soon Is Now? Medieval Texts, Amateur Readers, and the Queerness of Time.* Durham, NC: Duke University Press, 2012.

———. "A Kiss Is Just a Kiss: Heterosexuality and Its Consolations in *Sir Gawain and the Green Knight*." *Diacritics* 24, no. 2 (1994): 205–26.

Donaldson, E. Talbot. "Oysters, Forsooth: Two Readings in 'Pearl.'" *Neuphilologische Mitteilungen* 73, no. 1/3 (1972): 75–82.

Doyle, Anthony Ian. "English Books In and Out of Court from Edward III to Henry VII." In *English Court Culture in the Later Middle Ages*, edited by V. J. Scattergood and James Sherborne, 163–81. London: Gerald Duckworth, 1983.

Drimmer, Sonja. "Connoisseurship, Art History, and the Paleographical Impasse in Middle English Studies." *Speculum* 97, no. 2 (April 1, 2022): 415–68. https://doi.org/10.1086/718763.

Duffy, Eamon. *Marking the Hours: English People and Their Prayers 1240–1570*. New Haven, CT: Yale University Press, 2006.

Dwyer, Seamus. "Reading the Tied Letters of Cotton Nero A.x." *Review of English Studies* 74, no. 313 (February 2023): 16–30. https://doi.org/10.1093/res/hgac040.

Eagleton, Terry. *Literary Theory: An Introduction; with a New Preface*. Anniversary ed. Minneapolis: University of Minnesota Press, 2008.

Eberle, Patricia. "The Lovers' Glass: Nature's Discourse on Optics and the Optical Design of the *Romance of the Rose*." *University of Toronto Quarterly* 46, no. 3 (March 1, 1977): 241–62. https://doi.org/10.3138/utq.46.3.241.

Edwards, A. S. G. "The Manuscript: British Library MS Cotton Nero A.x." In *A Companion to the Gawain-Poet*, edited by Derek Brewer and Jonathan Gibson, 197–220. Arthurian Studies 38. Woodbridge, Suffolk, UK: D. S. Brewer, 1997.

Eldredge, Laurence. "Late Medieval Discussions of the Continuum and the Point of the Middle English *Patience*." *Vivarium* 17, no. 2 (1979): 90–115.

Epstein, Robert. "Literal Opposition: Deconstruction, History, and Lancaster." *Texas Studies in Literature and Language* 44, no. 1 (2002): 16–33.

Eyers, Tom. *Speculative Formalism: Literature, Theory, and the Critical Present*. Diaeresis. Evanston, IL: Northwestern University Press, 2017.

Falque, Ingrid. "'Daz Man Bild Mit Bilde Us Tribe': Imagery and Knowledge of God in Henry Suso's *Exemplar*." *Speculum* 92, no. 2 (April 2017): 447–92. https://doi.org/10.1086/690774.

Fein, Susanna, and David B. Raybin, eds. *Chaucer: Visual Approaches*. University Park: Pennsylvania State University Press, 2016.

Felski, Rita. *The Limits of Critique*. Chicago: University of Chicago Press, 2015.

Fish, Stanley. *Is There a Text in This Class? The Authority of Interpretive Communities*. Cambridge, MA: Harvard University Press, 1982.

Flanders, Eric. "Resetting *Pearl*, Disarming *Gawain*: A Manuscript-Oriented Reading of BL MS Cotton Nero A.x." MA thesis, University of Alaska Anchorage, 2018.

Fleming, John. "The Centuple Structure of *Pearl*." In *The Alliterative Tradition of the Fourteenth Century*, edited by Bernard S. Levy and Paul E. Szarmach, 99–130. Kent, OH: Kent State University Press, 1981.

Foys, Martin K. "Medieval Manuscripts: Media Archaeology and the Digital Incunable." In *The Medieval Manuscript Book*, edited by Michael Johnston and Michael Van Dussen, 1st ed., 119–39. Cambridge University Press, 2015. https://doi.org/10.1017/CBO9781107588851.007.

———. "The Remanence of Medieval Media." In *The Routledge Research Companion to Digital Medieval Literature*, edited by Jennifer Boyle and Helen Burgess, 9–30. London: Routledge, 2017.

Franklin-Brown, Mary. *Reading the World: Encyclopedic Writing in the Scholastic Age*. Chicago: University of Chicago Press, 2012.

Fredell, Joel. "The Pearl-Poet Manuscript in York." *Studies in the Age of Chaucer* 36, no. 1 (2014): 1–39. https://doi.org/10.1353/sac.2014.0004.

Frelick, Nancy M. "Introduction." In *The Mirror in Medieval and Early Modern Culture*, 25:1–29. Cursor Mundi. Turnhout, Belgium: Brepols Publishers, 2016. https://doi.org/10.1484/M.CURSOR-EB.5.111040.

Fuller, Mary C. *Lines Drawn across the Globe: Reading Richard Hakluyt's "Principal Navigations."* Montreal: McGill-Queen's University Press, 2023.

Garrison, Jennifer. "Liturgy and Loss: *Pearl* and the Ritual Reform of the Aristocratic Subject." *Chaucer Review* 44, no. 3 (January 1, 2010): 294–322. https://doi.org/10.5325/chaucerrev.44.3.0294.

Gayk, Shannon. *Image, Text, and Religious Reform in Fifteenth-Century England*. 1st ed. Cambridge: Cambridge University Press, 2010. https://doi.org/10.1017/CBO9780511659058.

George, Michael W. "Gawain's Struggle with Ecology: Attitudes toward the Natural World in *Sir Gawain and the Green Knight*." *Journal of Ecocriticism* 2, no. 2 (2010): 30–44.

Gilligan, Janet. "Numerical Composition in the Middle English *Patience*." *Studia Neophilologica* 61 (1989): 7–11.

Ginsberg, Warren. "Place and Dialectic in *Pearl* and Dante's *Paradiso*." *ELH* 55, no. 4 (1988): 731. https://doi.org/10.2307/2873134.

Gordon, E. V., and C. T. Onions. "Notes on the Text and Interpretation of 'Pearl.'" *Medium Ævum* 1, no. 2 (1932): 126–36. https://doi.org/10.2307/43625822.

Grabes, Herbert. *The Mutable Glass: Mirror-Imagery in Titles and Texts of the Middle Ages and the English Renaissance*. Cambridge: Cambridge University Press, 2009.

Gregory, Caspar René. "The Quires in Greek Manuscripts." *American Journal of Philology*, 1886. http://archive.org/details/jstor-287262.

Griffin, Carrie. "Instruction and Inspiration: Fifteenth-Century Codicological Recipes." *Exemplaria* 30, no. 1 (January 2, 2018): 20–34. https://doi.org/10.1080/10412573.2018.1436277.

Hadbawnik, David, ed. *Postmodern Poetry and Queer Medievalisms: Time Mechanics*. New Queer Medievalisms, volume 2. Berlin: De Gruyter, 2022.

Halberstam, Judith. *The Queer Art of Failure*. Durham, NC: Duke University Press, 2011.

Hamburger, Jeffrey F. *Ouvertures: La double page dans les manuscrits enluminés du Moyen Âge*. Collection "Amphi des arts." Dijon: Les Presses du réel, 2010.

———. *Script as Image*. Corpus of Illuminated Manuscripts, vol. 21. Leuven, Belgium: Peeters, 2014.

———. "Speculations on Speculation: Vision and Perception in the Theory and Practice of Mystical Devotion." In *Deutsche Mystik im abendländischen Zusammenhang*, edited by Walter Haug and Wolfram Schneider-Lastin, 353–408. Tübingen: Max Niemeyer Verlag, 2000. https://doi.org/10.1515/9783110928280.353.

Hanna, Ralph. "Unlocking What's Locked: Gawain's Green Girdle." *Viator* 14 (1983): 289–301.

Harwood, Britton. "Pearl as Diptych." In *Text and Matter: New Critical Perspectives of the Pearl-Poet*, edited by Robert J. Blanch, Miriam Youngerman Miller, and Julian N. Wasserman, 61–78. Troy, NY: Whitston, 1991.

Hatt, Cecilia A. *God and the Gawain-Poet: Theology and Genre in Pearl, Cleanness, Patience and Sir Gawain and the Green Knight*. Cambridge: D. S. Brewer, 2015.

Heng, Geraldine. "Feminine Knots and the Other *Sir Gawain and the Green Knight*." *PMLA* 106, no. 3 (May 1991): 500–514. https://doi.org/10.2307/462782.

Herman, J. M. "'With Lel Letteres Loken': *Sir Gawain and the Green Knight* Line 35." *Notes and Queries* 57, no. 3 (September 1, 2010): 311–13. https://doi.org/10.1093/notesj/gjq069.

Hieatt, A. Kent. "*Sir Gawain*: Pentangle, *Luf-Lace*, Numerical Structure." In *Silent Poetry: Essays in Numerological Analysis*, edited by Alastair Fowler, 116–40. London: Routledge and Kegan Paul, 1970.

Hill, Thomas D. "God's 'Inquits' and Exegetical Speech Theory in the Middle English *Patience*." *Journal of English and Germanic Philology* 116, no. 2 (April 1, 2017): 182–94. https://doi.org/10.5406/jenglgermphil.116.2.0182.

Hilmo, Maidie. "Creating a Visual Narrative of the Spiritual Journey to the New Jerusalem in the Pearl Manuscript." In *Medieval Images, Icons, and Illustrated English Literary Texts: From Ruthwell Cross to the Ellesmere Chaucer*, 138–59. Aldershot, UK: Ashgate, 2004.

———. "Did the Scribe Draw the Miniatures in British Library, MS Cotton Nero A.x (The Pearl-Gawain Manuscript)?" *Journal of the Early Book Society for the Study of Manuscripts and Printing History* 20 (2017): 111–36.

———. "The *Pearl* Manuscript." In *Opening up Middle English Manuscripts: Literary and Visual Approaches*, edited by Kathryn Kerby-Fulton, Linda Olson, and Maidie Hilmo, 172–89. Ithaca, NY: Cornell University Press, 2012.

———. "Re-Conceptualizing the Poems of the Pearl-Gawain Manuscript in Line and Color." *Manuscript Studies: A Journal of the Schoenberg Institute for Manuscript Studies* 3, no. 2 (2018): 383–420. https://doi.org/10.1353/mns.2018.0020.

Hines, Zachary. "'The Best Boke of Romance': The *Gawain* Manuscript and Composite Miscellaneity." *HLQ* 85, no. 4 (2022): 579–601.

Holsinger, Bruce. "'Historical Context' in Historical Context: Surface, Depth, and the Making of the Text." *New Literary History* 42, no. 4 (2011): 593–614. https://doi.org/10.1353/nlh.2011.0042.

———. "Of Pigs and Parchment: Medieval Studies and the Coming of the Animal." *PMLA: Publications of the Modern Language Association of America* 124, no. 2 (2009): 616–23. https://doi.org/10.1632/pmla.2009.124.2.616.

Hu, Hsin-Yu. "Delineating the Gawain-Poet: Myth, Desire, and Visuality." DPhil diss., Oxford University, 2014.

Hulbert, J. R. "Quatrains in Middle English Alliterative Poems." *Modern Philology* 48, no. 2 (1950): 73–81.

Ingham, Patricia Clare. *The Medieval New: Ambivalence in an Age of Innovation*. Middle Ages Series. Philadelphia: University of Pennsylvania Press, 2015.

Ingledew, Francis. *Sir Gawain and the Green Knight and the Order of the Garter*. Notre Dame, IN: University of Notre Dame Press, 2006.

Johnson, Eleanor. "Horrific Visions of the Host: A Meditation on Genre." *Exemplaria* 27, no. 1–2 (May 2015): 150–66. https://doi.org/10.1179/1041257315Z.00000000069.

———. *Staging Contemplation: Participatory Theology in Middle English Prose, Verse, and Drama*. Chicago: University of Chicago Press, 2018.

———. *Waste and the Wasters: Poetry and Ecosystemic Thought in Medieval England*. Chicago: University of Chicago Press, 2023.

Johnston, Michael, and Alex Mueller. "Kant in King Arthur's Court: Charges of Anachronism in Book Reviews." Accessed August 31, 2023. https://www.inthemedievalmiddle.com/2016/08/kant-in-king-arthurs-court-charges-of.html.

Kaluza, Max. "Strophische Gliederung in der mittelenglischen rein alliterirenden Dichtung." *Englische Studien* 16 (1892): 169–80.

Karnes, Michelle. *Imagination, Meditation, and Cognition in the Middle Ages*. Chicago: University of Chicago Press, 2011.

———. "Wonder, Marvels, and Metaphor in the 'Squire's Tale.'" *ELH* 82, no. 2 (2015): 461–90.

Käsmann, Hans. "Numerical Structure in Fitt III of *Sir Gawain and the Green Knight*." In *Chaucer and Middle English Studies in Honour of Rossell Hope Robbins*, edited by Beryl Rowland, 131–39. Kent, OH: Kent State University Press, 1974.

Kay, Sarah. "Analytical Survey 3: The New Philology." In *New Medieval Literatures*, vol. 3, edited by Rita Copeland, David Lawton, and Wendy Scase, 295–326. Oxford: Clarendon, 1999.

———. *Animal Skins and the Reading Self in Medieval Latin and French Bestiaries*. Chicago: University of Chicago Press, 2017.

———. "The *Roman de la Rose* and the Inverted Bouquet: Reflections of Love." In *Mythes à la cour, mythes pour la cour: Actes du XIIe Congrès de la société internationale de littérature courtoise*, 295–310. Publications romanes et françaises 248. Geneva: Droz, 2010.

Kaye, Joel. *Economy and Nature in the Fourteenth Century: Money, Market Exchange, and the Emergence of Scientific Thought*. 1st ed. Cambridge: Cambridge University Press, 1998. https://doi.org/10.1017/CBO9780511496523.

Kean, P. M. "Numerical Composition in *Pearl*." *Notes and Queries* 210 (1965): 49–51.

———. *The Pearl: An Interpretation*. London: Routledge, 1967.

Keiser, Elizabeth B. *Courtly Desire and Medieval Homophobia: The Legitimation of Sexual Pleasure in Cleanness and Its Contexts*. New Haven, CT: Yale University Press, 1997.

Kerby-Fulton, Kathryn, and Andrew W. Klein. "Rhymed Alliterative Verse in Mise En Page Transition: Two Case Studies in English Poetic Hybridity." In *The Medieval Literary: Beyond Form*, edited by Robert J. Meyer-Lee and Catherine Sanok, 1st ed., 87–118. Boydell and Brewer, 2018. https://doi.org/10.1017/9781787442191.005.

Kerby-Fulton, Kathryn, Linda Olson, and Maidie Hilmo. *Opening up Middle English Manuscripts: Literary and Visual Approaches*. Ithaca, NY: Cornell University Press, 2012.

Kinney, Clare. "The Best Book of Romance: *Sir Gawain and the Green Knight*." *University of Toronto Quarterly* 59, no. 4 (May 1, 1990): 457–74. https://doi.org/10.3138/utq.59.4.457.

Kline, Daniel T. "The Pearl, a Crayon, and a Lego." In *Essays in Medieval Studies* 15 (1998): 119–22.

Kossick, Shirley. "The Illustrations of the *Gawain* Manuscript." *De Arte* 25, no. 42 (September 1990): 21–37. https://doi.org/10.1080/00043389.1990.11761117.

Kottler, Barnet, and Alan Mouns Markman. *A Concordance to Five Middle English Poems: Cleanness, St. Erkenwald, Sir Gawain and the Green Knight, Patience [and] Pearl*. Pittsburgh, PA: University of Pittsburgh Press, 1966.

Kumler, Aden. *Translating Truth: Ambitious Images and Religious Knowledge in Late Medieval France and England*. New Haven, CT: Yale University Press, 2011.

Kurath, Hans, Sherman M. Kuhn, Robert E. Lewis, John Reidy, and Mary Jane Williams, eds. *Middle English Dictionary*. Ann Arbor: University of Michigan Press, 1952. http://bibpurl.oclc.org/web/2289.

Largier, Niklaus. *Figures of Possibility: Aesthetic Experience, Mysticism, and the Play of the Senses*. Stanford, CA: Stanford University Press, 2022.

———. *Spekulative Sinnlichkeit: Kontemplation und Spekulation im Mittelalter*. Mediävistische Perspektiven 7. Zurich: Chronos Verlag, 2018.

Lawton, David. "Englishing the Bible, 1066–1549." In *The Cambridge History of Medieval English Literature*, edited by David Wallace, 690–719. Cambridge: Cambridge University Press, 1999.

Lee, Jennifer. "The Illuminating Critic: The Illustrator of Cotton Nero A.x." *Studies in Iconography* 3 (1977): 17–46.

Leisegang, Hans. "La connaissance de Dieu au miroir de l'âme et de la nature." *Revue d'histoire et de philosophie religieuses* 17, no. 2 (1937): 145–71. https://doi.org/10.3406/rhpr.1937.2993.

Levine, Caroline. *Forms: Whole, Rhythm, Hierarchy, Network*. Princeton, NJ: Princeton University Press, 2015.

Levinson, Marjorie. "What Is New Formalism?" *PMLA* 122, no. 2 (2007): 558–69.

Lindberg, David C. *Theories of Vision from Al-Kindi to Kepler*. Chicago: University of Chicago Press, 1996.

Martinez, Ann M. "Bertilak's Green Vision: Land Stewardship in Sir Gawain and the Green Knight." *Arthuriana* 26, no. 4 (2016): 114–29.

McDermott, Ryan. "The Ordinary Gloss on Jonah." *PMLA* 128, no. 2 (2013): 424–38.

McGillivray, Murray, and Christina Duffy. "New Light on the *Sir Gawain and the Green Knight* Manuscript: Multispectral Imaging and the Cotton Nero A.x. Illustrations." *Speculum* 92, no. S1 (October 2, 2017): S110–44. https://doi.org/10.1086/693361.

McNamer, Sarah. "Feeling." In *Middle English*, edited by Paul Strohm, 241–57. Oxford Twenty-First Century Approaches to Literature. Oxford: Oxford University Press, 2007.

———. "The Literariness of Literature and the History of Emotion." *PMLA* 130, no. 5 (October 2015): 1433–42. https://doi.org/10.1632/pmla.2015.130.5.1433.

Melchior-Bonnet, Sabine. *The Mirror: A History*. Translated by Katherine H. Jewett. London: Routledge, 2001.

Meyer-Lee, Robert J. *The Problem of Literary Valuing*. Manchester: Manchester University Press, 2022.

Meyer-Lee, Robert J., and Catherine Sanok, eds. *The Medieval Literary: Beyond Form*. 1st ed. Boydell and Brewer, 2018. https://doi.org/10.1017/9781787442191.004.

Minnis, Alastair. "Unquiet Graves: Pearl and the Hope of Reunion." In *Truth and Tales: Cultural Mobility and Medieval Media*, edited by Fiona Somerset and Nicholas Watson, 117–34. Interventions: New Studies in Medieval Culture. Columbus: Ohio State University Press, 2015.

Molstad, Caleb D. "Adaptation, Autobiography, and Divine Passibility in *Patience*." *Neophilologus* 106, no. 4 (December 2022): 669–81. https://doi.org/10.1007/s11061-022-09730-z.

Newman, Barbara. "The Artifice of Eternity: Speaking of Heaven in Three Medieval Poems." *Religion and Literature* 37, no. 1 (2005): 1–24.

Nolan, Maura. "Beauty." In *Middle English: Oxford Twenty-First Century Approaches to Literature*, edited by Paul Strohm, 207–21. Oxford: Oxford University Press, 2007.

———. "Lydgate's Worst Poem." In *Lydgate Matters*, edited by Lisa H. Cooper and Andrea Denny-Brown, 71–87. New York: Palgrave Macmillan US, 2008. https://doi.org/10.1057/9780230610293_5.

———. "Medieval Habit, Modern Sensation: Reading Manuscripts in the Digital Age." *Chaucer Review* 47, no. 4 (April 1, 2013): 465–76. https://doi.org/10.5325/chaucerrev.47.4.0465.

Olson, Glending. *Literature as Recreation in the Later Middle Ages*. Ithaca, NY: Cornell University Press, 1982.

Osborne, Marijane. "The Squire's 'Steed of Brass' as an Astrolabe: Some Implications for the Canterbury Tales." In *Hermeneutics and Medieval Culture*, 121–31. Albany: State University Press of New York, 1989.

Otter, Samuel. "An Aesthetics in All Things." *Representations* 104, no. 1 (November 1, 2008): 116–25. https://doi.org/10.1525/rep.2008.104.1.116.

Outhwaite, Patrick. "Sir Gawain's Penitential Development from Attrition to Contrition." *Chaucer Review* 56, no. 2 (April 1, 2021): 153–70. https://doi.org/10.5325/chaucerrev.56.2.0153.

Palmén, Ritva. *Richard of St. Victor's Theory of Imagination*. Vol. 8. Investigating Medieval Philosophy. Leiden: Brill, 2014.

Parkes, M. B. *Pause and Effect: An Introduction to the History of Punctuation in the West*. Berkeley: University of California Press, 1993.

Payne, Roberta L. *The Influence of Dante on Medieval English Dream Visions*. Vol. 63. American University Studies. New York: Lang, 1989.

Petti, Anthony G. *English Literary Hands from Chaucer to Dryden*. London: Arnold, 1977.

Phillips, Noelle D. "Meeting One's Maker: The Jeweler in Fitt V of Pearl." In *Glossator 9: Pearl*, edited by Nicola Masciandaro and Karl Steel, 91–108. Open Humanities Press, 2015.

Pierson Prior, Sandra. *The Fayre Formez of the Pearl Poet*. East Lansing: Michigan State University Press, 1996.

Pollock, Sheldon. "Future Philology? The Fate of a Soft Science in a Hard World." *Critical Inquiry* 35, no. 4 (January 2009): 931–61. https://doi.org/10.1086/599594.

Putter, Ad. "Adventures in the Bob-and-Wheel Tradition: Narratives and Manuscripts." In *Medieval Romance and Material Culture*, edited by Nicholas Perkins, 147–63. Studies in Medieval Romance 18. Cambridge University Press, 2015.

———. *An Introduction to the Gawain-Poet*. 1st ed. Longman Medieval and Renaissance Library. New York: Addison Wesley Longman, 1996.

———. *"Sir Gawain and the Green Knight" and French Arthurian Romance*. Oxford: Oxford University Press, 1995.

Queen, Christopher D. "Negative Affect, Queer Aesthetics, and the Illuminations of *Cleanness*." *Exemplaria* 33, no. 2 (April 3, 2021): 109–36. https://doi.org/10.1080/10412573.2021.1914983.

Raschko, Mary. *The Politics of Middle English Parables: Fiction, Theology, and Social Practice*. 1st ed. Manchester Medieval Literature and Culture. Manchester: Manchester University Press, 2019.

Reichardt, Paul F. "'Counted . . . Bi a Clene Noumbre': The Design of the Pearl Manuscript." *Manuscripta* 38, no. 2 (July 1994): 116–37.

———. "Paginal Eyes: Faces among the Ornamented Capitals of MS Cotton Nero A.x, Art. 3." *Manuscripta* 36, no. 1 (March 1992): 22–36. https://doi.org/10.1484/J.MSS.3.1390.

———. "'Several Illuminations, Coarsely Executed': The Illustrations of the 'Pearl' Manuscript." *Studies in Iconography* 18 (1997): 119–42.

Rentz, Ellen K. "'Holsum to Haue in Memory': An Added Tale in an English Book of Hours." *Chaucer Review* 54, no. 2 (April 2019): 191–215. https://doi.org/10.5325/chaucerrev.54.2.0191.

Rhodes, Jim. "The Dreamer Redeemed: Exile and the Kingdom in the Middle English Pearl."

Studies in the Age of Chaucer 16, no. 1 (1994): 119–42. https://doi.org/10.1353/sac.1994.0005.

Richards, Christopher T. "Picturing Desire and Desiring Pictures: The Ovidian Manuscript Tradition." PhD diss., New York University, 2023.

Ritchey, Sara Margaret. *Holy Matter: Changing Perceptions of the Material World in Late Medieval Christianity*. Ithaca, NY: Cornell University Press, 2014.

Roberts, Jane. "The Hand and Script." In *London, British Library MS Cotton Nero A.x. (Art. 3): A Digital Facsimile and Commented Transcription*, edited by Murray McGillivray. Publications of the Cotton Nero A.x., Project 3. Calgary: Cotton Nero A.x. Project, 2012.

Rozenski, Steven. "Authority and Exemplarity in Henry Suso and Richard Rolle." In *The Medieval Mystical Tradition in England: Exeter Symposium VIII: Papers Read at Charney Manor, July 2011*, edited by E. A. Jones, 93–108. Cambridge: D. S. Brewer, 2013.

———. *Wisdom's Journey: Continental Mysticism and Popular Devotion in England, 1350–1650*. South Bend, IN: University of Notre Dame Press, 2022.

Rudd, Gillian. "'The Wilderness of Wirral' in 'Sir Gawain and the Green Knight.'" *Arthuriana* 23, no. 1 (2013): 52–65.

Russell, Arthur J. "Praying by Hand: Meditations on Reading with Feeling in Late Medieval England." *Postmedieval* 12 (December 2021): 199–217. https://doi.org/10.1057/s41280-021-00218-8.

Russell, J. Stephen. "Sir Gawain and the White Monks: Cistercian Marian Spirituality and *Sir Gawain and the Green Knight*." *Journal of Medieval Religious Cultures* 39, no. 2 (July 1, 2013): 207–26. https://doi.org/10.5325/jmedirelicult.39.2.0207.

Rust, Martha Dana. "The Arma Christi and the Ethic of Reckoning." In *The Arma Christi in Medieval and Early Modern Material Culture*, edited by Lisa H. Cooper and Andrea Denny-Brown, 143–69. Routledge, 2013. https://doi.org/10.4324/9781315241296.

———. *Imaginary Worlds in Medieval Books*. New York: Palgrave Macmillan US, 2007. https://doi.org/10.1007/978-1-137-06192-8.

———. "'Straunge' Letters and Strange Loops in Bodleian Library MS Arch. Selden. B.24." In *Imaginary Worlds in Medieval Books*, 81–116. New York: Palgrave Macmillan US, 2007. https://doi.org/10.1007/978-1-137-06192-8.

Sawyer, Daniel. *Reading English Verse in Manuscript c. 1350–c. 1500*. 1st ed. Oxford English Monographs. Oxford: Oxford University Press, 2020.

Scala, Elizabeth. *Absent Narratives, Manuscript Textuality, and Literary Structure in Late Medieval England*. New Middle Ages. New York: Palgrave, 2002.

Scarry, Elaine. *On Beauty and Being Just*. Princeton, NJ: Princeton University Press, 2001.

Schmidt, A. V. Carl. "'Kynde Craft' and the 'Play of Paramorez': Natural and Unnatural Love in Purity." In *Genres, Themes, and Images in English Literature: From the Fourteenth to the Fifteenth Century: The J. A. W. Bennett Memorial Lectures, Perugia, 1986*, edited by Piero Boitani and Anna Torti, 105–24. Tübinger Beiträge zur Anglistik 11. Tübingen: Gunter Narr Verlag, 1988.

Schmidt, Margot. "Miroir." In *Dictionnaire de Spiritualité*. Vol. 10. Paris: Beauchesne, 1980.

Scott, Kathleen L. *Later Gothic Manuscripts, 1390–1490*. 2 vols. Part 6 of *A Survey of Manuscripts Illuminated in the British Isles*. London: H. Miller, 1996.

Seaman, Myra. *Objects of Affection: The Book and the Household in Late Medieval England*. Manchester Medieval Literature and Culture. Manchester: Manchester University Press, 2021.

Shoaf, R. A. "*Purgatorio* and *Pearl*: Transgression and Transcendence." *Texas Studies in Literature and Language* 32, no. 1 (1990): 152–68.

Simpson, James. "Not Yet: Chaucer and Anagogy." *Studies in the Age of Chaucer* 37, no. 1 (2015): 31–54. https://doi.org/10.1353/sac.2015.0012.

Smith, Kathryn A. *The Taymouth Hours: Stories and the Construction of the Self in Late Medieval England*. London: British Library, 2012.

Solberg, Emma Maggie. "Imagining the Bob and Wheel." *PMLA* 137, no. 1 (January 2022): 52–69. https://doi.org/10.1632/S0030812921000663.

Spearing, A. C. *The Gawain-Poet: A Critical Study*. Cambridge: Cambridge University Press, 1970.

———. "*Patience* and the Gawain-Poet." *Anglia* 84, no. Jahresband (1966): 305–29. https://www.degruyter.com/document/doi/10.1515/angl.1966.1966.84.305/html.

———. "Poetic Identity." In *A Companion to the Gawain-Poet*, edited by Derek Brewer and Jonathan Gibson, 35–51. Arthurian Studies 38. Woodbridge, Suffolk, UK: D. S. Brewer, 1997.

———. "The Subtext of Patience: God as Mother and the Whale's Belly." *Journal of Medieval and Renaissance Studies* 29, no. 2 (1999): 293–323.

———. "What Is a Narrator?: Narrator Theory and Medieval Narratives." *Digital Philology: A Journal of Medieval Cultures* 4, no. 1 (2015): 59–105. https://doi.org/10.1353/dph.2015.0003.

Spivak, Gayatri Chakravorty. *An Aesthetic Education in the Era of Globalization*. Cambridge, MA: Harvard University Press, 2013.

Spyra, Piotr. *The Epistemological Perspective of the Pearl-Poet*. Farnham, Surrey, England: Ashgate, 2014.

———. "The God of the Middle English *Cleanness* and His Erotic Exhortations of Purity." *Studia Anglica Posnaniensia* 47, no. 4 (December 2012): 133–45. https://doi.org/10.2478/v10121-012-0015-7.

Staley Johnson, Lynn. "'Patience' and the Poet's Use of Psalm 93." *Modern Philology* 74, no. 1 (1976): 67–71.

———. "The *Pearl* Dreamer and the Eleventh Hour." In *Text and Matter: New Critical Perspectives of the "Pearl"-Poet*, edited by Robert J. Blanch, Miriam Youngerman Miller, and Julian N. Wasserman, 3–15. Troy, NY: Whitston, 1991.

———. *The Voice of the Gawain-Poet*. Madison: University of Wisconsin Press, 1984.

Stanbury, Sarah. *Seeing the Gawain-Poet: Description and the Act of Perception*. Philadelphia: University of Pennsylvania Press, 1991. http://www.jstor.org/stable/j.ctv4s7fx3.

———. *The Visual Object of Desire in Late Medieval England*. Middle Ages Series. Philadelphia: University of Pennsylvania Press, 2008.

Staples, James C. "Poynts and Spots: Molecular Revolutions, Mystical Desires, and the Pearl-Poet." PhD diss., New York University, 2019.

———. "Pure Pleasure: *Cleanness* and Fourteenth-Century Sexual Liberation." *Exemplaria* 34, no. 1 (January 2, 2022): 40–65. https://doi.org/10.1080/10412573.2021.2020992.

Stern, Milton R. "An Approach to 'The Pearl.'" *Journal of English and Germanic Philology* 54, no. 4 (1955): 684–92.

Strohm, Paul. "Historicity without Historicism?" *Postmedieval: A Journal of Medieval Cultural Studies* 1, no. 3 (December 2010): 380–91. https://doi.org/10.1057/pmed.2010.34.

———, ed. *Middle English: Oxford Twenty-First Century Approaches to Literature*. Oxford: Oxford University Press, 2007.

Tomasch, Sylvia. "A 'Pearl' Punnology." *Journal of English and Germanic Philology* 88, no. 1 (1989): 1–20.

Treharne, Elaine. *Perceptions of Medieval Manuscripts: The Phenomenal Book*. 1st ed. Oxford: Oxford University Press, 2021. https://doi.org/10.1093/oso/9780192843814.001.0001.

Trigg, Stephanie. *Shame and Honor: A Vulgar History of the Order of the Garter*. 1st ed. Philadelphia: University of Pennsylvania Press, 2012.

Wakelin, Daniel. *Immaterial Texts in Late Medieval England: Making English Literary Manuscripts, 1400–1500*. 1st ed. Cambridge: Cambridge University Press, 2022. https://doi.org/10.1017/9781009119313.

———. *Scribal Correction and Literary Craft: English Manuscripts 1375–1510*. 1st ed. Cambridge: Cambridge University Press, 2014. https://doi.org/10.1017/CB09781139923279.

Wallace, David, ed. *The Cambridge History of Medieval English Literature*. Cambridge: Cambridge University Press, 1999.

———. "*Cleanness* and the Terms of Terror." In *Text and Matter: New Critical Perspectives of the Pearl-Poet*, edited by Robert J. Blanch, Miriam Youngerman Miller, and Julian N. Wasserman, 93–104. Troy, NY: Whitston, 1991.

Warner, Lawrence. "Notes on *Sir Gawain and the Green Knight*." *Chaucer Review* 56, no. 2 (2021): 125–52.

Warren, Michelle R. *Holy Digital Grail: A Medieval Book on the Internet*. Stanford Text Technologies. Stanford, CA: Stanford University Press, 2022.

Wasserman, Julian, and Liam O. Purdon. "Sir Guido and the Green Light: Confession in *Sir Gawain and the Green Knight* and *Inferno* XXVII." *Neophilologus* 84, no. 4 (2000): 649–68. https://doi.org/10.1023/A:1004748613400.

Watson, Nicholas. "Desire for the Past." *Studies in the Age of Chaucer* 21, no. 1 (1991): 59–97. https://doi.org/10.1353/sac.1991.0047.

———. "The Gawain-Poet as Vernacular Theologian." In *A Companion to the Gawain-Poet*, edited by Derek Brewer and Jonathan Gibson, 293–313. Arthurian Studies 38. Woodbridge, Suffolk, UK: D. S. Brewer, 1997.

———. "The Phantasmal Past: Time, History, and the Recombinative Imagination." *Studies in the Age of Chaucer* 32, no. 1 (2010): 1–37. https://doi.org/10.1353/sac.2010.a402774.

Weiskott, Eric. "Alliterative Metre and the Textual Criticism of the *Gawain* Group." *Yearbook of Langland Studies* 29 (January 2015): 151–75. https://doi.org/10.1484/J.YLS.5.110098.

———. *English Alliterative Verse: Poetic Tradition and Literary History*. Cambridge Studies in Medieval Literature. Cambridge: Cambridge University Press, 2016.

———. "Stanza-Linking in *Sir Gawain and the Green Knight*: The Phenomenology of Narrative." *Neophilologus* 105, no. 3 (September 2021): 457–61. https://doi.org/10.1007/s11061-021-09677-7.

West, Martin Litchfield. *Textual Criticism and Editorial Technique Applicable to Greek and Latin Texts*. Stuttgart: B. G. Teubner, 1973.

Wright, C. E. *English Vernacular Hands from the Twelfth to the Fifteenth Centuries*. Oxford: Clarendon Press, 1960.

INDEX

Page numbers in italics refer to illustrations.